Biblespeak

The Epistles

Nelson P. Miller

Biblespeak—the epistles.

Miller, Nelson P.

Published by:

Crown Management LLC – May 2018

1527 Pineridge Drive
Grand Haven, MI 49417
USA

ISBN-13: 978-1-7322387-1-8

All Rights Reserved
© 2018 Nelson P. Miller
c/o 111 Commerce Avenue S.W.
Grand Rapids, MI 49503
(616) 560-0632
millern57@gmail.com

*For Glen, Laura, Charles, Larry, Ross, Todd,
and other church elders everywhere.*

Table of Contents

Introduction 1

Part I: Light 5

Father	6
Son	13
Spirit	20
Light	23
Creation	25
Gospel	27
Word	30
Crucifixion	32
Resurrection	35
Kingdom	39
Confession	41
Faith	43
Baptism	48
Communion	49
Promise	51
Children	53
Grace	55
Peace	58
Redemption	60
Glory	63
Power	66
Heaven	70
Calling	72
Freedom	75
Inheritance	76
Sanctification	78
Return	82
Eternity	85

Part II: Darkness 87

Satan	88
Sin	90
Death	95
Law	99
Circumcision	103
Deceivers	105
Desertion	109
Idols	112
Persecution	114
Traditions	116

Quarrels	120
Slavery	122
World	124
Riches	126
Flesh	128
Curse	130
Spirits	132
Doubt	133
Favoritism	134
Judgment	135

Part III: Direction 139

Obedience	140
Authority	143
Discipline	145
Repentance	146
Humility	148
Forgiveness	151
Unity	153
Action	155
Service	157
Fellowship	161
Elders	165
Church	168
Love	172
Joy	175
Sowing	177
Teaching	179
Building	185
Discerning	187
Wisdom	190
Trials	192
Rulers	196
Encouragement	197
Families	199
Body	203
Gifts	206
Giving	208
Prayer	210
Gratitude	213

Conclusion 215
Abbreviations 218
Appendices 219

Authors	220
Audiences	229

Introduction

When God speaks through his word the Bible, readers don't hear mere whispers, hints, suggestions, myths, or comforts. The Bible, far and away the most-widely published book in history, instead tells the world's story in unparalleled clarity, antiquity, scope, import, originality, and perspective. And God's word is exactly as it should be, fully worthy of its inestimable author, with every verse perfectly crafted in its proper place.

For all its perfection and unmatchable significance, though, the Bible does not tell its story easily. One even finds hard telling a new reader where to begin. Some say to go to John's gospel first, or to Paul's letter to the Romans, or to Hebrews, or Luke's gospel. Others say to start from the beginning, with Genesis, but as any Bible reader knows, Genesis passes quickly through Exodus and into difficult books of law and national treaty, histories, writings, and prophecy, a very long way from the climactic Gospels. The Bible can put off the most intrepid of readers when they do not read with the Spirit's discernment. Plenty of books, indeed rafts of exquisite commentaries, explain the Bible. Yet wouldn't reading the Bible's own words be especially valuable, if one could organize those words into fully coherent story?

The letters, or if you prefer *epistles*, give us that opportunity. The Bible's sixty-six books include history, law, teaching, genealogy, prophecy, wisdom writing, song, revelation, and, yes, letters. The Bible places the letters in a New Testament series, after the Gospels and the history of the early church in Acts but before the concluding book Revelation. The letters play a critical role in confirming, clarifying, and encompassing the doctrine that the Bible's other books spread across complex histories, events, and prophecies. The epistles provide an invaluable confirmation of the gospel story, an absolute treasure, spelling out the gospel's concepts and meanings in relatively plain language, while leaving no doubt as to the lessons to draw. Without the epistles, a reader would have to infer the correct meaning of many widely varying Bible histories, trends, tendencies, patterns, peoples, conflicts, characters, and events, indeed would have to infer that they carry any special meaning. The reader would also have to wrestle applications and lessons from that meaning. The four Gospels and Acts of course provide the gospel foundation, but the letters clarify critical understandings, commitments, concepts, and doctrine. If you want to think, walk, and talk Bible, *biblespeak,* having God's word dwell in you most richly, which is a profound desire, then you must know the letters.

Yet the challenge of grasping the Bible's profound meaning is nearly as great when reading the letters as it is when reading the Bible's history, law, teaching, genealogy, prophecy, wisdom writing, song, and revelation. Many readers, even the inveterate well-read, lack the conceptual skill, perseverance, and spiritual discernment to draw those inferences and lessons. The problem is that the letters are, well, *letters*, correspondence on mixed topics, in no comprehensive order, stating important things throughout but not organizing those things into coherence. To learn broadly about any specific topic, whether heaven, the devil, the Spirit, prayer, or dozens of other critical concepts, one must flit from letter to letter. The letter's several authors, including at least Paul, James, Peter, John, and Jude, did not write a coherent work ready to incorporate into the Bible to serve that role. Rather, each author wrote most of the individual letters to a church, community, person, or small group of individuals, about concerns specific to that audience. Placing the letters together in one place within the Bible, while convenient for locating them, does not make them into a whole.

Many outstanding commentaries are available on the epistles, explaining the context for and intended meaning of each verse, verse by verse, indeed word by word. Yet commentaries inevitably mix our voice with God's voice. In truth, no one comments on the Bible. Instead, the Bible always comments on us. God's people hold a passion for the Word that we recognize as alive within us, indeed as the author of life. We wish to hear God speak in all events and through each of us. Bible verses come to mind, and in them, we hear God's voice. Yet we promptly mix God's voice with our own voice, as we listen, reason, and discern, on our own or through preachers and theologians. When we speak Bible verses to ourselves or others, we may speak God's word into our life or theirs, or, mixing it with our own words, we may misspeak it into circumstances to which God would not have it apply. We wish to know more of God's word, yet as God's word dwells in us, our own voice and reason speak on. What would hearing more of his word and less of our own words be like? How would it purify and uplift us, guide and inform us?

The following sections reorganize the letters' verses, verse by verse and in some cases by parts of verses, into their most-common topics. While each letter standing alone addresses specific concerns, the letters taken together tell the full story. One sees in reorganizing the letters verse by verse according to topic, that the story's first part, that of the light of God, tells of God's nature and creation, loving call, and invitation to reason with him. The first part calls us to live in gospel kingdom and context, saved by his Son, freed of sin's burden, sanctified in the Spirit, and anticipating a resurrection and glorified end, witnessing to the Son and glorifying the Father. Taken individually, the epistles give profound counsel to the churches and audiences to whom their authors wrote them, in snippets and snatches relevant to their context. Taken together, reorganized by theme, the letters become a symphony to the Messiah, beginning with his great light, warning us against an opposed darkness, and ending with persistent direction. The following writings are close paraphrases and, in some cases, modest generalizations of the cited verses, drawn from different Bible translations.

You might wonder whether a good concordance in the back of a Bible or as a separate book, or even a simple search function of an electronic Bible, would have sufficed instead of this book. I, too, appreciate concordances and used them frequently until giving way to the more-convenient search function of an electronic Bible. Concordances and search functions certainly have their place. One challenge, though, in using a concordance or search is that it picks up only your specific search term, when the Bible and its letters may use several terms to describe the same concept or related concepts. If you search *sanctification*, then you miss the many verses on the related concept *righteousness*. If you search *death*, then you miss *dead, die,* and *dying*. If you search Jesus's *return*, then you miss his *second coming* and the *last day* or *day of judgment*. Concordances also require you to cast back and forth through the Bible or the letters, from verse to verse, with your thumb on one page and forefinger on another. Collecting in one place all verses on each major topic thus has its own value. Moreover, I tried to reorganize the many verses on each topic into more sensible and readable order within the topic. My organization of the verses within each topic helps the verses flow sensibly from one to another and from subtopic to subtopic.

I hope that you glean some insight from this reorganized presentation of the letters. I did. I had read the letters, start to finish in their New Testament order, around thirty times, so often that I tired of keeping count. Yet the reorganizing here stunned me at how much the letters said about so many topics, most of which the reorganization brought into greater emphasis and clarity, and how little the letters said about other topics. The reading, editing, and writing taught me a lot, which intense interaction with the divine text always does. The introductions to each topic capture a little of what I learned, while the book's conclusion captures other patterns that the reorganizing revealed. You, though, will likely have other, better insights, which again is the nature of God's holy word, living and active, dividing, testing, and guiding the heart, mind, and soul. Read God's word with God's Spirit. Discover again the life of Christ.

> After this letter has been read to you, see that it is also read in the church of the Laodiceans and that you in turn read the letter from Laodicea. *Col 4:16*

Part I: Light

    Father. Son. Spirit. Light. Creation. Gospel. Word. Crucifixion. Resurrection. Kingdom. Faith. Baptism. Communion. Promise. Children. Grace. Peace. Redemption. Glory. Power. Heaven. Calling. Freedom. Inheritance. Sanctification. Return. Eternity.

The Bible tells the great story of light coming into the world as the life of humankind. That light is the good-news story, that glorious bit of meaning making every bit of difference to the conduct and outcome of our lives. The story begins with God creating the world and placing humankind in it, knowing that we would reject him to follow our own way. But the good news is that God sent, sacrificed, and resurrected his glorious Son to show us how much God loves us and wants us back with him. The story unfolds that our faith in God's Son justifies us as God's children through his rich mercy and grace. We thus turn in repentance from that which harms us. His Spirit carries his blessing, calling us apart from the world's slavery to a righteous freedom enjoying God's increasing kingdom, while we eagerly await Jesus's full return. We will live with him forever. See how the letters address the great light surrounding us. Do you know and follow the light?

Father

The letters confirm God revealing himself to us in Father, Son, and Spirit forms. The letters begin with relationship, that God is both Father to our Lord Jesus and our own Father, making us his sons and daughters whom he himself seeks. Yet the letters add that the Father also gave us the exquisite gifts of his Spirit and his word. The letters also confirm the Father's attributes as divine, unchanging, unknowable but revealed, and judging but patient, forgiving, compassionate, loving, and giving of the one great gift of our Lord Jesus Christ, along with many other good and perfect gifts. See how the letters reveal the Father to us. Do you tremble at the mention of his name?

God. The Lord Almighty says that God is a Father to us, and we are his sons and daughters.$_{2Co\ 6:18}$ We kneel before the Father, from whom every family in heaven and on earth derives its name.$_{Eph\ 3:14-15}$ Those who did not seek God found him because he revealed himself to those who did not ask for him.$_{Ro\ 10:20}$ God our Savior wants all people saved and to know the truth.$_{1Ti\ 2:3-4}$ God chose you out of nowhere to be royal and holy, his special possession, calling you out of darkness into his wonderful light.$_{1Pe\ 2:9-10}$ Give joyful thanks to the Father, who has qualified you to share with his holy people in the kingdom of light.$_{Col\ 1:12}$ God continuously held out his hands to a disobedient and obstinate chosen people.$_{Ro\ 10:21}$ We don't give to God in that he must repay us because everything is from him, through him, and for him.$_{Ro\ 11:35-36}$ God called you to eternal life when you confessed before many witnesses.$_{1Ti\ 6:12}$ You cannot please God without faith because you must believe that God exists and rewards those who earnestly seek him.$_{Heb\ 11:6}$ Our common faith as a family of believers is in grace and peace from God the Father and Christ Jesus our Savior.*Tit 1:4* Every family in heaven derives its name from the Father.*Eph 3:14-15*

King. God to you is not like the dark, gloomy, and stormy mountain burning with fire, a harsh trumpet blast, or frightening voice the commands from which you cannot bear, terrifying you so that you tremble with fear.*Heb 12:18-21* You have instead come to the city of the living God, the heavenly Jerusalem, with millions of angels in joyful assembly.*Heb 12:22* You have come to the church of the firstborn whose names God wrote in heaven.*Heb 12:23* Before he created the world, God chose us in him to be holy and blameless in his sight.*Eph 1:4* God prepares a city for those in whom he has no shame when others call him their God.*Heb 11:16* The Father shares his kingdom of light.*Col 1:12* God brings us into the kingdom of the Son whom he loves.*Col 1:13* God calls you into his kingdom.*1Th 2:12* God will count you worthy of his kingdom for which you suffer.*2Th 1:5* Remain in view of God's kingdom.*2Ti 4:1* The Lord will bring us safely to his heavenly kingdom.*2Ti 4:18* God's kingdom is not about eating and drinking but righteousness, peace, and joy in the Holy Spirit.*Ro 14:17* Draw near to God with faith's full assurance.*Heb 10:22* You are a child of God who can cry to your Father.*Ro 8:15* You have a Master in heaven.*Col 4:1* Thank the Father, who has qualified you to share in the inheritance of his holy people.*Col 1:12*

Creator. God finished his works when creating the world.*Heb 4:3* God rested from all his works on the seventh day of creation.*Heb 4:4* Creation eagerly waits for God to reveal his children.*Ro 8:19* God delays so he can liberate creation from its decay, bringing it into the freedom and glory of God's children.*Ro 8:21* Creation groans as in childbirth just as we who have the Spirit's firstfruits groan as we wait eagerly for God to adopt us as his children and redeem our bodies.*Ro 8:22-23* Don't you, a mere person, talk back to your creator God, who though all-powerful still leaves you to your own will.*Ro 9:19-20* God has the right to create both the special and common.*Ro 9:21* The Father made us his creation's firstfruits.*Jas 1:18* You have put on the new self that God renews in knowledge in his image as Creator.*Col 3:10* Everything God created is good, not to reject but to receive with thanksgiving.*1Ti 4:4* God calls into being things that were not.*Ro 4:17* God gives life to the dead.*Ro 4:17* The God of peace, through the blood of the eternal covenant, raised from the dead our Lord Jesus, the great Shepherd of the sheep.*Heb 13:20* God sees everything in all creation, uncovered and laid bare before him to whom we must give account.*Heb 4:13*

Word. God's word brings to us mysteries God shared by revelation.*Eph 3:3* In reading God's word, we understand insight into the mystery of Christ that God disclosed to people in prior generations, as his Spirit revealed it through holy apostles and prophets.*Eph 3:4-5* The Father gave us spiritual birth through the word of truth.*Jas 1:17-18* Carry the Spirit's sword, which is the word of God.*Eph 6:17* Accept God's word from one another not as a human word but as it is, the word of God, which works in you who believe.*1Th 2:13* Receive anything consecrated by the word of God.*1Ti 4:5* While someone might chain a gospel witness, no one chains God's word.*2Ti 2:9* God breathed all Scripture for teaching, rebuking, correcting, and training in righteousness.*2Ti 3:16-17* God enriches us in him in every way including all kinds of speech and with all knowledge, confirming testimony about Christ in us.*1Co 1:5-6* The law is still the very words of God.*Ro 2:2* God's word did not originate with you, and you are not the only people it has reached.*1Co 14:36* God's word lives actively, like a sharp blade penetrating to divide soul from spirit, joints from marrow, judging the heart's thoughts and attitudes.*Heb 4:12*

Son. God chose Christ before creating the world but only revealed him recently for your sake.*1Pe 1:20* God's Son Jesus is from heaven.*1Th 1:10* In the Son, God created everything in heaven and on earth, visible and invisible, rulers and authorities, through the Son and for him.*Col 1:16* The Son is before everything, holding everything together.*Col 1:17* God named Jesus his Son and said he was his Father.*Heb 1:5* God appointed Jesus the Son of God through the Spirit of holiness.*Ro 1:4* God called Jesus Son and said he was his Father.*Heb 5:5-6* God did not put angels over the world to come but put the Son of Man, Jesus Christ, leaving nothing over which he will not rule, even though we do not yet see all that he will rule.*Heb 2:5-8* God exalted Jesus over everyone for his glory as the Father.*Php 2:11* At Jesus's baptism, God the Father gave Jesus glory from heaven.*2Pe 1:17* When God did not spare his own Son but gave him up for us, he showed that he graciously gives us everything.*Ro 8:32* God presented Christ as a sacrifice of atonement, through the shedding of his blood.*Ro 2:25-26* God delivered Jesus over to death for our sins.*Ro 4:25* Jesus Christ, the Righteous One, is not only your advocate with the Father.*1Jn 2:1-2* The Father sent his Son as the world's Savior.*1Jn 4:13-14* Anyone who acknowledges Jesus as God's Son lives in God and God in them.*1Jn 4:15* When we are like Jesus, God makes love complete among us so that we may pass his judgment.*1Jn 4:17* Approach God's throne with confidence for mercy and grace when in need.*Heb 4:16*

Spirit. God poured his love into our hearts through the Holy Spirit, whom he gave to us.*Ro 5:5* If God's Spirit lives in you, then you pursue the Spirit rather than the flesh. Those whom the Spirit of God leads are the children of God.*Ro 8:14* The Spirit does not make you fearful slaves but makes you a child of God who can cry to your Father.*Ro 8:15* The Spirit testifies with our spirit that we are God's children who, if we suffer with Christ, inherit Christ's glory with him.*Ro 8:16-17* God who searches our hearts knows the Spirit's mind as the Spirit intercedes for God's people in God's will.*Ro 8:27* God gives to each one the Spirit's manifestation for the common good.*1Co 12:7* To one God gives wisdom through the Spirit, to another knowledge by the same Spirit, to another faith by the same Spirit, to another gifts of healing by that one Spirit, to others miraculous powers, prophecy, distinguishing between spirits, speaking in different tongues, or interpretation of tongues.*1Co 12:8-10*

Reconciler. God makes us stand firm in Christ, having anointed us.*2Co 1:21* Grace to you from God our Father and the Lord Jesus Christ.*Php 1:2* We receive grace, mercy and peace from God the Father through Jesus Christ, in truth and love.*2Jn 3* Grace to each of you from God our Father and the Lord Jesus Christ.*Gal 1:3* God brings us to fullness in Christ.*Col 2:10* God the Father loves us, keeping us for Jesus Christ while blessing us with abundant mercy, peace, and love.*Jude 1-2* God made Christ who had no sin to be sin for us, so that in Christ we would show God's righteousness.*2Co 5:21* God our Father asked Jesus to give himself for our sins to rescue us from how evil things are these days.*Gal 1:4* God reconciled us to himself through Christ, giving us the ministry of reconciliation.*2Co 5:18* God reconciled the world to himself in Christ, not counting people's sins against them, as he commits the reconciliation message to us.*2Co 5:19* When Jesus returns, God will punish with permanent destruction those who do not obey the Lord Jesus's gospel.*2Th 1:8-10* The living God is the Savior of all people, especially those who believe.*1Ti 4:10* Peace to you from God our Father.*Col 1:2* Peace to those in God the Father and the Lord Jesus Christ.*1Th 1:1* Peace from God the

Father and the Lord Jesus Christ.*2Th 1:1-2* Peace is from God the Father and Christ Jesus our Lord.*2Ti 1:2*

Resurrector. Because the glory of the Father raised Jesus Christ from the dead, we also live a new life.*Ro 6:3-4* If the Spirit of God who raised Jesus from the dead lives in you, then God who raised Christ from the dead will also give your body life because of his Spirit who lives in you.*Ro 8:11* God the Father raised Jesus Christ from the dead.*Gal 1:1* God raised Jesus from the dead.*Ro 4:22-24* God delivered Jesus over to death for our sins and raised him to life for our justification.*Ro 4:25* God appointed Jesus the Son of God through the Spirit of holiness and resurrected him from the dead as Jesus Christ our Lord.*Ro 1:4* We should thank God the Father of our Lord Jesus Christ for his great mercy giving us new birth into living hope through Jesus's resurrection from the dead.*1Pe 1:3* If the Spirit of God who raised Jesus from the dead lives in you, then God who raised Christ from the dead will also give your body life because of his Spirit who lives in you.*Ro 8:11* God made us alive in Christ when we were dead in our sins.*Col 2:13* God raised you with Christ.*Col 3:1* You died, and your life now hides with Christ in God.*Col 3:3* Wait for God's Son Jesus, whom God raised from the dead.*1Th 1:10* Thank God for victory through our Lord Jesus Christ.*1Co 15:57*

Savior. God's power for believers is the same as the mighty strength he exerted when he raised Christ from the dead and seated him at his right hand in the heavenly realms, over all rule, authority, power, and dominion, and every name not only now but in the future.*Eph 1:19-21* You choose, but whoever believes in the Son of God accepts God's testimony, while whoever does not believe makes God out to be a liar.*1Jn 5:10* The testimony is that God gave us eternal life in his Son and only in his Son.*1Jn 5:11-13* Our Lord Jesus Christ and God our Father by his grace gave us good hope of eternity.*2Th 2:16-17* Praise to the God and Father of our Lord Jesus Christ, the Father of compassion, and the God of all comfort.*2Co 1:3* When God brought his firstborn Son Jesus into the world, God said that the angels would worship Jesus.*Heb 1:6* God's oath appointed the Son, whom God made perfect forever.*Heb 7:28* God loves having all his fullness dwell in the Son.*Col 1:19* Through the Son, God reconciles to himself all things on earth and in heaven.*Col 1:20* God said to the Son to sit at his right hand until God made his enemies a footstool for his feet.*Heb 1:13* God gave Jesus Christ our Lord glory, majesty, power, and authority.*Jude 24-25* God favors us now and saves us now.*2Co 6:2*

Giver. When you believed, God marked you in him with the seal of the promised Holy Spirit, who guarantees our inheritance until God redeems those whom he possesses.*Eph 1:13-14* God saved us through rebirth's washing and renewal by the Holy Spirit whom he poured out on us generously through Jesus Christ our Savior.*Tit 5:6* God gives you his Holy Spirit with instruction.*1Th 4:8* The Spirit God gave us does not leave us timid but gives us power, love, and self-discipline.*2Ti 1:7* When leading others to obey God, you act through the Spirit of God's power.*Ro 15:18-19* God revealed to us by his Spirit things that he prepared for those who love him, that no eye had seen, ear heard, or mind conceived.*1Co 2:9-10* The Spirit searches everything, even God's deep things.*1Co 2:10* No one knows God's thoughts except God's Spirit, just as only one's own spirit knows one's own thoughts.*1Co 2:11* We received God's Spirit, not the world's spirit, so that we can understand what God freely gave us.*1Co 2:12* Your body is a temple of the Holy Spirit, who is in you and whom you received from God.*1Co 6:19* God makes us ministers of the Spirit's new covenant through which the Spirit gives life.*2Co 3:6* God gave us the Spirit as a deposit to guarantee life to come.*2Co 5:5* The Holy Spirit testifies that God put his laws in our hearts and minds, and no longer remembers our sins and lawless acts.*Heb 10:16*

Character. We see and understand God's invisible qualities including his eternal power and divine nature from what he made.*Ro 1:20* No one knows the Lord's mind or can give him counsel.*Ro 11:34* Time differs to the Lord to whom a day is like a thousand years and thousand years like a day.*2Pe 3:8* The Father in heaven, who does not change, gives the good and perfect gifts from above.*Jas 1:17* The wisdom and knowledge of God are deeply rich.*Ro 11:33* God makes his angels spirits and his servants flames of fire.*Heb 1:7* God destroys the wise's wisdom and frustrates the intelligent's intelligence, but the cross is God's power to us whom God saves.*1Co 1:18-19* God who calls you is faithful.*1Th 5:24* That the Father calls us his children shows his lavish love for us.*1Jn 3:1-2* You have come to the God who is the Judge of all and to spirits of the righteous he made perfect.*Heb 12:23* God is pure light without any darkness.*1Jn 1:5* The gospel reveal's God's righteousness, which we live out by faith.*Ro 1:17* The gospel declares that God judges people's secrets through Jesus

Christ.*Ro 2:16* God is the blessed, honored, mighty, eternal, and only Ruler, the King of kings and Lord of lords, who alone is immortal, living in unapproachable light, whom no one has seen or can see.*1Ti 6:15-16* God gives life to the dead.*Ro 4:17* When God said to let light shine out of darkness, he shined his light into our hearts, lighting our knowledge of God's glory in Christ's face.*2Co 4:6* Worship God with reverence and awe as you would a consuming fire.*Heb 12:28-29* Praise God the Father of our Lord Jesus Christ, who brings us every spiritual blessing in Christ.*Eph 1:3*

Son

Whether expressed or implied, every letter focuses on Jesus, the Son of God and our Savior. Jesus is the authors' reason to write, without whom our faith means nothing but with whom the world takes its ordained course. The letters' authors saw, heard, and knew Jesus, or heard hundreds who did see, hear, and know Jesus, and who witnessed his resurrection. The authors knew that history hinged on the Son of God, and their letters said so. The letters repeatedly confirm Jesus in each of the roles by which we know him, as God, God's Son, Lord, High Priest, and Savior. The letters capture his suffering, crucifixion, and resurrection, declaring him eternal. The letters also describe his gifts. See how consistently and richly the letters testify to Jesus. Do you with your whole spirit hail the Son?

God. The Messiah Jesus is God over all, forever praised.*Ro 9:5* The Son is the invisible God's image, the firstborn over all creation.*Col 1:15* The Son radiates God's glory, exactly representing his being, while sustaining all things by his powerful word.*Heb 1:3* Christ is the Deity's fullness living in bodily form.*Col 2:9* God loves having all his fullness dwell in the Son.*Col 1:19* Jesus Christ was the same in the past as he is today and will be forever.*Heb 13:8* Jesus Christ our Lord is the one before all ages to whom God gave glory, majesty, power, and authority.*Jude 24-25* Christ is the head over every power and authority.*Col 2:10* Our ancestors all ate the same spiritual food and drank the same spiritual drink from the spiritual rock Christ who accompanied them.*1Co 10:3-4* We know about our Lord Jesus Christ's coming not as a cleverly devised story but from eyewitnesses to his majesty.*2Pe 1:16* God spoke to our ancestors through the prophets, but in these last days he has spoken to us by his Son, who is his heir through whom he made the universe.*Heb 1:2* Everything is garbage next to the surpassing worth of knowing Christ Jesus our Lord, for whose sake we should lose all things.*Php 3:8* The Son of God came as the true God and eternal life that we may know him and be in him who is true.*1Jn 5:20*

Son. God named Jesus Son and said he was his Father.*Heb 1:5* God's oath appointed the Son, whom God made perfect forever.*Heb 7:28* When God brought his firstborn Son into the world, he said that the angels would worship him.*Heb 1:6* To the Son God says his throne, as God, will last forever, with a scepter of justice for his kingdom.*Heb 1:8* The Son is the beginning and firstborn from among the dead, supreme in everything.*Col 1:18* As God's Son, Jesus is without father or mother or genealogy, without beginning or end.*Heb 7:1-17* Christ, as God's Son, is far superior to the angels.*Heb 1:4-5* Through the Son, God reconciles to himself all things on earth and in heaven.*Col 1:20* God said his Son loved righteousness and hated wickedness, and so had set the Son above, anointing him with the oil of joy.*Heb 1:9* God said to the Son, not the angels, to sit at his right hand until God made his enemies a footstool for his feet.*Heb 1:13* Jesus is the Son of God and our great high priest who ascended into heaven.*Heb 4:14* As to his earthly life, God's Son Jesus descended from David.*Ro 1:3* God appointed Jesus the Son of God through the Spirit of holiness.*Ro 1:4* At Jesus's baptism, God the Father gave Jesus honor and glory from heaven, saying, with the same voice from heaven that disciples heard on the sacred mountain, that Jesus is his Son whom he loves and with whom he is well pleased.*2Pe 1:17-18*

Lord. Jesus our Lord came from the order of the king of peace and righteousness.*Heb 7:1-17* God exalted Jesus to the highest place, giving him the name above every other name that every knee in heaven, on earth, and under earth should bow and every tongue acknowledge that Jesus Christ is Lord.*Php 2:9-11* Revere Christ as Lord.*1Pe 3:15* We need no longer teach one another to know the Lord because we all, from least to greatest, know him.*Heb 8:11* Jesus Christ became a stumbling stone to those who pursued righteousness by law and works but salvation to those who believed in him.*Ro 9:32-33* We must all appear before Christ's judgment seat.*2Co 5:10* God did not put angels over the world to come but the Son of Man, Jesus Christ, leaving nothing over which he will not rule, even though we do not yet see all that he will rule.*Heb 2:5-8* Learn more of the grace of our Lord and Savior Jesus Christ to whom we give glory now and forever.*2Pe 3:17-18* The Lord waits patiently to return, wanting everyone to repent rather than any to perish.*2Pe 3:9* The Lord is near.*Php 4:5* Christ must reign until all enemies are under his feet.*1Co 15:25* The last enemy Christ destroys is death.*1Co 15:26* God has put everything under Christ's feet other than God himself.*1Co 15:27* When the Son finishes, the Son will subject himself to the Father who put everything under him, so that God is everything in all.*1Co 15:28* Come, Lord.*1Co 16:22* When times reach fulfillment, God will unify everything in heaven and on earth under Christ.*Eph 1:8-10*

Priest. Jesus is the great priest over God's house.*Heb 10:21* Our high priest Jesus empathizes with our weaknesses, like us tempted in every way, but without sin.*Heb 4:15* Christ did not proclaim for himself the glory of a high priest, but God instead called him Son and said he was his Father, making Christ a priest forever.*Heb 5:5-6* God designated Jesus to be high priest in long-established order.*Heb 5:10* Jesus our Lord is an indestructible priest forever rather than from the Levitical priesthood that administered the law.*Heb 7:1-17* Our forerunner Jesus entered the inner sanctuary for us as our high priest forever from long-established order.*Heb 6:19-20* The Lord swore not to change his mind that Jesus is a priest forever.*Heb 7:20-21* Other priests die, ending their office, but Jesus lives forever in permanent priesthood.*Heb 7:23-24* Jesus thus saves completely those who come to God through him, because he lives forever interceding for them.*Heb 7:25* The high priest Jesus thus truly meets our need, as holy, blameless, pure, set apart from sinners, and exalted above the heavens.*Heb 7:26* Jesus needs no daily sacrifices for his own sins or the people's sins because he sacrificed once for all, offering himself.*Heb 7:27* We have a high priest who sat down at the right hand of the Majesty's throne in heaven, who serves in the Lord's own inner sanctuary, and not as a mere human.*Heb 8:2* Every high priest offers gifts and sacrifices, and so Jesus also offered, but not as a priest serving the law would offer.*Heb 8:3-4*

Suffering. Even though Jesus was God's Son, Jesus learned obedience from what he suffered*Heb 5:8* Once Jesus's suffering made him perfect, he became eternal salvation's source for all who obey him.*Heb 5:9* Jesus came under the sign of water baptism and to give his blood—both water and blood—the Spirit confirming that truth as God's own testimony about his own Son.*1Jn 5:6-9* Christ is our sacrificed Passover lamb.~1Co 5:6-7~ Jesus, who did nothing wrong and never lied, just took it when accusers hurled insults at him because he trusted the just God.~1Pe 2:22-23~ The mediator Christ Jesus gave himself as ransom for all.~1Ti 2:5~ Non-believers killed the Lord Jesus and the prophets, and so they may also drive you out, even though they displease God and are hostile to all while trying to keep you from saving others.~1Th 2:15-16~

Crucifixion. Rulers crucified the Lord of glory.~1Co 2:8~ Men crucified Christ in weakness, but Christ lives by God's power.~2Co 13:4~ Christ triumphed over evil powers and authorities by the cross.~Col 2:15~ Christ endured the cross for the joy before him, scorning the cross's shame, to sit down at the right hand of God's throne.~Heb 12:2~ Christ's purpose on the cross was to reconcile in him one new peaceful humanity out of the divided two sides, putting to death their hostility.~Eph 2:15-16~ God reconciles to himself all things on earth and in heaven, by making peace through the Son's blood, shed on the cross.~Col 1:20~ Our old self's crucifixion with Christ killed the sinful body, setting us free from sin and making us no longer slaves to sin.~Ro 6:6-7~ We submit to crucifixion with Christ so that we no longer live on our own, but by our faith, Christ, who loved us and gave himself for us, lives in us.~Gal 2:20~ The cross of our Lord Jesus Christ crucified the world to us and us to the world.~Gal 6:14~

Resurrection. Christ rose on the third day after burial, as the Scriptures also say.~1Co 15:3~ God raised our Lord Jesus from the dead.~Heb 13:20~ The risen Christ appeared to Peter, then the twelve disciples, then more than five hundred brothers and sisters at the same time, most of whom were still living when authors wrote about it.~1Co 15:5-6~ Christ next appeared to his brother James, then to the apostles, and last to the apostle Paul, as one abnormally born.~1Co 15:7-8~ The Spirit of God raised Jesus from the dead.~Ro 8:11~ God the Father raised Jesus Christ from the dead.~Gal 1:1~ God raised Jesus from the dead.~Ro 4:22-24~ God raised Jesus to life for our justification.~Ro 4:25~ God resurrected Jesus from the dead as Christ our Lord.~Ro 1:4~ God the Father of our Lord Jesus Christ gave us new birth through Jesus's resurrection from the dead.~1Pe 1:3~ We hope in God for raising Christ from the dead.~1Pe 1:21~ Jesus Christ's resurrection saves you because he is in heaven at God's right hand with angels.~1Pe 3:21-22~ God exerted mighty strength when he raised Christ from the dead.~Eph 1:19-21~ God raised Christ from the dead.~Col 2:12~ Wait for God's Son Jesus, whom God raised from the dead.~1Th 1:10~ Christ died and returned to life so that he might be the Lord of both the dead and the living.*Ro 14:9* By his power, God raised the Lord from the dead and will also raise us.*1Co 6:14* God has raised Christ from the dead as the first among those who have died.*1Co 15:20* We know that God who raised the Lord Jesus from the dead will also raise us with Jesus, presenting us to himself.*2Co 4:14*

Eternal. Because God raised Christ from the dead, he cannot die again, and death no longer has mastery over him.*Ro 6:9* Our Savior Christ Jesus destroyed death and brought immortality.*2Ti 1:10* Those who die with Christ will also live with him.*2Ti 2:11* Those of the earth are as the earthly man was, but those of heaven are as the heavenly man is.*1Co 15:48* Thank God for victory through our Lord Jesus Christ.*1Co 15:57* The covenant under which God raised our Lord Jesus from the dead is eternal.*Heb 13:20* We receive the promised eternal inheritance, now that Christ has died as a ransom to set us free from the sins committed under the first covenant.*Heb 9:15* Christ's one sacrifice made perfect forever, you whom God is making holy.*Heb 10:14* Wait for the mercy of our Lord Jesus Christ to bring you to eternal life.*Jude 20-21* Our Lord Jesus Christ and God our Father gave us good hope of eternity.*2Th 2:16-17* Those who believe in Christ Jesus receive eternal life.*1Ti 1:16* The elect, obtaining salvation in Christ Jesus, receive eternal glory.*2Ti 2:10* Grace brings eternal life through Jesus Christ our Lord.*Ro 5:21* God's gift is eternal life in Christ Jesus our Lord.*Ro 6:21-22* The Son's throne, as God, will last forever.*Heb 1:8* The earth and heavens will perish, wearing out like garments, but the Lord will remain.*Heb 1:11* The Lord will roll up earth and heavens like a robe, changing them like a garment, but the Lord will remain the same, for never-ending years.*Heb 1:12*

Savior. Adam, the first to sin, was a pattern of the one to come, the sinless Jesus.*Ro 5:14* After the Son provided purification for sins, he sat down at the right hand of the Majesty in heaven.*Heb 1:3* When Christ as high priest offered for all time one sacrifice for sins, he sat down at God's right hand, waiting for his enemies to be his footstool.*Heb 10:12-13* Although Christ Jesus is in very nature God in human likeness, Christ did not use equality with God to his own advantage but instead made himself nothing in the very nature of a servant, humbly obedient even to death on a cross.*Php 2:6-8* You choose, but whoever believes in the Son of God accepts God's testimony, while whoever does not believe makes God out to be a liar.*1Jn 5:10* The testimony is that God gave us eternal life in his Son and only in his Son.*1Jn 5:11-13* As you approach the living stone Jesus, whom God chose as precious but humans rejected, God is building you like living stones into a spiritual house and ministry, offering sacrifices God accepts through Jesus.*1Pe 2:4-5* The Bible says that God laid his chosen and precious cornerstone Jesus in Israel so that those who trust in him will never find shame.*1Pe 2:6* We see Jesus, whom God lowered beneath angels for a little while before crowning him with glory and honor, dying by God's grace for everyone.*Heb 2:9* You have come to Jesus, the new covenant's mediator, under the sprinkled blood that speaks a better word than Abel's blood.*Heb 12:24*

Gifts. God the Father loves us, keeping us for Jesus Christ while blessing us with abundant mercy, peace, and love.*Jude 1-2* God hides in Christ all the treasures of wisdom and knowledge.*Col 2:3* Do not lose connection with the head, Christ, from whom the whole body grows as God causes it to grow.*Col 2:19* The promise of life is in Christ Jesus.*2Ti 1:1* Remember Jesus Christ, raised from the dead, descended from David.*2Ti 2:8* Remain in view of Christ's appearing.*2Ti 4:1* For anyone in Christ, the old creation is gone and the new creation here.*2Co 5:17* God reconciled us to himself through Christ, giving us the ministry of reconciliation.*2Co 5:18* God reconciled the world to himself in Christ, not counting people's sins against them, as he commits the reconciliation message to us.*2Co 5:19* Jesus keeps safe from the evil one those born of God who thus do not continue to sin.*1Jn 5:18* We receive grace, mercy and peace from God the Father and from Jesus Christ, in truth and love.*2Jn 3* In Christ and through faith in him we approach God with freedom and confidence.*Eph 3:12* We are Christ's ambassadors, God as if appealing through us, imploring on Christ's behalf to reconcile to God.*2Co 5:20* God made Christ who had no sin to be sin for us, so that in Christ we would show God's righteousness.*2Co 5:21* Through Jesus, continually offer God a sacrifice of praise, openly professing his name.*Heb 13:15* Our Lord Jesus is the great Shepherd of the sheep.*Heb 13:20*

Return. The Lord will indeed return.*2Pe 3:9* Christ will return in just a little while and will not delay.*Heb 10:37* When the Lord comes down from heaven, with a loud command, with the voice of the archangel and with the trumpet call of God, those who died in Christ will rise first.*1Th 4:16* Then, God will catch up in the clouds together with the rising dead, the living who remain, to meet the Lord in the air to be with him forever.*1Th*

4:17 The Lord's return will not surprise believers, who know the truth.*1Th 5:4* God will reveal the Lord Jesus from heaven in blazing fire with his powerful angels.*2Th 1:7* We indeed look forward to the Lord's promised righteous new heaven and new earth after Christ's return.*2Pe 3:13* Christ's second appearance will not be to bear sin but to bring salvation to those awaiting him.*Heb 9:27-28* When Christ returns, dear children of God, we do not yet know what we will be, but we know we will be like him, seeing him as he is.*1Jn 3:2* We know that God who began a good work in us will continue until the day Christ Jesus returns.*Php 1:6* When Christ appears, you will appear with him in glory.*Col 3:4* Be blameless and holy in the presence of our God and Father when our Lord Jesus returns with all his holy ones.*1Th 3:13* The Lord Jesus in the splendor of his return will overthrow and destroy the lawless one.*2Th 2:7-8* Christ comes first, then when he comes, those who belong to him.*1Co 15:23*

Spirit

The letters celebrate God's Holy Spirit as the intimate presence of God, leading his children to salvation and eternal life in the Son of God, Jesus Christ. While the Spirit is ours as God's guarantee of eternal life to come, the Spirit also brings us abundant present gifts in the loving, discerning, and sanctifying character of Christ. See how the letters articulate the Spirit's nature, presence, benefits, and role. Do you know the Spirit with the intimacy that he desires?

God. God poured his love into our hearts through the Holy Spirit, whom he gave to us.*Ro 5:5* If God's Spirit lives in you, then you pursue the Spirit rather than the flesh. If the Spirit of God who raised Jesus from the dead lives in you, then God who raised Christ from the dead will also give your body life because of his Spirit who lives in you.*Ro 8:11* Those whom the Spirit of God leads are the children of God.*Ro 8:14* The Spirit does not make you fearful slaves but makes you a child of God who can cry to your Father.*Ro 8:15* When you believed, God marked you in him with the seal of the promised Holy Spirit, who guarantees our inheritance until God redeems those whom he possesses.*Eph 1:13-14* God gives you his Holy Spirit with instruction.*1Th 4:8* God revealed to us by his Spirit things that he prepared for those who love him, that no eye had seen, ear heard, or mind conceived.*1Co 2:9-10* The Spirit searches everything, even God's deep things.*1Co 2:10* No one knows God's thoughts except God's Spirit, just as only one's own spirit knows one's own thoughts.*1Co 2:11* We received God's Spirit, not the world's spirit, so that we can understand what God freely gave us.*1Co 2:12* Do not grieve the Holy Spirit of God.*Eph 4:30* God makes us ministers of the Spirit's new covenant through which the Spirit gives life.*2Co 3:6* God gave us the Spirit as a deposit to guarantee life to come.*2Co 5:5*

Christ. God has given us his Spirit, through whom we see and testify that the Father sent his Son as the world's Savior.~1Jn 4:13-14~ Anyone without the Spirit of Christ does not belong to Christ.~Ro 8:9~ If Christ is in you, then even though your body dies because of sin, the Spirit gives life because of righteousness.~Ro 8:10~ If the Spirit of God who raised Jesus from the dead lives in you, then God who raised Christ from the dead will also give your body life because of his Spirit who lives in you.~Ro 8:11~ The Spirit testifies with our spirit that we are God's children who, if we suffer with Christ, inherit Christ's glory with him.~Ro 8:16-17~ God who searches our hearts knows the Spirit's mind as the Spirit intercedes for God's people in God's will.~Ro 8:27~ Know the Spirit's gifts.~1Co 12:1~ No one who speaks by God's Spirit can curse Jesus, just as no one claims Jesus as Lord other than by the Holy Spirit.~1Co 12:3~ God saved us through rebirth's washing and renewal by the Holy Spirit, whom he poured out on us generously through Jesus Christ our Savior.~Tit 5:6~ The Spirit vindicated Christ.~1Ti 3:16~ The Lord is the Spirit, and with the Lord's Spirit comes freedom.~2Co 3:17~ The Lord's glory comes from the Lord who is the Spirit.~2Co 3:18~

Gifts. The same Spirit distributes different gifts.~1Co 12:4~ God gives to each one the Spirit's manifestation for the common good.~1Co 12:7~ To one God gives wisdom through the Spirit, to another knowledge by the same Spirit, to another faith by the same Spirit, to another gifts of healing by that one Spirit, to others miraculous powers, prophecy, distinguishing between spirits, speaking in different tongues, or interpretation of tongues.~1Co 12:8-10~ The same Spirit distributes each gift to each one, just as he determines.~1Co 12:11~ The Spirit helps us in our weakness, interceding for us with groans when we don't know for what we should pray.~Ro 8:26~ The Spirit's fruit is love, joy, peace, patience, kindness, goodness, faithfulness, gentleness, and self-control, none of which law prohibits.~Gal 5:22-23~ We live by the Spirit, keeping in step with the Spirit.~Gal 5:25~ The Spirit does not leave us timid but gives us power, love, and self-discipline.~2Ti 1:7~ The Holy Spirit lives in you, helping you hold to sound teaching.~2Ti 1:13-14~ May you overflow with hope by the Holy Spirit's power.~Ro 15:13~ Do not quench the Spirit.~1Th 5:19~ Let the Spirit fill you so that you speak to one another with psalms, hymns, and songs from the Spirit.~Eph 5:18-19~ We love in the Spirit.~Col 1:8~

Sanctification. The Spirit's sanctifying work saves believers.~2Th 2:13~ The Holy Spirit sanctifies hearers of the proclaimed gospel.~Ro 15:16~ The name of our Lord Jesus Christ and Spirit of our God washed, sanctified, and justified you.~1Co 6:11~ Your body is a temple of the Holy Spirit, who is in you and whom you received from God.~1Co 6:19~ The Spirit's ministry bringing righteousness is far more glorious than the ministry that brought condemnation.~2Co 3:8-9~ The Holy Spirit says that if you hear his voice, then do not harden your hearts in rebellion.~Heb 3:7-8~ The Holy Spirit testifies that God put his laws in our hearts and minds, and no longer remembers our sins and lawless acts.~Heb 10:16~ True godliness springs from the great mystery that Christ received the Spirit's vindication and ascended in glory.~1Ti 3:16~ Conduct yourselves appropriately in purity, understanding, patience, and kindness, in the Holy Spirit.~2Co 6:6-7~ God's kingdom is not about eating and drinking but righteousness, peace, and joy in the Holy Spirit.~Ro 14:17~

Wisdom. When leading others to obey God, you act through the Spirit of God's power.~Ro 15:18-19~ The message we speak is not human wisdom but as the Spirit taught us, explaining spiritual realities with Spirit-taught words.~1Co 2:13~ The person without the Spirit rejects things from God's Spirit, considering them foolishness because one discerns them only through the Spirit.~1Co 2:14~ The person with the Spirit judges all things with Christ's mind, while not subject to merely human judgments because no one knows the Lord's mind to instruct.~1Co 2:15-16~ We pray for the wisdom and understanding that the Spirit gives.~Col 1:9~ The Spirit clearly warns against abandoning the faith.~1Ti 4:1~ We serve in the Spirit's new way rather than the written code's old way.~Ro 7:6~ The Holy Spirit shares with us from heaven, matters into which even angels long to look.~1Pe 1:12~ The gospel came not simply with words but also the Holy Spirit and deep conviction.~1Th 1:5~ You are a letter from Christ, the result of another's ministry, written not with ink but with the Spirit of the living God, not on stone tablets but on tablets of human hearts.~2Co 3:3~

Light

The letters recognize God as both light and life, set against and overcoming opposing death in darkness. Jesus is the true light, bringing life and immortality. Through Christ, we join in God's life, invited into his glorious kingdom of light. Night is nearly over and day nearly here. See how the letters celebrate God's pure light and holy life. Has your spirit embraced God's light and life?

God. God is the blessed, honored, mighty, eternal, and only Ruler, the King of kings and Lord of lords, who alone is immortal, living in unapproachable light, whom no one has seen or can see.*1Ti 6:15-16* Witnesses who heard, saw, and touched God's Son, who existed from the start and is the eternal Word of Life, joyfully proclaim their experience so that we can share with them the Father and his Son Jesus Christ.*1Jn 1:1-4* The message that they share is that God is pure light without any darkness.*1Jn 1:5* The message is both an old one from the beginning and a new one, with darkness passing, that we see and shine truth in Jesus Christ, the true light who already shines.*1Jn 2:7-8* Christ Jesus brought life and immortality to light.*2Ti 1:10* Everything light exposes becomes visible, and everything illuminated becomes a light.*Eph 5:13* Light and darkness have nothing in common.*2Co 6:14*

You. God chose you out of nowhere to be royal and holy, his special possession, calling you out of darkness into his wonderful light.*1Pe 2:9-10* When God said to let light shine out of darkness, he shined his light into our hearts, lighting our knowledge of God's glory in Christ's face.*2Co 4:6* The book of life has the names of those who contend in the gospel's cause.*Php 4:3* You who were once darkness are now light in the Lord and so should live as children of light in all goodness, righteousness, and truth, pleasing the Lord.*Eph 5:8-10* Shine in a corrupt world like stars in the sky as you hold firmly to the word of life.*Php 2:15-16* You who claim light remain in darkness if you hate a fellow follower, and will stumble around in your darkness, while you who love followers are in the light and will not stumble.*1Jn 2:9-11* Wake up, rising from the dead so that Christ shines on you.*Eph 5:14* Christ is your life with whom you will appear in glory.*Col 3:4* The night is nearly over and day almost here, so time to put aside dark deeds to put on light's armor.*Ro 13:12* We are all children of the light and children of the day, not belonging to the night or darkness.*1Th 5:5* We belong to the day.*1Th 3:8* Give joyful thanks to the Father, who has qualified you to share with his holy people in the kingdom of light.*Col 1:12*

Creation

The letters confirm God as the universe's creator. The letters reveal, though, that God first chose Christ and only then created everything in heaven and on earth. Indeed, God created through Christ and for Christ. The letters confirm that we, too, are God's creation, in his image. Yet God's creation groans for its restoration, just as we groan, eagerly waiting God to restore. See how magnificently the letters treat God's creation. Do you esteem creation and Creator as the letters recommend?

God. God calls into being things that were not._{Ro 4:17} Everything God created is good, not to reject but to receive with thanksgiving._{1Ti 4:4} God finished his works when creating the world._{Heb 4:3} God rested from all his works on the seventh day of creation._{Heb 4:4} Creation eagerly waits for God to reveal his children._{Ro 8:19} God delays so he can liberate creation from its decay, bringing it into the freedom and glory of God's children._{Ro 8:21} Creation groans as in childbirth just as we who have the Spirit's first fruits groan as we wait eagerly for God to adopt us as his children and redeem our bodies._{Ro 8:22-23} God has the right to create both the special and common._{Ro 9:21}

Christ. God chose Christ before creating the world and revealed him only recently for your sake._{1Pe 1:20} In the Son, God created everything in heaven and on earth, visible and invisible, rulers and authorities, through the Son and for him._{Col 1:16} The Lord laid the earth's foundations, and the heavens are his hands' work._{Heb 1:10} The Son is before everything, holding everything together._{Col 1:17} The Son is the invisible God's image, the firstborn over all creation._{Col 1:15} The Son radiates God's glory, exactly representing his being, while sustaining all things by his powerful word._{Heb 1:3} Christ is the Deity's fullness living in bodily form.*Col 2:9* God's oath appointed the Son, whom God made perfect forever.*Heb 7:28* When God brought his firstborn Son into the world, he said that the angels would worship him.*Heb 1:6* The Son is the beginning and firstborn from among the dead, supreme in everything.*Col 1:18* As God's Son, Jesus is without father or mother or genealogy, without beginning or end.*Heb 7:1-17* God made Christ who had no sin to be sin for us.*2Co 5:21* God made the first man out of the earth's dust but makes the second man of heaven.*1Co 15:47*

You. The Father made us his creation's first fruits.*Jas 1:18* Even though we praise our Lord and Father, we somehow turn right around and immediately curse others whom God made in his likeness.*Jas 3:9-12* Don't you, a mere person, talk back to your creator God who, though all-powerful, still leaves you to your own will.*Ro 9:19-20* You have put on the new self that God renews in knowledge in his image as Creator.*Col 3:10* Since the world's creation, we have seen and understood God's invisible qualities including his eternal power and divine nature from what he made, so that people are without excuse.*Ro 1:20* God, to whom we must give account, sees everything in all creation, uncovered and laid bare before him.*Heb 4:13*

Gospel

The letters reflect the gospel message throughout but also treat of it specifically in certain verses and passages. The letters show that the good news first requires God as Savior. God must then sacrifice his glorious Son to open our path back to him. We, though, accept God's salvation only by professing our faith. When we do accept salvation, we not only share in Christ's glory and receive other priceless benefits, but we should also yearn to joyously share the precious gospel message. See how the letters treat the gospel message of a Savior God whose own sacrifice offers salvation. Have you fully embraced the inestimable gospel message?

Savior. God, our kind and loving Savior, mercifully appeared to save us.*Tit 3:3-5* God kept the gospel's mystery, the glorious riches of Christ in you, hidden for ages and generations before disclosing it to the Lord's people.*Col 1:26-27* The gospel is not of human origin but Christ's revelation.*Gal 1:11-12* God promised the gospel in the Holy Scriptures beforehand through his prophets.*Ro 1:2* The prophets learned that their prophesying was to serve us in receiving the gospel that the Holy Spirit shares with us from heaven, into which even angels long to look.*1Pe 1:12* Salvation is through our Lord Jesus Christ.*1Th 3:9* Do not sin, but if you do, then know that Jesus Christ, the Righteous One, is not only your advocate with the Father but also the atoning sacrifice for the whole world's sins.*1Jn 2:1-2* The living God is the Savior of all people, especially those who believe.*1Ti 4:10* God revealed the gospel so that all might obey through faith.*Ro 16:26* God favors us now and saves us now.*2Co 6:2*

Sacrifice. Christ died for us when we were powerless sinners, demonstrating his extraordinary love for us because no one dies for sinners, even if one might die for the good.~Ro 5:6-8~ Christ justified us by his blood, saving us from God's wrath through him.~Ro 5:9~ Jesus bore our sins on the cross, so that we who were going astray would die to sin, live for righteousness, and return to him, his wounds healing us.~1Pe 2:24-25~ The death of God's Son reconciled us to God while we were still God's enemies, just as Christ now saves us through his life.~Ro 5:10~ We boast in God through our Lord Jesus Christ, having this reconciliation.~Ro 5:11~ Christ culminates the law so that everyone who believes has God's righteousness.~Ro 10:4~ We have one mediator between God and us, the man Christ Jesus, who gave himself as ransom for all.~1Ti 2:5~ Suffering is for the gospel, by the power of God.~2Ti 1:8~ Christ Jesus destroyed death and brought life and immortality through the gospel.~2Ti 1:10~

Salvation. For salvation, you need only declare "Jesus is Lord" and believe that God raised him from the dead.~Ro 10:9~ Your believing heart justifies you, while your professing mouth saves you, just as Scripture says.~Ro 10:10-11~ The gospel has been growing and bearing fruit throughout the world and among you since you first learned it from faithful ministers of Christ.~Col 1:6-7~ God our Savior wants all people saved and to know the truth.~1Ti 2:3-4~ Rely on and fully accept that Christ Jesus came into the world to save sinners, of whom we may be the worst.~1Ti 1:15~ Sinners break the law and are lawless, but the sinless Christ came to take away our sins in that anyone living in him stops sinning.~1Jn 3:4-6~ In forgiving our sins, God canceled the indebtedness that stood against and condemned us.~Col 2:14~ When we walk in the light the way Jesus is in the light, his blood purifies us from sin.~1Jn 1:7~ Anyone who acknowledges Jesus as God's Son lives in God and God in them.~1Jn 4:15~ Remember the gospel preached to you, which you received and on which you stand.~1Co 15:1~ This gospel saved you, if you hold firmly to the preached word, but otherwise, you will have believed in vain.~1Co 15:2~

Sharing. We are servants of the gospel.~Col 1:23~ Delight to share God's gospel.~1Th 2:7-8~ Speak to non-believers so that they may be saved.~1Th 2:16~ Be co-workers in God's service of spreading Christ's gospel.~1Th 3:2~ We know that we live in him and he in us because he has given us his Spirit, through whom we see and testify that the Father sent his Son as the world's Savior.~1Jn 4:13-14~ God calls and sets apart leaders for his gospel.~Ro 1:1~ Have no shame over the gospel because its power of God brings salvation to everyone who believes.~Ro 1:16~ Fully proclaim

Christ's gospel.~Ro 15:19~ Make your ambition to preach Christ's gospel where not known, so that you do not build on someone else's foundation, and those whom no one told about Christ may see, hear, and understand.~Ro 15:20-21~ The gospel is the message we proclaim about Jesus Christ, in keeping with the revelation of the mystery hidden for long ages past but revealed in the prophetic writings by the eternal God's command.~Ro 16:25-26~ Pass on the most-important gospel message that you receive, that Christ died for our sins as the Scriptures say, but then, after burial, he rose on the third day as the Scriptures also said.~1Co 15:3~ The priestly duty is to proclaim God's gospel so that non-believers may become offerings God accepts, sanctified by the Holy Spirit.~Ro 15:16~

Benefits. When we are like Jesus, God makes love complete among us so that we may pass his judgment.~1Jn 4:17~ Love drives out fear of God's punishment.~1Jn 4:18~ You love and believe in Jesus without even seeing him, your faith rewarding you with salvation.~1Pe 1:8-9~ You who once were far away have been brought near by the blood of Christ.~Eph 2:13~ God brings us to fullness in Christ.~Col 2:10~ The gospel reveal's God's righteousness, which we live out by faith.~Ro 1:17~ The gospel declares that God judges people's secrets through Jesus Christ.~Ro 2:16~ The gospel came not simply with words but also power, the Holy Spirit, and deep conviction.~1Th 1:5~ The hope of salvation is our helmet.~1Th 3:8~ Jesus gave himself for our sins to rescue us from how evil things are these days, just as God our Father asked of him.~Gal 1:4~ When Jesus returns, God will punish with permanent destruction those who do not obey the Lord Jesus's gospel.~2Th 1:8-10~ The gospel calls us to share in our Lord Jesus Christ's glory.~2Th 2:14~ The gospel concerns the blessed God's glory.~1Ti 1:11~

Word

The letters exalt God's word as a living and active revelation of his mysteries, on which we should entirely rely. The letters also credit God's holy Scriptures for foretelling and recording Christ's coming, and then reporting and promoting the gospel message. What veneration God's people hold for God's Holy Word! See how the letters reflect that veneration. Are you accepting God's word as the letters present it?

God. God's word does not fail.*Ro 9:6* God's word brings to us mysteries God shared by revelation.*Eph 3:3* God's word lives actively, like a sharp blade penetrating to divide soul from spirit, joints from marrow, judging the heart's thoughts and attitudes.*Heb 4:12* The Father gave us spiritual birth through the word of truth.*Jas 1:17-18* Carry the Spirit's sword, which is the word of God.*Eph 6:17* Accept God's word from one another not as a human word but as it is, the word of God, which works in you who believe.*1Th 2:13* Receive anything consecrated by the word of God.*1Ti 4:5* God breathed all Scripture for teaching, rebuking, correcting, and training in righteousness.*2Ti 3:16-17* The law is still the very words of God.*Ro 2:2* Everything in the Scriptures is to teach us, so that we draw hope from the endurance the Scriptures depict and encouragement they provide.*Ro 15:4* As written, in faith's same spirit, we believe and so speak.*2Co 4:13* God's word did not originate with you, and you are not the only people it has reached.*1Co 14:36*

Christ. In reading God's word, we gain insight into the mystery of Christ that God had disclosed to people in prior generations, as his Spirit revealed it through holy apostles and prophets.*Eph 3:4-5* Christ said that he had come to do God's will, just as the Scriptures wrote about him.*Heb 10:7* Faith comes from hearing the word about Christ.*Ro 10:17* The word about

Christ reaches everyone to the ends of the world.*Ro 10:18* While someone might chain a gospel witness, no one chains God's word.*2Ti 2:9* The Holy Scriptures are the source for what makes us wise for salvation through faith in Christ Jesus.*2Ti 3:14-15* The Scriptures say that Christ died for our sins, just as the Scriptures said that after burial Christ would rise on the third day.*1Co 15:3* If you think the Spirit has gifted you, then acknowledge the Lord's command because if you ignore the command, then others will ignore you.*1Co 14:37-38* Everything written for you, you should be able to read and understand.*2Co 1:13* You are a letter from Christ, the result of another's ministry, written not with ink but with the Spirit of the living God, not on stone tablets but on tablets of human hearts.*2Co 3:3*

Crucifixion

The letters address directly the historical fact of Christ's crucifixion, authorities nailing the Lord of Glory to a rude cross. Yet the letters also confirm the crucifixion's profound import: Christ's sacrifice meant our atonement, escape to God from the slavery of our sins. The letters also state directly some of the crucifixion's glorious results. See how the letters represent the crucifixion. Do you know the love Christ's crucifixion expressed?

Cross. Rulers crucified the Lord of glory._{1Co 2:8} Men crucified Christ in weakness, but Christ lives by God's power._{2Co 13:4} God nailed our indebtedness to the cross._{Col 2:14} Christ triumphed over evil powers and authorities by the cross._{Col 2:15} Many live as enemies of Christ's cross._{Php 3:18} The cross of our Lord Jesus Christ crucified the world to us and us to the world._{Gal 6:14} Christ's purpose on the cross was to reconcile in him one new peaceful humanity out of the divided two sides, putting to death their hostility._{Eph 2:15-16} The cross's message is foolishness to those who perish because God destroys the wise's wisdom and frustrates the intelligent's intelligence, but the cross is God's power to us whom God saves._{1Co 1:18-19} Don't be foolish, letting others bewitch you into abandoning the crucifixion's truth._{Gal 3:1} Those who fall away from God's heavenly gift mean to crucify God's Son all over again, subjecting him again to public disgrace._{Heb 6:6} Do not follow other teachers whom no one crucified, when Christ himself is not so divided._{1Co 1:11-15} We who belong to Christ Jesus have crucified the flesh's passions and desires._{Gal 5:24}

Meaning. God presented Christ as a sacrifice of atonement, through the shedding of his blood._{Ro 2:25-26} God delivered Jesus over to death for our sins._Ro 4:25_ Christ's love convinces us that he died for all and thus all died with him._2Co 5:14_ Christ is our sacrificed Passover lamb._1Co 5:6-7_ We submit to crucifixion with Christ so that we no longer live on our own, but by our faith, Christ, who loved us and gave himself for us, lives in us._Gal 2:20_ Wise and eloquent preaching must not empty Christ's cross of its power._1Co 1:17_ The thanksgiving cup for which we give thanks participates in Christ's blood, while the bread we break participates in Christ's body, just as eating the sacrifices participates in the altar._1Co 10:16,18_ God reconciles us by Christ's physical body, through death, to present you holy, without blemish, and free from accusation, in his sight._Col 1:22_ Christ redeems us through his blood, the forgiveness of sins, as God lavished his grace's riches on us._Eph 1:7-8_ The perfect lamb Christ's precious blood, not perishable things like precious metals, redeemed you from the empty life your family handed down to you._1Pe 1:18-19_ Jesus shared in our humanity because we are human, so that by his death he would break the devil's power of death._Heb 2:14_ Christ redeemed us from law's curse when crucifixion cursed Christ who died for us._Gal 3:13_ Proclaim God's testimony not with eloquence or human wisdom but instead knowing only Jesus Christ crucified, and that in weakness with great fear and trembling._1Co 2:1-3_ Jews demand signs and Greeks look for wisdom, but we preach Christ crucified, a stumbling block to Jews and foolishness to other non-believers but God's power and wisdom to those whom God called._1Co 1:22-24_

Result. God reconciles to himself all things on earth and in heaven, by making peace through the Son's blood, shed on the cross._Col 1:20_ Christ endured the cross for the joy before him, scorning the cross's shame, to sit down at the right hand of God's throne._Heb 12:2_ Christ entered the Most Holy Place not by animal blood but once for all by his own blood, for eternal redemption._Heb 9:12_ When God did not spare his own Son but gave him up for us, he showed that he graciously gives us everything._Ro 8:32_ Our old self's crucifixion with him killed the sinful body, setting us free from sin and making us no longer slaves to sin._Ro 6:6-7_ You died, and your life now hides with Christ in God._Col 3:3_ Christ died for all, so that we should no longer live for ourselves but for him who died for us and rose again._2Co 5:15_ Jesus suffered outside the city gate to make the people holy through his own blood._Heb 13:12_ Go to Jesus outside the camp, bearing the disgrace he bore, because we have no enduring city here, instead looking for the city to come._Heb 13:14_ Christ's one sacrifice made perfect forever those whom God is making holy.*Heb 10:14* Be confident entering the Most Holy Place by Jesus's blood, the new and living way he opened for us through the curtain, that is, his body.*Heb 10:19-20* Jesus frees those held in slavery by their fear of death.*Heb 2:15*

Resurrection

Christ's story surely did not end with crucifixion. The letters depict the cross as only a momentary waystation, testifying at length instead to the resurrection's following power. Christ rose from the dead, conquering death and bringing eternal life not only for himself but for those who believe. The letters assure us that God supplies each of us a resurrected body to enjoy in heaven. See how powerfully the letters depict the resurrection. Are you fully anticipating your own resurrection, in great joy as you should?

Risen. While Christ died for our sins as the Scriptures say, he rose on the third day after burial, as the Scriptures also say._{1Co 15:3} The God of peace, through the blood of the eternal covenant, raised from the dead our Lord Jesus, the great Shepherd of the sheep._{Heb 13:20} The risen Christ appeared to Peter, then the twelve disciples, then more than five hundred brothers and sisters at the same time, most of whom were still living when authors wrote about it._{1Co 15:5-6} Christ next appeared to his brother James, then to the apostles, and last to the apostle Paul, as one abnormally born._{1Co 15:7-8} God the Father raised Jesus Christ from the dead._{Gal 1:1} God raised Jesus from the dead._{Ro 4:22-24} God appointed Jesus the Son of God through the Spirit of holiness and resurrected him from the dead as Jesus Christ our Lord._{Ro 1:4} God raised Christ from the dead._{Col 2:12} Without resurrection, Christ is still in the grave._{1Co 15:13} And if Christ never rose, then preaching and faith are useless, and we witness falsely about God._{1Co 15:14-15} If no one rises, then Christ hasn't either, your faith is futile, you remain sinful, and those already dead are lost._{1Co 15:16-18} If only for this life we hope in Christ, pity us the most._{1Co 15:19} But God has raised Christ from the dead as the first among those who have died._{1Co 15:20}

Life. God gives life to the dead.*Ro 4:17* Because God raised Christ from the dead, he cannot die again, and death no longer has mastery over him.*Ro 6:9* Christ died once for all and so lives to God.*Ro 6:10* The Lord Jesus died for us so that, whether we are alive or dead, we may live together with him.*1Th 3:10* Those who die with Christ will also live with him.*2Ti 2:11* Christ died and returned to life so that he might be the Lord of both the dead and the living.*Ro 14:9* Our Savior Christ Jesus destroyed death and brought immortality.*2Ti 1:10*

Meaning. God delivered Jesus over to death for our sins and raised him to life for our justification.*Ro 4:25* Desire to know the power of Christ's resurrection and participation in his sufferings, becoming like him in his death and so attaining to resurrection from death.*Php 3:10-11* We should thank God the Father of our Lord Jesus Christ for his great mercy, giving us new birth into living hope through Jesus's resurrection from the dead.*1Pe 1:3* Through Christ you believe in God and place your hope in God, for raising Christ from the dead and glorifying him.*1Pe 1:21* Jesus Christ's resurrection saves you because he is in heaven at God's right hand with angels, authorities, and powers submitting to him.*1Pe 3:21-22* We neither live nor die for ourselves alone but live and die for the Lord, either way belonging to the Lord.*Ro 14:7-8* Because death came through a man, resurrection also comes through a man.*1Co 15:21* In Adam all died so that in Christ all could live.*1Co 15:22* Without resurrection, baptism means nothing.*1Co 15:29* Without resurrection, we may as well not endanger ourselves every hour.*1Co 15:30* Without resurrection, one may as well give up fighting for Christ and instead just eat and drink today, to die tomorrow.*1Co 15:32*

You. Because the glory of the Father raised Jesus Christ from the dead, you also live a new life.*Ro 6:3-4* God made you alive in Christ when you were dead in your sins.*Col 2:13* God raised you with Christ.*Col 3:1* Because you joined him in a death like his, you will certainly also join with him in a resurrection like his.*Ro 6:5* Because you died with Christ, you believe that you will also live with him.*Ro 6:8* If Christ is in you, then even though your body dies because of sin, the Spirit gives life because of righteousness.*Ro 8:10* If the Spirit of God who raised Jesus from the dead lives in you, then God who raised Christ from the dead will also give your body life because of his Spirit who lives in you.*Ro 8:11* You died to the law so that you could belong to Christ raised from the dead, bearing fruit for God.*Ro 7:4*

Body. Don't worry foolishly about how resurrection happens.*1Co 15:35-36* The plant must die to sow the seed that comes to life.*1Co 15:36* Sowing is not planting what will be but instead planting only the seed of what will be.*1Co 15:37* God gives the seed a body as he determines, giving each seed its own body.*1Co 15:38* Not all flesh is alike, because people have one kind of flesh, animals another, birds another, and fish another.*1Co 15:39* Heavenly bodies differ in splendor than earthly bodies.*1Co 15:40* The sun has one kind of splendor, the moon another, and the stars another, while star differs from star in splendor.*1Co 15:41* Resurrection is the same way, the body sown perishable but raised imperishable.*1Co 15:42* God sows the body in dishonor but raises it in glory, sows it in weakness but raises it in power.*1Co 15:43* God sows a natural body but raises a spiritual body because to have a natural body is to anticipate a spiritual body.*1Co 15:44*

Result. God's power for believers is the same as the mighty strength he exerted when he raised Christ from the dead and seated him at his right hand in the heavenly realms, over all rule, authority, power, and dominion, and every name not only now but in the future.*Eph 1:19-21* The resurrection of the dead has not yet taken place.*2Ti 2:18* We have yet to obtain resurrection through faith, which is our goal, but we press on to that goal for which Christ Jesus embraced us.*Php 3:12-13* Our Savior the Lord Jesus Christ will by his complete power transform our lowly bodies to be like his glorious body.*Php 3:20-21* Wait for God's Son Jesus, whom God raised from the dead.*1Th 1:10* By his power God raised the Lord from the dead and will also raise us.*1Co 6:14* We know that God who raised the Lord Jesus from the dead will also raise us with Jesus, presenting us to himself.*2Co 4:14* To live is Christ even though in dying we gain.*Php 1:20-21* Whether to live or die tears us because living means fruitful labor while departing means to be with Christ, which is far better.*Php 1:22-23*

Heaven. The Scriptures say that the first man Adam lived, and so Christ, the last Adam, brings a living spirit.*1Co 15:45* The spiritual follows the natural.*1Co 15:46* God made the first man out of the earth's dust but makes the second man of heaven.*1Co 15:47* Those of the earth are as the earthly man was, but those of heaven are as the heavenly man is.*1Co 15:48* We begin as the earthly man's image but end bearing the heavenly man's image.*1Co 15:49* The mystery is that we will not all die, but we will all be changed._1Co 15:51_ Our change will be in a flash, the twinkling of an eye, when the last trumpet sounds for God to raise the dead imperishable._1Co 15:52_ The perishable must clothe itself with the imperishable, the mortal with immortality._1Co 15:53_ When the perishable puts on the imperishable, and the mortal immortality, then the Scriptures' saying that victory swallowed up death will be true._1Co 15:54_ Death has no victory or sting when death's sting is sin and sin's power is the law._1Co 15:55-56_ Thank God for victory through our Lord Jesus Christ._1Co 15:57_ Just stand firm, nothing moving you, while always giving yourselves fully to the Lord's work, because you know that your labor in the Lord is not in vain._1Co 15:58_

Kingdom

While Jesus spoke often and at length about God's kingdom, the letters attend briefly to Jesus's kingdom message. God shares his kingdom with those who may be poor in material things but are rich in faith and love. See how the letters depict God's kingdom. Are you living kingdom life?

Invitation. God calls you into his kingdom.*1Th 2:12* God will count you worthy of his kingdom for which you suffer.*2Th 1:5* The Lord will bring us safely to his heavenly kingdom.*2Ti 4:18* Remain in view of God's kingdom.*2Ti 4:1* You receive God's kingdom that does not shake.*Heb 12:28-29* The Father shares his kingdom of light.*Col 1:12* God brings us into the kingdom of the Son whom he loves.*Col 1:13* Our Lord and Savior Jesus Christ offers us a rich welcome into his eternal kingdom.*2Pe 1:10-11* The kingdom we seek to inherit is of Christ and God.*Eph 5:5* The poor who are rich in faith and love God inherit his promised kingdom.*Jas 2:5* The pure inherit the kingdom of Christ and God.*Eph 5:5* God's kingdom is not about eating and drinking but about righteousness, peace, and joy in the Holy Spirit.*Ro 14:17* God's kingdom is not a matter of talk but of power.*1Co 4:20* Only free children, not slave children, share our inheritance from God.*Gal 4:30-31*

Worthy. Those who sin do not inherit God's kingdom.*Gal 5:19-21* Wrongdoers, the sexually immoral, idolaters, adulterers, men who have sex with men, thieves, the greedy, drunkards, slanderers, and swindlers do not inherit God's kingdom.*1Co 6:9-10* Idolaters do not inherit the kingdom of Christ and God.*Eph 5:5* Flesh and blood do not inherit God's kingdom, just as the perishable does not inherit the imperishable.*1Co 15:50* The Son has a scepter of justice for his kingdom.*Heb 1:8* Do your best to confirm your calling and election so that you receive a rich welcome into our Lord and Savior Jesus Christ's eternal kingdom.*2Pe 1:10-11* Welcome and comfort co-workers for God's kingdom when they visit.*Col 4:10-11* Thank God that you receive his kingdom.*Heb 12:28-29* Give joyful thanks to the Father for sharing in the kingdom of light.*Col 1:12*

Confession

The letters briefly treat one's confession, just as they note Christ Jesus's own good confession. Other sections on faith, repentance, and teaching show more of how the letters emphasize confession's role in the gospel message. See here what the letters say about confession, profession, and testimony. Have you confirmed your confession?

Christ Jesus while testifying before Pontius Pilate made the good confession.*1Ti 6:13* God called you to eternal life when you confessed before many witnesses.*1Ti 6:12* Do not be ashamed of the testimony about our Lord or of fellow believers.*2Ti 1:8* Those who confess the Lord's name must turn away from wickedness."*2Ti 2:19* Confess your sins to each other.*Jas 5:16-18* Do not show contempt for the riches of God's kindness, forbearance and patience, because he intends his kindness to lead you to repentance.*Ro 2:4* We enter God's rest by believing.*Heb 4:3* The gifts by which you prove yourself lead others to praise God for your obedience in confessing Christ's gospel and generosity in sharing with them and everyone else.*2Co 9:13* Your believing heart justifies you, while your professing mouth saves you, just as Scripture says.*Ro 10:10-11* Through Jesus, continually offer God a sacrifice of praise, openly professing his name.*Heb 13:15* Hold unswervingly to the hope you profess, for God is faithful.*Heb 10:23* God has given us his Spirit, through whom we see and testify that the Father sent his Son as the world's Savior.*1Jn 4:13-14* Celebrate when followers testify about one another's faithfulness to the truth.*3Jn 3-4* Proclaim God's testimony not with eloquence or human wisdom but instead knowing only Jesus Christ crucified, and that in weakness with great fear and trembling.*1Co 2:1-3* Be bold for having hope.*2Co 3:12* We believe and so speak.*2Co 4:13* God prepares a city for those in whom he has no shame when others call him their God.*Heb 11:16*

We don't want non-believers to shame us but instead to have enough courage to always exalt Christ whether in living or dying.*Php 1:20*

Faith

The letters treat the topic of faith more extensively than nearly any other topic, confirming its central role in the gospel message. The letters define faith, give many faith examples, list faith heroes, and especially address the faith of Moses and of Abraham, whom we know as the father of faith. Yet the letters also emphasize Christ's faith on which we ultimately rely. We should pursue faith in the company of fellow believers, against all opposition, but our faith is not in our strength, rather the victory of Jesus Christ. See how richly the letters treat the topic of faith. Where do you stand in your faith?

Defined. Faith is to confidently hope for what you do not see, to the point of assurance.*Heb 11:1* Our faith explains how the observed universe came out of nothing by God's command.*Heb 11:3* You cannot please God without faith because you must believe that God exists and rewards those who earnestly seek him.*Heb 11:6* God tests our heart.*1Th 2:4* God is our witness.*1Th 2:5* God who calls you is faithful.*1Th 5:24* Sincere faith promotes love.*1Ti 1:5* Your hoped-for righteousness is from faith.*Gal 5:2-5* Your good deeds should prove your faith.*Jas 2:18* The Lord is faithful to strengthen and protect you.*2Th 3:3* The Lord directs our heart into God's love and Christ's perseverance.*2Th 3:5* Let the faith's truths nourish you.*1Ti 4:6* Fan into flame the gift of God, in you through the laying on of hands.*2Ti 1:6* We live out the gospel of righteousness by faith.*Ro 1:17* To hope is not to see and have but instead to wait patiently for something we don't yet have.*Ro 8:24-25* Draw near to God with faith's full assurance.*Heb 10:22*

Heroes. The Bible's faith heroes were still living by faith when they died without receiving the promised things that they only saw and welcomed from a distance, while they accepted that earth was foreign and strange to them.*Heb 11:13* The world has not been worthy of our faith heroes who wandered in deserts and mountains, living in caves and holes in the ground.*Heb 11:38* God commended all for their faith, yet none received what God promised, because God planned something better for us, so that only together with us would God make them perfect.*Heb 11:39-40*

Examples. Faith led Abel to offer God a better sacrifice than Cain offered, so that God commended Abel as righteous, Abel's life still speaking to us even though he is dead.*Heb 11:4* Enoch's faith pleased God so much that God took him away before death.*Heb 11:5* God commended the ancients for this faith.*Heb 11:2* Noah's faith led him to build an ark to save his family when warned about the coming flood, condemning the world and inheriting the righteousness that comes from faith.*Heb 11:7* Isaac's faith led him to bless Jacob and Esau for their future.*Heb 11:20* Jacob's faith led him, when dying, to bless Joseph's sons and to worship leaning on his staff.*Heb 11:21* Joseph's faith, when he was dying, led him to foretell the Israelites' exodus from Egypt and to instruct concerning the burial of his bones.*Heb 11:22* Jericho's walls fell by faith, after the army marched around them for seven days.*Heb 11:30* The prostitute Rahab's faith led her to welcome the spies, saving her life when the Israelites killed the disobedient.*Heb 11:31* Gideon, Barak, Samson, Jephthah, David, Samuel, and the prophets were other heroes whose faith conquered kingdoms, administered justice, gained the promise, shut the lions' mouths, quenched the flames, and escaped the sword, whose weakness became strength and who became powerful in battle and routed foreign armies.*Heb 11:32-34* Adopt the faith of your leaders who spoke God's word to you.*Heb 13:7*

Abraham. Abraham's faith led him to obey the call to go to the place he would later inherit, even though he had no idea where he was going.*Heb 11:8* Abraham's faith also led him to live in the promised land like a stranger in a foreign country, in tents, as did Isaac and Jacob who inherited the same promise.*Heb 11:9* Sarah's faith in the faithful God who promised, enabled her to bear children when it was too late, so that countless descendants could come from Abraham, who was also already as good as dead.*Heb 11:11-12* Abraham's faith led him to offer his only son Isaac as a sacrifice when God tested him, even though God had said that Isaac would have the reckoned offspring.*Heb 11:17-18* Abraham had faith that God could raise the dead, as in a way God brought Isaac back from death.*Heb 11:19* God justifies us through our faith and blesses us when we rely on faith, just as God justified and blessed Abraham, the man of faith, through Abraham's faith.*Gal 3:8-9* Abraham himself, our ancestor, had nothing to boast before God from his works but instead got God's credit for righteousness, because Abraham believed God.*Ro 4:1-3* Abraham and his offspring received God's promise through righteousness from faith.*Ro 4:13* Faith invokes the promise of inheritance. *Ro 4:14-15* The promise comes by faith, so that grace guarantees inheritance to all those who have faith like Abraham, who is our father in the sight of God in whom he believed.*Ro 4:16-17* Against all hope, when he was as good as dead, Abraham never wavered but instead had stronger faith, believed God's power and promise, and so became the father of many nations, just as God said.*Ro 4:18-21*

Moses. The faith of Moses' parents led them to hide Moses for three months after his birth, because they saw he was no ordinary child, and they did not fear the king's edict.*Heb 11:23* Moses's faith, when he had grown, led him to refuse to be the son of Pharaoh's daughter and instead to be mistreated along with God's people, rather than to enjoy sin's fleeting pleasures.*Heb 11:24-25* Moses regarded disgrace for Christ's sake as more valuable than Egypt's treasures because he looked ahead to his reward.*Heb 11:26* By faith Moses left Egypt, not fearing the king's anger, because he saw the invisible God.*Heb 11:27* Moses's faith led him to keep the Passover, applying blood so that the destroyer would not touch Israel's firstborn.*Heb 11:28* The people's faith led them to pass through the Red Sea as on dry land, when the Egyptians drowned.*Heb 11:29* Moses was a faithful servant in God's house, witnessing what God would say in the future.*Heb 3:5*

Christ. Jesus was faithful to God who appointed him, just as Moses was faithful in God's house.*Heb 3:2* Christ is the faithful Son over God's house, where we are God's house, if we hold firmly to our confidence and the hope in which we glory.*Heb 3:6* Our common faith as a family of believers is in grace and peace from God the Father and Christ Jesus our Savior.*Tit 1:4* If we are faithless, Christ remains faithful, for he cannot disown himself.*2Ti 2:13* Faith is for his name's sake.*Ro 1:5* Christ dwells in your heart through faith.*Eph 3:16-17* Jesus Christ establishes you in the gospel.*Ro 16:25-26* Keep living in Christ Jesus after having received him.*Col*

$_{2:6}$ Remain rooted and built up in Christ, strengthened in faith and overflowing with thankfulness.$_{Col\ 2:7}$ Faith justified us, giving us peace with God through our Lord Jesus Christ.$_{Ro\ 5:2}$ God is faithful for having called you into fellowship with his Son, Jesus Christ our Lord.$_{1Co\ 1:9}$ God makes us stand firm in Christ, having anointed us.$_{2Co\ 1:21}$ Have one husband, Christ, and be faithful to him.$_{2Co\ 11:2}$ Examine and test yourself to see if you are in the faith, confirming that Christ Jesus is in you unless you fail the test.$_{2Co\ 13:5}$ Don't fail the test.$_{2Co\ 13:6}$ Hold firmly to the faith that we have in Jesus, Son of God and great high priest who has ascended into heaven.$_{Heb\ 4:14}$ Our hope anchors our soul, firm and secure in the inner sanctuary behind the curtain our forerunner Jesus opened for us.$_{Heb\ 6:19-20}$

Pursuit. Look for a country of your own, like these faith heroes who instead of thinking of what they were leaving, longed for a better heavenly country.$_{Heb\ 11:14-16}$ Faith gave women back their dead, raised to life again.$_{Heb\ 11:35}$ Faith enabled others to endure torture, face jeers and flogging, and suffer chains and imprisonment, refusing release to gain an even better resurrection.$_{Heb\ 11:35-36}$ Faith enabled others to face death by sword, stoning, or sawing in two, and others to go about in sheepskins and goatskins, destitute, persecuted, and mistreated.$_{Heb\ 11:37}$ Look to Jesus, who pioneered and perfected our faith.$_{Heb\ 12:2}$ God's righteous live by faith.$_{Heb\ 10:38}$ We live by faith, not by sight.$_{2Co\ 5:7}$ Those with faith obey the good news proclaimed to us, while those who do not share the faith do not obey.$_{Heb\ 4:2}$ Faith comes from hearing the message through the word about Christ.$_{Ro\ 10:17}$ Hold unswervingly to the hope you profess, for God is faithful.$_{Heb\ 10:23}$ While we share salvation, we must still contend for the faith that God once for all entrusted to his holy people.$_{Jude\ 3}$ Continue in your faith, established and firm in the hope that the gospel holds out.$_{Col\ 1:23}$ Wear faith as a breastplate.$_{1Th\ 3:8}$ Persevere in faith through persecutions and trials.$_{2Th\ 1:4}$ Rest your faith not on human wisdom but on God's power.$_{1Co\ 2:5}$ Those given a trust must prove faithful.$_{1Co\ 4:2}$ In faith's same spirit, we believe and so speak.$_{2Co\ 4:13}$

Opposition. The tempter tempts you to destroy your faith.$_{1Th\ 3:5}$ Do not let loving money tempt you to wander from the faith.$_{1Ti\ 6:10}$ Wicked and evil people have no faith.$_{2Th\ 3:2}$ Faith's righteousness rejects the law's constant calculation of who gets to heaven or goes to hell, which attempts to take Christ's place.$_{Ro\ 10:6-7}$ Faith's righteousness instead says that the necessary word you need about faith is right in your mouth and heart.*Ro 10:8* Faith justifies a person apart from works of the law.*Ro 2:28* Faith does not nullify the law but instead upholds it.*Ro 2:31* Hold on to faith and a good conscience, which some reject and so suffer shipwreck with regard to the faith.*1Ti 1:19* The Spirit warns against abandoning the faith.*1Ti 4:1* The unfaithfulness of some does not nullify God's faithfulness because God remains true when every person is a liar.*Ro 2:3-4*

Others. Supply what is lacking in others' faith.*1Th 3:10* Strive together as one for gospel faith.*Php 1:27* Let co-workers in God's service encourage you in your faith.*1Th 3:2* Love one another in the faith.*Tit 3:15* Take joy in others' faith.*1Th 3:9* Pray that you may supply what others lack in faith.*1Th 3:10* Always thank God for brothers and sisters whose faith grows more and more.*2Th 1:3* We are a family in the faith.*1Ti 1:2* God saves women who continue in faith, love, and holiness with propriety.*1Ti 2:15* Be an example in faith for believers.*1Ti 4:11* To not provide for one's own household is to deny the faith.*1Ti 5:8* Believers in God should pursue faith.*1Ti 6:11* Fight faith's good fight.*1Ti 6:12* Recall the sincere faith of others.*2Ti 1:5* Pursue faith with those who call on the Lord out of a pure heart.*2Ti 2:22* The faith of some, others will report all over the world.*Ro 1:8* God justifies all through the same faith.*Ro 2:29-30* Accept the one with weak faith, without quarreling over disputable matters.*Ro 14:1* Just because your faith is strong, don't treat with contempt the one who has weak faith, indeed don't judge them at all, because God accepts them.*Ro 14:2-3* You are no one to judge another's servant, when each servant depends on their own master's judgment, and the Lord will help the one of weak faith stand.*Ro 14:4* Don't lord it over another's faith, but work with others for their joy, because by faith you stand firm.*2Co 1:24* Imitate those who through faith and patience inherit the promised reward.*Heb 6:12*

Baptism

The letters briefly address the Israelites' baptism under cloud and through sea, Christ's baptism giving him heaven's glory, and our baptism into the faith. The letters also describe baptism's benefit that it cleanses our conscience and clothes us with Christ. See how the letters address baptism, even as you remember and confirm your own.

Our ancestors were all under the cloud and passed through the sea, baptized into Moses in the cloud and in the sea.*1Co 10:1-2* At Jesus's baptism, God the Father gave Jesus glory from heaven.*2Pe 1:17* All those baptized into Christ Jesus were buried with him through baptism into death so that just as the glory of the Father raised Christ from the dead, we also live a new life.*Ro 6:3-4* Baptism buried us with Christ while raising us with him through our faith in God's working.*Col 2:12* All who receive baptism into Christ are clothed with Christ.*Gal 3:27* Baptism in water symbolizes not removing dirt from the body but cleansing one's conscience toward God.*1Pe 3:21* Do not quarrel among you by claiming to follow different teachers whom no one crucified and in whose name no one baptized you, when Christ himself is not so divided.*1Co 1:11-15* You have only one Lord, one faith, and one baptism.*Eph 4:5* One Spirit baptized all, whether insider or outsider, slave or free, to form one body, giving each the same Spirit to drink.*1Co 12:13* Without resurrection, baptism means nothing.*1Co 15:29*

Communion

The letters briefly address the meaning of communion, our mysterious and profound partaking of the body and blood of Jesus Christ in his remembrance. The letters also caution how a fellowship of believers should treat communion. See how the letters address communion, even as you continue to partake, while searching your soul and conscience as the letters admonish.

Meaning. On the night a disciple betrayed him, the Lord Jesus took bread, gave thanks, and broke it, saying that the bread was his body for you and that you should do as he did in his remembrance.*1Co 11:23-24* Likewise, after supper he said the cup is the new covenant in his blood to drink in remembrance of him.*1Co 11:25* The bread we break participates in Christ's body.*1Co 10:16* The thanksgiving cup for which we give thanks participates in Christ's blood, while the bread we break participates in Christ's body, just as eating the sacrifices participates in the altar.*1Co 10:16,18* Whenever you eat the bread and drink the cup, you proclaim the Lord's death until he comes.*1Co 11:26* Our ancestors all ate the same spiritual food and drank the same spiritual drink from the spiritual rock Christ who accompanied them.*1Co 10:3-4*

Manner. Although a fellowship of believers takes communion together, some are not eating the Lord's Supper together, instead having their own private suppers, leaving one hungry while another gets drunk.*1Co 11:20-21* Eat and drink in your own homes if you must, but don't despise God's church by humiliating those who have nothing.*1Co 11:22* When you gather to eat, you should all eat together.*1Co 11:33* Anyone who is hungry should eat at home so as to avoid judgment when you gather.*1Co 11:34* Examine yourself before eating the bread and drinking from the cup.*1Co 11:28* You cannot drink the Lord's cup and the demons' cup, too, taking part in both the Lord's table and demons' table.*1Co 10:21* Those who unworthily eat the Lord's bread or drink the Lord's cup sin against the Lord's body and blood.*1Co 11:27* Those who eat and drink without discerning Christ's body judge themselves.*1Co 11:29* Many among you are weak and sick, and a number of you have fallen asleep, for this reason.*1Co 11:30*

Promise

The letters confirm a core construct of faith in Christ, which is that we rely on God's welcome new covenant of grace, replacing a condemning old covenant of law. God keeps his promises. His loving promise, one that his Son put into effect and mediates, is to put his Spirit in our hearts and his laws on our minds so that he no longer sees our sins, and he can guarantee our inheritance. See how the letters treat God's wondrously generous promise. Have you given his promise its due full embrace?

Covenant. Hold unswervingly to the hope you profess, for God who promised is faithful._{Heb 10:23} Abraham received the blessing that God promised, God's oath confirming the promise while ending any argument._{Heb 6:13-16} God's oath confirmed to his heirs the unchanging nature of his promise's purpose._{Heb 6:17} God confirmed his unchangeable promise to greatly encourage us who hold to his hope._{Heb 6:18} You were once separate from Christ, excluded from holy citizenship and foreigners to the promise, without hope and without God in the world._{Eph 2:12} The eternal covenant was for God to raise our Lord Jesus from the dead._{Heb 13:20} God's revealed mystery is that through the gospel we are heirs together with his chosen people, members of one body, sharing the promise in Christ Jesus._{Eph 3:6} Christ became a servant of the Jews on behalf of God's truth, so that God could confirm the promises God made to the patriarchs._{Ro 15:8-9} Because of God's promises, we should revere God by keeping ourselves from anything contaminating body or spirit, perfecting holiness._{2Co 7:1} Be careful not to fall short of God's standing promise of entering his rest._{Heb 4:1}

Old. Christ said that God had not desired sacrifices and offerings, which did not please God, even though our ancestors offered according to the law.*Heb 10:8* When Christ said instead that he was here to do God's will, Christ set aside the first covenant to establish the second.*Heb 10:9* Jesus's ministry is superior to the former ministry just as the covenant he mediates is superior to the former covenant, because the new covenant has better promises.*Heb 8:6* If the first covenant had nothing wrong in it, then God would not have established another.*Heb 8:7* But finding fault with the people, God said that he would make a new covenant with the people.*Heb 8:8* The new covenant is not like the old covenant God made with the ancestors whom God led out of Egypt, but who did not remain faithful to the old covenant, so that God turned away from them.*Heb 8:9* God called the covenant new because he made the first covenant obsolete, while the obsolete and outdated will soon disappear.*Heb 8:13*

New. God's new covenant is to put his laws in our hearts and minds, to be our God and for us to be his people.*Heb 8:10* God forgives our wickedness and remembers our sins no more.*Heb 8:12* Jesus is the new covenant's mediator.*Heb 12:24* Jesus became the guarantor of a better covenant.*Heb 7:22* The Holy Spirit testifies that after Christ's sacrifice, God covenanted that he would put his laws in our hearts, writing them on our minds, and then would no longer remember our sins and lawless acts.*Heb 10:16* Christ mediates a new covenant, that those whom God calls may receive the promised eternal inheritance, now that Christ has died as a ransom to set us free from the sins committed under the first covenant.*Heb 9:15* The Son of God, Jesus Christ, preached among you, has always been yes rather than yes and no.*2Co 1:19* No matter how many promises God made, they are yes in Christ, so that we can say amen to God's glory.*2Co 1:20* God set his seal of ownership on us, putting his Spirit in our hearts as a deposit for what he guarantees will come.*2Co 1:22* No one can deny or add to God's promise, which not even the law that God gave hundreds of years later contradicts.*Gal 3:15-17*

Children

A Father, especially such a loving Creator Father, must have children. The letters repeatedly confirm that we who receive God's Spirit in witness to God's Son are God's children. God chooses us as Christ's brothers and sisters, in the Son's image. We then receive an inheritance as God's children, although we should then behave as God's children. See how the letters speak of God's children. Do you know in your heart, mind, soul, and spirit that you are God's child?

Spirit. Those whom the Spirit of God leads are the children of God.$_{Ro\ 8:14}$ The Spirit does not make you fearful slaves but makes you a child of God who can cry to your Father.$_{Ro\ 8:15}$ Creation groans as in childbirth just as we who have the Spirit's first fruits groan as we wait eagerly for God to adopt us as his children.$_{Ro\ 8:22-23}$ That the Father calls us his children shows his lavish love for us.$_{1Jn\ 3:1-2}$ God chooses and loves those whom one would not expect, calling them his children.$_{Ro\ 9:24-26}$ The children of God's promise, not the children of physical descent, receive the promised benefit.$_{Ro\ 9:7-9}$ Our inheritance is as free children of God rather than slave children who do not inherit.$_{Gal\ 4:30-31}$ Because you are God's child rather than his slave any longer, God makes you an heir to his promise.$_{Gal\ 4:7}$ Once we were his children, God could then send the Spirit of his Son into our hearts, the Spirit who calls God Father.$_{Gal\ 4:6}$ We know that we are children of God.$_{1Jn\ 5:19}$ We appeal for those who join us as children in the family of faith, who were formerly useless to us but have become useful to all.$_{Phm\ 9-11}$

Christ. Those whom God knew in advance he also predestined to conform to his Son's image so that the Son would be the firstborn among many brothers and sisters.$_{Ro\ 8:29}$ Jesus presents himself to God with the children God gave him.~Heb 2:13~ Jesus bears no shame calling us brothers and sisters because the one making holy and ones made holy are the same family.~Heb 2:12~ Jesus declares your name to his brothers and sisters, singing your praises in the assembly.~Heb 2:12~ The Spirit testifies with our spirit that we are God's children who, if we suffer with Christ, inherit Christ's glory with him.~Ro 8:16-17~ Through our faith in Christ Jesus we are all children of God.~Gal 3:26~ Belonging to Christ makes us Abraham's seed and heirs to God's promise.~Gal 3:29~ Before Christ came, we were underage heirs, awaiting the promise's fulfillment while still subject to the world's elemental spiritual forces.~Gal 4:1-3~ But the time God set finally came for a woman to bear his Son under the law, to redeem us from under the law, so that God could adopt us as children.~Gal 4:4-5~

Distinction. The difference between God's children and children of the devil is easy: God's children love one another and stop sinning, while the devil's children do not.~1Jn 3:9~ Just because your ancestors were holy doesn't make you holy.~Ro 9:6~ Be blameless and pure children of God without fault in this warped and crooked generation.~Php 2:15~ Follow God's example as dearly loved children by walking in love's way, like Christ loved and gave himself up for us as a fragrant offering and sacrifice to God.~Eph 5:1~ We are all children of the light and children of the day, not belonging to the night or darkness.~1Th 5:5~ As obedient children of God, reject the evil desires you had when you didn't know God, and instead be holy in all you do, like God is holy.~1Pe 1:14-16~ Be people who live by the Spirit rather than who are still worldly—mere infants in Christ.~1Co 3:1~ When Christ returns, dear children of God, we do not yet know what we will be, but we know we will be like him, seeing him as he is.~1Jn 3:2~

Grace

The letters emphasize God's abundant grace and bountiful mercy. God the Father and our Lord Jesus Christ offer you unmerited favor, blessings that you did not earn. The letters further confirm that God's mercy against judgment is also available, indeed necessary because of our sin. Yet God offers us mercy and grace only through Christ's gift. Indeed, God would judge our sin but for the mercy he extends through Christ's gift. See how the letters describe God's grace. Do you know the grace that God has for you?

Offer. Grace to you from God our Father.$_{Col\ 1:2}$ Grace to those in God the Father and the Lord Jesus Christ.$_{1Th\ 1:1}$ Grace to you from God our Father and the Lord Jesus Christ.$_{Php\ 1:2}$ Grace from God the Father and the Lord Jesus Christ.$_{2Th\ 1:1-2}$ Grace to you from God our Father and the Lord Jesus Christ.$_{1Co\ 1:3}$ Grace to you from God our Father and the Lord Jesus Christ.$_{Ro\ 1:7}$ Grace to each of you from God our Father and the Lord Jesus Christ.$_{Gal\ 1:3}$ God the Father and Christ Jesus our Lord bring grace and mercy.$_{1Ti\ 1:2}$ The grace of the Lord Jesus be with you.$_{1Co\ 16:23}$ The grace of our Lord Jesus be with you.$_{Ro\ 16:20}$ May the grace of the Lord Jesus Christ be with you.$_{2Co\ 13:14}$ Grace to you from God our Father and the Lord Jesus Christ.$_{2Co\ 1:2}$ The grace of our Lord Jesus Christ be with you.$_{1Th\ 5:28}$ The grace of our Lord Jesus Christ be with you all.$_{2Th\ 3:18}$ Grace be with you.$_{Col\ 4:18}$ Grace be with you.$_{Heb\ 13:25}$ Grace be with you all.$_{1Ti\ 6:21}$ The Spirit is a Spirit of grace.$_{Heb\ 10:29}$ God saved us out of his grace, not because of anything we have done.$_{2Ti\ 1:9}$ God cannot base his grace on your works, or it would no longer be grace.$_{Ro\ 11:6}$ Grace be with you all.$_{2Ti\ 4:22}$ God justifies all freely by his grace.$_{Ro\ 2:24}$ God gives grace to the churches.$_{2Co\ 8:1}$

Sin. Sin is not your master because you are under grace, not law.*Ro 6:14* Do not sin, because you are under grace rather than law.*Ro 6:15* God gave the law to increase sin so that grace would increase even more.*Ro 5:20* Jesus is different from Adam in that many died from Adam's sin while many live from the gift of God's grace in Jesus Christ.*Ro 5:15* The penalty of Adam's sin differs from God's gift of grace in that judgment's condemnation followed sin, but grace's justification followed many sins.*Ro 5:16* Grace reigns through righteousness.*Ro 5:21* Stand steady in God's true grace.*1Pe 5:12* God's grace teaches us to reject ungodliness and worldly passions, while living self-controlled, upright, and godly lives.*Tit 2:12* God gives everyone to disobedience so that he can show them all mercy.*Ro 11:32* Plead for relief from the Lord, but the Lord may answer that his grace is sufficient for you, his power made perfect in your weakness.*2Co 12:8* Let no one fall short of God's grace.*Heb 12:15* Let grace strengthen your heart.*Heb 13:9*

Christ. God's grace offers salvation to all.*Tit 2:11* We understand the gospel to be God's grace.*Col 1:6* God gave us grace in Christ Jesus before the beginning of time.*2Ti 1:9* Through our Lord Jesus Christ we gained access to the grace in which we now stand.*Ro 5:2* God's abundant grace reigns in life through Jesus Christ's gift.*Ro 5:17* Because of his great love for us, our merciful God brought us alive with Christ, grace saving us when we were still dead in transgressions.*Eph 2:4-5* God raised us up with Christ and seated us with him in the heavenly realms so that he might soon show us the incomparable riches of his grace, expressed in his kindness to us in Christ Jesus.*Eph 2:6-7* Through Christ we received grace.*Ro 1:5* For grace saved us, through faith, not from ourselves, and not by our works so that we can boast, but by God's gift.*Eph 2:8-9* Do not set aside God's grace because if righteousness came through law, then Christ would have died for nothing.*Gal 2:21* God has given each one of us grace just as Christ apportioned it.*Eph 4:7* Grace to all who have undying love for our Lord Jesus Christ.*Eph 6:24* Let the Lord Jesus Christ's grace be with your spirit.*Php 4:23* Our Lord Jesus Christ and God our Father by his grace gave us good hope of eternity.*2Th 2:16-17* Our Lord pours out his grace abundantly, along with the faith and love that are in Christ Jesus.*1Ti 1:14* Be strong in the grace that is in Christ Jesus.*2Ti 2:1*

Mercy. Christ became a servant of the Jews on behalf of God's truth, so that the Gentiles could glorify God for his mercy.*Ro 15:8-11* God has mercy on whom he has mercy, and compassion for whom he has compassion.*Ro 9:14-15* Salvation depends on God's mercy, not human desire or effort.*Ro 9:16* God has mercy on whom he wants to have mercy.*Ro 9:18* Be merciful, as the law that gives freedom and has mercy triumph over judgment requires, because God will judge without mercy those who are unmerciful.*Jas 2:12-13* God has mercy on the believing ill and their believing family and friends, saving the ill from death to spare sorrow upon sorrow.*Php 2:27* God will show mercy to a blasphemer, persecutor, and violent person who acts in ignorance and unbelief.*1Ti 1:13* God has shown mercy to the worst of sinners so that Christ Jesus might display his immense patience, as an example for those who would believe in him and receive eternal life.*1Ti 1:16* Grace and mercy are from God the Father and Christ Jesus our Lord.*2Ti 1:2* The Lord shows mercy to households that seek and refresh, rather than turn away from, suffering believers.*2Ti 1:16-18* Because God is merciful, offer your body as a living sacrifice, holy and pleasing to God, as your true and proper worship.*Ro 12:1* God's mercy grants us a teaching ministry.*2Co 4:1* Approach God's throne with confidence for mercy and grace when in need.*Heb 4:16*

Peace

The letters highlight that along with his abundant grace, God also brings peace. As with all things, we receive God's peace through our Lord Jesus Christ. God's peace brings much-needed rest. While we receive God's peace and rest by believing, we must remain in the Spirit of unity, accepting, seeking, and teaching peace. See how the letters describe the God of peace. Are you abiding in and sharing God's peace?

Blessing. God the Father blesses us with abundant peace.*Jude 1-2* God the Father chose his elect to receive peace in abundance.*1Pe 1:2* Peace to you from God our Father.*Col 1:2* The God of peace sanctifies.*1Th 5:23* We receive peace from God the Father and from Jesus Christ.*2Jn 3* Peace to each of you from God our Father and the Lord Jesus Christ.*Gal 1:3* Peace to you from God our Father and the Lord Jesus Christ.*Php 1:2* Peace to you from God our Father and the Lord Jesus Christ.*1Co 1:3* Peace to you from God our Father and the Lord Jesus Christ.*2Co 1:2* Peace to you from God our Father and the Lord Jesus Christ.*Ro 1:7* Peace to those in God the Father and the Lord Jesus Christ.*1Th 1:1* Peace from God the Father and the Lord Jesus Christ.*2Th 1:1-2* Peace is from God the Father and Christ Jesus our Lord.*2Ti 1:2* God the Father and Christ Jesus our Lord bring peace.*1Ti 1:2* Peace is the Spirit's fruit.*Gal 5:22-23* The Lord of peace may give you peace at all times and in every way when with you.*2Th 3:16* May the God of hope fill you with all peace as you trust in him.*Ro 15:13* The God of peace be with you.*Ro 15:33*

Christ. The God who raised Jesus from the dead is the God of peace.*Heb 13:20* God makes peace through the Son's blood.*Col 1:20* Christ's purpose on the cross was to reconcile in him one new peaceful humanity out of the divided two sides, putting to death their hostility.*Eph 2:15-16* Our common faith as a family of believers is in peace from God the Father and Christ Jesus our Savior.*Tit 1:4* Our peace is Christ, who has destroyed the barrier, the dividing wall of hostility.*Eph 2:14-15* Christ came preaching peace.*Eph 2:17* Peace to all of you who are in Christ.*1Pe 5:14* Peace with faith from God the Father and the Lord Jesus Christ, to the brothers and sisters.*Eph 6:23* Apostles of Christ Jesus bring a message of peace from God our Father and the Lord Jesus Christ.*Eph 1:1-2* Faith's justification gave us peace with God through our Lord Jesus Christ.*Ro 5:2* With prayer, God's peace, transcending all understanding, will guard your heart and mind in Christ Jesus.*Php 4:7* We will receive peace in abundance knowing God, our Lord Jesus.*2Pe 1:1-2*

Rest. God rested from all his works on the seventh day of creation.*Heb 4:4* God has a Sabbath rest for his people.*Heb 4:9* Be careful not to fall short of God's standing promise of entering his rest.*Heb 4:1* We enter God's rest by believing.*Heb 4:3* Anyone entering God's rest also rests from their work, just as God did from his.*Heb 4:10* Make every effort to enter God's rest, so that no one will perish in disobedience.*Heb 4:11* Those who disobey in unbelief will never enter God's rest.*Heb 3:17-19* Some are yet to enter God's rest, while others who heard the good news rejected God's rest out of disobedience.*Heb 4:6* We belong to the truth and set our condemning hearts at rest when we acknowledge that God is greater than our hearts and knows everything.*1Jn 3:19-20*

Seeking. Make every effort to do what leads to peace and mutual edification.*Ro 14:19* Make every effort to be at peace with the patient God as you await the end of all things.*2Pe 3:14-16* Everyone who does good may expect peace.*Ro 2:10* Those who have no fear of God will not know peace.*Ro 2:17-18* Keep the Spirit's unity through the bond of peace.*Eph 4:3* Let the peace of Christ rule in your hearts because as members of one body God called you to peace.*Col 3:15* Make every effort to live in peace with everyone.*Heb 12:14* Live peacefully with each other.*1Th 3:13* Wish to one another peace from God our Father and the Lord Jesus Christ.*Phm 1-3* Teach the people to be peaceable.*Tit 3:1-2* If you want to enjoy life with good days, then seek peace.*1Pe 3:10-11* Practice what you learn so that the God of peace is with you.*Php 4:9* Stand firm with your feet fitted with the readiness that comes from the gospel of peace.*Eph 6:14-15* Pray for all people including those in authority that you may live peaceful lives.*1Ti 2:1-2* Live in peace, and the God of love and peace will be with you.*2Co 13:11*

Redemption

The letters make clear the extraordinary result of our accepting God's loving sacrifice of his own Son, which is our redemption from all that corrupts and burdens us. Astonishingly, God restores us to his presence and favor. The letters confirm that no less than Jesus's blood, his terrible yet ultimately loving sacrifice, suffices to reconcile and redeem, so great was the extent of our appalling wickedness. The letters also remind us of the fabulous result of our redemption, that we are Christ's own brothers and sisters in his glory. See how the letters describe God redeeming us out of our sinful nature and sin-filled world. Do you know the power of your redemption?

Justification. God justifies, and no one else.$_{Ro\ 8:33}$ God justifies all freely through the redemption that came by Christ Jesus.$_{Ro\ 2:24}$ God presented Christ as a sacrifice of atonement, for us to receive by faith in Jesus, God justifying us.$_{Ro\ 2:25\text{-}26}$ God delivered Jesus over to death for our sins and raised him to life for our justification.$_{Ro\ 4:25}$ Creation groans as in childbirth just as we who have the Spirit's first fruits groan, as we wait eagerly for God to adopt us as his children and redeem our bodies.$_{Ro\ 8:22\text{-}23}$ God reconciles us by Christ's physical body through death to present you holy, without blemish, and free from accusation, in his sight.$_{Col\ 1:22}$ Jesus Christ our Lord keeps us from stumbling, to present us before his glorious presence without fault.$_{Jude\ 24\text{-}25}$ God will redeem those whom he possesses, marked and guaranteed by his Holy Spirit.$_{Eph\ 1:13\text{-}14}$ Christ redeemed us to bless those of us who through faith receive the promise of the Spirit.$_{Gal\ 3:14}$ God sealed you with the Holy Spirit for the day of redemption.$_{Eph\ 4:30}$

Blood. Christ redeems us through his blood, the forgiveness of sins, as God lavished his grace's riches on us.*Eph 1:7-8* The perfect lamb Christ's precious blood, not perishable things like precious metals, redeemed you from the empty life your family handed down to you.*1Pe 1:18-19* Christ entered the Most Holy Place not by animal blood but once for all by his own blood, for eternal redemption.*Heb 9:12* The high priest carried animal blood into the Most Holy Place as a sin offering but burned the bodies outside the camp.*Heb 13:11* And so Jesus also suffered outside the city gate to make the people holy through his own blood.*Heb 13:12* Go to Jesus outside the camp, bearing the disgrace he bore, because we have no enduring city here and instead look for the city to come.*Heb 13:14* Christ's one sacrifice made perfect forever those whom God is making holy.*Heb 10:14* Be confident entering the Most Holy Place by Jesus's blood, the new and living way he opened for us through the curtain, that is, his body.*Heb 10:19-20* Christ Jesus is our redemption.*1Co 1:30*

Sin. Some of you were wrongdoers, sexually immoral, idolaters, adulterers, thieves, greedy, drunkards, slanderers, and swindlers, but the name of the Lord Jesus Christ and Spirit of our God washed and justified you.*1Co 6:9-11* We wait for our blessed hope, which is that we would see our great God and Savior Jesus Christ, who gave himself to redeem us from all wickedness and purify for himself a people that are his own, eager to do good.*Tit 2:13-14* Our redemption and forgiveness of sins is in Jesus Christ.*Col 1:14* Jesus shared in our humanity because we are human, so that by his death he would break the devil's power of death.*Heb 2:14* Jesus frees those held in slavery by their fear of death.*Heb 2:15* Jesus doesn't help angels but us, Abraham's descendants.*Heb 2:16* Jesus had to become like us, fully human in every way, to become a merciful and faithful high priest in service to God, atoning for our sins.*Heb 2:17* Jesus suffered when tempted, making him able to help us when facing temptation.*Heb 2:18*

Result. God enriches us in him in every way including all kinds of speech and with all knowledge, confirming testimony about Christ in us.*1Co 1:5-6* Draw near to God with sincere heart, faith's full assurance, hearts sprinkled to cleanse our guilty conscience, and our bodies washed with pure water.*Heb 10:22* To bring many sons and daughters to glory through salvation, God, for and through whom everything exists, fittingly made salvation's pioneer Jesus Christ perfect through his suffering.*Heb 2:10*

Jesus declares your name to his brothers and sisters, singing your praises in the assembly.*Heb 2:12* Jesus presents himself to God with the children God gave him.*Heb 2:13* Better things having to do with salvation convince us.*Heb 6:9* Jesus bears no shame calling us brothers and sisters because the one making holy and ones made holy are the same family.*Heb 2:12* God is just, remembering your work and the love you show him as you help his people.*Heb 6:10* Show the same diligence to the very end, so that you realize that for which you hope.*Heb 6:11* Do not be lazy, but instead imitate those who through faith and patience inherit the promised reward.*Heb 6:12*

Glory

The letters remind us not only of God's astounding glory but also that God shared his glory with his perfect Son. The letters also call substantial attention to an extraordinary privilege that accompanies our redemption: we share in God's glory. Indeed, our ambition should be to pursue his glory. What a loss when we do not daily see and pursue his glory! See how often and richly the letters refer to God's glory. Do you know and embrace your own access to that glory?

God. God exalted Jesus over everyone for his glory as the Father.*Php 2:11* That God will redeem those of us whom he possesses is to his glory's praise.*Eph 1:13-14* Be overjoyed at seeing his glory.*1Pe 4:13* To God be the power forever.*1Pe 5:11* God chose you with the purpose that you declare his praises.*1Pe 2:9-10* We praise our Lord and Father.*Jas 3:9* God adopted us through Jesus Christ for the praise of his glorious grace.*Eph 1:5-6* Your righteousness is to God's glory and praise.*Php 1:11* To our God and Father be glory forever.*Php 4:20* Now to God, who can do immeasurably more than all we ask or imagine by his power at work within us, be glory in the church and in Christ Jesus forever.*Eph 3:20-21* The gospel concerns the blessed God's glory.*1Ti 1:11* The King eternal, immortal, invisible, the only God, has honor and glory forever.*1Ti 1:17* To the Lord be glory forever.*2Ti 4:18* Praise the Lord, everyone, with everyone extolling him.*Ro 15:11* Give God the glory forever.*Ro 11:36* Glorify God for his mercy.*Ro 15:8-9* Glory forever through Jesus Christ to the only wise God.*Ro 16:27* Glory to God forever.*Heb 13:21*

Jesus. At Jesus's baptism, God the Father gave Jesus glory from heaven.*2Pe 1:17* Jesus Christ our Lord is the one before all ages to whom God gave glory, majesty, power, and authority, to present you before his glorious presence.*Jude 24-25* The prophets searched for salvation, the grace that was to come to us, to discover through Christ's Spirit when and how the Messiah would come, suffer, and receive his glory.*1Pe 1:10-11* Rulers crucified the Lord of glory.*1Co 2:8* To Jesus Christ be glory forever.*Gal 1:5* The Lord's holy people who believed in Jesus, including you, will glorify Jesus on his return.*2Th 1:10-11* We who hope in Christ as we hear the true message of gospel salvation should praise his glory.*Eph 1:11-13* Everyone should praise God through Jesus Christ, who has glory and power forever.*1Pe 4:11* God took up Christ in glory.*1Ti 3:16*

Shared. God called us to share in our Lord Jesus Christ's glory.*2Th 2:14* The Spirit testifies with our spirit that we are God's children who, if we suffer with Christ, inherit Christ's glory with him.*Ro 8:16-17* Our suffering does not compare with the glory that God will reveal in us.*Ro 8:18* Those whom God justified, he also glorified.*Ro 8:30* God showed his wrath and power to us, while patiently bearing those who rejected him to their destruction, to let those of us whom he prepared in advance for glory know the riches of his glory.*Ro 9:22-23* Praise God the Father of our Lord Jesus Christ, who brings us every spiritual blessing in Christ.*Eph 1:3* The gospel of Christ in you is the hope of glory.*Col 1:27* When Christ appears, you will appear with him in glory.*Col 3:4* God calls you into his glory.*1Th 2:12* Fellow believers are your glory when our Lord Jesus comes.*1Th 2:19-20* May we glorify the name of our Lord Jesus and receive his glory, by the grace of God and the Lord Jesus Christ.*2Th 1:12* The elect obtaining salvation in Christ Jesus receive eternal glory.*2Ti 2:10*

Pursuit. God gives eternal life to those who seek glory by persistent good works.*Ro 2:7* Do everything for God's glory.*1Co 10:31* Everyone who does good may expect glory and honor.*Ro 2:10* We boast in the hope of the glory of God even while we glory in our sufferings.*Ro 5:3* Glory in Christ Jesus in your service to God.*Ro 15:17* Thanksgiving overflows to God's glory, as grace reaches ever more people.*2Co 4:15* Our eternal glory far outweighs our troubles that achieve that glory for us.*2Co 4:17* When Jesus returns, God will shut out from the glory of the Lord's might those who do not know God.*2Th 1:8-10* All sin, falling short of God's glory.*Ro 2:23* The ministry that brought death, engraved in letters on tablets, came with so much glory that the Israelites could not look at Moses, transitory though it was.*2Co 3:7* The Spirit's ministry bringing righteousness is even more glorious than the ministry that brought condemnation.*2Co 3:8-9* What was glorious has no glory compared to the surpassing glory.*2Co 3:10* If the transitory had glory, then the eternal has much greater glory.*2Co 3:11* Those with dulled minds still read the old covenant with veiled faces because only in Christ does the veil fall away.*2Co 3:14* A veil covers their hearts as they read Moses.*2Co 3:15* You have no need to cover your face like Moses so that others cannot see the old glory pass away.*2Co 3:13* Whenever anyone turns to the Lord, he takes the veil away.*2Co 3:16* The Lord transforms into his image with growing glory, all who with unveiled faces contemplate the Lord's glory, which comes from the Lord who is the Spirit.*2Co 3:18*

Power

The letters emphasize at length God's power, on which we should rely over any human wisdom. God resurrected Jesus from the dead, granting Jesus all his power. Jesus's resurrection defeated all other powers including the power of evil and death. You live within God's power, as heroes of the faith have lived in God's power. Let the Spirit strengthen you in God's power. See how the letters describe God's power. Do you stand in awe of, and are you fully relying on, God's power?

God. We see and understand God's eternal power and divine nature from what he made._{Ro 1:20} God showed his wrath and power to us, to let those of us whom he prepared in advance for glory know the riches of his glory._{Ro 9:22-23} By his power, God raised the Lord from the dead and will also raise us._{1Co 6:14} Rest your faith not on human wisdom but on God's power._{1Co 2:5} God's power shields us in our faith until the salvation comes that he will reveal in the last time._{1Pe 1:5} God's power for believers is the same as the mighty strength he exerted when he raised Christ from the dead and seated him at his right hand in the heavenly realms, over all rule, authority, power, and dominion._{Eph 1:19-21} Suffering is for the gospel, by the power of God._{2Ti 1:8} Have no shame over the gospel because its power of God brings salvation to everyone who believes._{Ro 1:16} The gospel came not simply with words but also power, the Holy Spirit, and deep conviction._{1Th 1:5} We preach Christ crucified, a stumbling block to Jews and foolishness to other non-believers but God's power and wisdom to those whom God called._{1Co 1:22-24} God hardens whom he wants to harden, to display his power and see his name proclaimed in all the earth._{Ro 9:17-18} God's kingdom is not a matter of talk but of power._{1Co 4:20} Now to God, who can do immeasurably more than all we ask or imagine by his power at work within us, be glory in the church and in

Christ Jesus forever._{Eph 3:20-21} To God be the power forever._{1Pe 5:11} We become the gospel's servants by the gift of God's grace given us through his power._{Eph 3:7} Pray that the Spirit may enlighten our heart that we may know God's hope, his glorious inheritance in us, and his incomparably great power for us who believe._{Eph 1:18-19}

Christ. God gave Jesus Christ our Lord glory, majesty, power, and authority._{Jude 24-25} God will reveal the Lord Jesus from heaven in blazing fire with his powerful angels._{2Th 1:7} Christ is the head over every power and authority._{Col 2:10} Jesus Christ our Lord is the one before all ages to whom God gave glory, majesty, power, and authority._{Jude 24-25} Praise God through Jesus Christ, who has glory and power forever._{1Pe 4:11} Assemble with the Lord Jesus's power present, to hand wrongdoers among you over to Satan to destroy the flesh, so that God may save the disobedient one's spirit on the Lord's day._{1Co 5:4-5} Jesus Christ sustains all things by his powerful word._{Heb 1:3} The cross is God's power to us whom God saves._{1Co 1:18-19} Men crucified Christ in weakness, but Christ lives by God's power._{2Co 13:4} Christ triumphed over evil powers and authorities by the cross._{Col 2:15} Wise and eloquent preaching must not empty Christ's cross of its power._{1Co 1:17} Desire to know the power of Christ's resurrection and participation in his sufferings, becoming like him in his death and so attaining to resurrection from death._{Php 3:10-11} Our Savior the Lord Jesus Christ will by his complete power transform our lowly bodies to be like his glorious body._{Php 3:20-21} Christ is not weak but powerful in dealing with you._{2Co 13:1-3} We have the gospel treasure in jars of clay to show that all-surpassing power is from God and not us._{2Co 4:7}

Evil. Lawlessness's secret power already works, even though the Lord Jesus will overthrow and destroy the lawless one._{2Th 2:7-8} All are under sin's power._{Ro 2:8-11} Jesus shared in our humanity because we are human, so that by his death he would break the devil's power of death._{Heb 2:14} The lawless one comes in the wicked way that Satan works, using all sorts of powerfully deceiving displays._{2Th 2:9} God permits those who reject the truth and instead delight in wickedness, to suffer the powerful delusion that condemns them as they believe the lie._{2Th 2:11-12} We struggle not against flesh and blood but against rulers, authorities, and powers of this dark world and spiritual forces of evil in the heavenly realms._{Eph 6:12} Death has no victory or sting, when death's sting is sin and sin's power is the law._{1Co 15:55-56} The law had no power to free us from sin, but God sent his own Son to meet the law's righteous requirement in those of us who live by the Spirit rather than the flesh.*Ro 8:3-4* Neither death nor life, angels nor demons, nor any powers, nor anything else in all creation, can separate us from God's love in Christ Jesus our Lord.*Ro 8:38-39* Christ disarmed and triumphed over evil powers and authorities, making a public spectacle of them.*Col 2:15*

You. Be strong in the Lord in his mighty power.*Eph 6:10* Although men crucified Christ, Christ lives by God's power, just as you are weak in him but live by God's power in dealing with the sin of one another.*2Co 13:4* The Lord's grace is sufficient for you because he makes his power perfect in your weakness.*2Co 12:8* Boast all the more gladly about weaknesses, so that Christ's power rests on you.*2Co 12:9* God, though all-powerful, still leaves you to your own will.*Ro 9:19-20* Christ died for us when we were powerless sinners, demonstrating his extraordinary love for us because no one dies for sinners even if for the good.*Ro 5:6-8* The Spirit God gave you does not leave you timid but gives you power, love, and self-discipline.*2Ti 1:7* When leading others to obey God, you act through the Spirit of God's power.*Ro 15:18-19* May you overflow with hope by the Holy Spirit's power.*Ro 15:13* God makes us worthy of his calling, by his power granting our every desire for goodness and every deed prompted by faith.*2Th 1:11* Because we know his glory and goodness, God by his great and precious promises and power gives us everything for a godly life, to participate in his divine nature and escape the world's corruption that evil desires cause.*2Pe 1:3-4* Conduct yourselves appropriately in purity, understanding, patience, and kindness, in God's power and with weapons of righteousness in both hands.*2Co 6:6-7* Speak of no service other than what Christ accomplished through you, through the Spirit of God's power.*Ro 15:18-19* We proclaim Christ with all wisdom and all the energy Christ so powerfully works in us.*Col 1:28* In prayer, receive God's strength with all power according to his glorious might so that you endure with great patience.*Col 1:10-11* Constantly pray for one another that our God make us worthy of his calling and by his power grant our every desire for goodness and every deed prompted by faith.*2Th 1:11*

Others. God gives some miraculous powers.*1Co 12:8-10* Fight with weapons not of the world but having divine power to demolish strongholds.*2Co 10:4* Angels are stronger and more powerful than the arrogant non-believers who heap abuse on them, but angels still let the

Lord judge them.*1Pe 2:10-11* Abraham believed God's power and promise, and so became the father of many nations.*Ro 4:18-21* Heroes' faith conquered kingdoms, routed armies, and escaped the sword by making those heroes powerful in battle.*Heb 11:32-34* Jesus Christ's resurrection saves you because he is in heaven at God's right hand with angels, authorities, and powers submitting to him.*1Pe 3:21-22* God sows the body in dishonor but raises it in glory, sows it in weakness but raises it in power.*1Co 15:43* Jesus Christ is in heaven at God's right hand with angels, authorities, and powers submitting to him.*1Pe 3:21-22* The end will come when Christ hands God's kingdom to the Father after destroying all dominion, authority, and power.*1Co 15:24* The prayer of a righteous person is powerful and effective.*Jas 5:16-18* We pray that out of God's glorious riches he strengthens you in your inner being with power through his Spirit, so that Christ dwells in your heart through faith.*Eph 3:16-17*

Heaven

The letters highlight heaven, the divine place where God and his Son Jesus Christ reside together and where angels tread. You, too, will reside in heaven, taken up by Christ, before whom every knee in heaven will bow. See how the letters describe God's heaven. Do you confidently anticipate joining our Lord in heaven?

Father. God's word created the heavens and the earth.*2Pe 3:5* The unchanging Father in heaven gives heaven's good and perfect gifts.*Jas 1:17* God makes his angels spirits, and his servants flames of fire.*Heb 1:7* The Holy Spirit shares matters with us from heaven, into which even angels long to look.*1Pe 1:12* Every family in heaven derives its name from the Father.*Eph 3:14-15* You have a Master in heaven.*Col 4:1* God reveals his wrath from heaven.*Ro 1:18* God warns you from heaven with a warning that you cannot escape.*Heb 12:25* God promises that his voice will shake earth and heaven, leaving only what does not shake.*Heb 12:26-27* God intends that the church make his wisdom known to the rulers and authorities in the heavenly realms.*Eph 3:10-11* Every creature under heaven hears proclamation of the gospel.*Col 1:23* Set your mind on things above, not on earthly things.*Col 3:2*

Christ. God's Son Jesus is from heaven.*1Th 1:10* Christ, as God's Son, is far superior to the angels.*Heb 1:4-5* When God brought his firstborn Son into the world, he said that the angels would worship him.*Heb 1:6* God the Father gave Jesus honor and glory from heaven at Jesus's baptism.*2Pe 1:17-18* Christ did not just enter the human tabernacle but entered heaven itself to appear for us in God's presence.*Heb 9:24* Christ did not enter heaven to offer himself repeatedly, the way a human high priest entered the Most Holy Place every year with animal blood.*Heb 9:25* When God raised Christ from the dead, he seated him at his right hand in the heavenly realms, over all rule, authority, power, and dominion.*Eph 1:19-21* The Son sits at the right hand of the Majesty in heaven.*Heb 1:3* Jesus Christ is in heaven at God's right hand with angels, authorities, and powers submitting to him.*1Pe 3:21-22* When times reach fulfillment, God will unify everything in heaven and on earth under Christ.*Eph 1:8-10* When Christ ascended, he took many captives, while giving gifts to his people.*Eph 4:8* Christ, who also descended to the lower, earthly regions, ascended higher than heaven, so high as to fill the whole universe.*Eph 4:9-10* Christ ascended in glory.*1Ti 3:16* Every knee in heaven will bow with every tongue acknowledging that Jesus Christ is Lord.*Php 2:9-11*

You. God calls us heavenward in Christ Jesus.*Php 3:13-14* Make your citizenship heaven, eagerly awaiting heaven's Savior the Lord Jesus Christ.*Php 3:20-21* God raised us up with Christ and seated us with him in the heavenly realms so that he might soon show us the incomparable riches of his grace.*Eph 2:6-7* God keeps in heaven for us an inheritance that can never perish, spoil or fade.*1Pe 1:4* On his return, the Lord will come down from heaven and, with a loud command in the archangel's voice and with God's trumpet call, will catch up living and dead believers together in the clouds to meet him in the air and be with him in heaven forever.*1Th 4:17* The Lord will bring us safely to his heavenly kingdom.*2Ti 4:18* If the earthly tent in which we live suffers destruction, God gives us an eternal house in heaven, not built by human hands.*2Co 5:1* In our earthly tent, we groan with burden, fearing deadly exposure while wanting heaven's protection from death.*2Co 5:4* You receive God's kingdom that does not shake.*Heb 12:28-29* We long to be in our heavenly dwelling, which will not leave us exposed.*2Co 5:2-3* We look forward to the Lord's promised righteous new heaven and new earth.*2Pe 3:13* Our faith and love spring from the hope stored up for us in heaven, about which we hear in the true gospel message.*Col 1:5* Set your heart on things above where Christ sits at God's right hand.*Col 3:1*

Calling

The letters emphasize that God chose a people, indeed chose an elect group to be his people, carrying his message to the world. Moreover, God chose you, calling you to his heaven through his Son Jesus Christ. God chooses, and he chose you. See how the letters depict God's call. Do you hear and pursue God's call?

People. God chooses those whom he loves.*1Th 1:4* God foreknew his chosen people and, despite an appeal to reject them, preserved a remnant who had remained faithful to him.*Ro 11:1-3* Only the elect among God's chosen people obtained what they all so earnestly sought, because God hardened the others.*Ro 11:7* Likewise, God today chooses a remnant by grace.*Ro 11:5* God's chosen people did not stumble beyond recovery but just enough to open rich salvation to all.*Ro 11:11* God's holy chosen people made the believing remnant holy, which made later believers holy.*Ro 11:16* Believers should not consider themselves superior to God's chosen people, who were the supporting holy root for the believers' own salvation.*Ro 11:18* God will take in again his chosen people if they believe, because, unlike you, they were his holy root, the original tree.*Ro 11:23-24* God hardened his chosen people in part until all others who would be saved were saved, after which God will save his chosen people.*Ro 11:25-26* God's chosen people are enemies of the gospel for your sake but are still God's elect, loved on the patriarchs' account.*Ro 11:28* God brought reconciliation to the world when he rejected his chosen people, whose acceptance now means life from the dead.*Ro 11:15* God's full inclusion of his chosen people will bring much greater riches.*Ro 11:12*

You. God called you into fellowship with his Son, Jesus Christ our Lord.*1Co 1:9* God chose the world's foolish things.*1Co 1:27* God chose the world's lowly things, despised things, and even things that are not.*1Co 1:28-29* You were once disobedient to God but received his mercy because of the disobedience of his chosen people.*Ro 11:30* God's chosen people are now disobedient so that they too may now receive God's mercy out of God's mercy to you.*Ro 11:31* God calls for his own purpose those who love him, for whom he now works in all things for their good.*Ro 8:28* God elects us before we do anything good or bad, and not by right but by grace, to show that his call, not our works, makes the difference.*Ro 9:10-12* God is still just, favoring those whom he favors.*Ro 9:14-15* God calls both insiders and outsiders, choosing and loving those whom one would not expect and calling them his children.*Ro 9:24-26* Many descend from the chosen, but few receive salvation.*Ro 9:27* Before he created the world, God chose us in him to be holy and blameless in his sight.*Eph 1:4* When God calls, we must not consult others about whether to follow his call.*Gal 1:16* God chose believers as first fruits.*2Th 2:13* You are God's chosen people, holy and dearly loved.*Col 3:12* God called you to eternal life when you confessed before many witnesses.*1Ti 6:12*

Christ. God calls persons to belong to Jesus Christ.*Ro 1:6* Those whom God knew in advance he also predestined to conform to his Son's image so that the Son would be the firstborn among many brothers and sisters.*Ro 8:29* Those whom God predestined he also called, and those he called he also justified, while those he justified he also glorified.*Ro 8:30* In Christ God chose us, predestined as he planned, God working out everything to conform to his will.*Eph 1:11-12* God sets us apart from our mother's womb, calling us by his grace, pleased to reveal his Son in us so that we might share him among those who don't know him.*Gal 1:15-16* God the Father chose his elect with foreknowledge, to obey Jesus Christ through the Spirit's sanctifying work and under his sprinkled blood.*1Pe 1:2* Do you best to confirm your calling and election so that you never stumble and instead receive a rich welcome into our Lord and Savior Jesus Christ's eternal kingdom.*2Pe 1:10-11* As the Lord's prisoners, we urge one another to live worthy of the calling we have received.*Eph 4:1* God appointed us not to suffer wrath but to receive salvation through our Lord Jesus Christ.*1Th 3:9*

Pursuit. God called us to holy life.*1Th 4:7* God's gifts and call are irrevocable.*Ro 11:29* God makes us worthy of his calling, by his power granting our every desire for goodness and every deed prompted by faith.~2Th 1:11~ God called us through the gospel to share in our Lord Jesus Christ's glory.~2Th 2:14~ God our Savior and Christ Jesus choose leaders in the faith.~1Ti 1:1~ Christ Jesus our Lord appoints teachers to his service.~1Ti 1:12~ God appoints some as heralds and apostles, as true and faithful teachers.~1Ti 2:7~ God called us to a holy life out of his own purpose and grace.~2Ti 1:9~ Endure everything so that the elect may also obtain salvation in Christ Jesus.~2Ti 2:10~ God's solid foundation stands firm because the Lord knows who are his.~2Ti 2:19~ God calls apostles from among Christ Jesus's servants.~Ro 1:1~ Christ appointed apostles to call non-believers.~Ro 1:5~ God calls his holy people.~Ro 1:7~ God's will calls apostles of Christ Jesus.~1Co 1:1~ Remember what you were like when God first called you, neither wise nor influential, and not many of noble birth.~1Co 1:26~ Remain in the situation you were in when God called you.~1Co 7:20~ Remain in the same situation you were in when God called you, as responsible to God.~1Co 7:24~ Live as the Lord assigns and God calls you, as a rule in all the churches.~1Co 7:17~

Freedom

The letters remind us of our freedom in Christ, more precious than we often realize. No matter our earthly circumstances, whether bound or not, we are free and fulfilled, indeed free of all need, in Christ. See how the letters describe our freedom. Do you value and live out your freedom?

God called us to freedom, not to indulge ourselves but instead to serve one another humbly in love.*Gal 5:13* For we fulfill the entire law by loving our neighbor as we love ourselves.*Gal 5:14* Live as God's slaves, which is to live free of evil.*1Pe 2:16* No one condemns because Christ Jesus, who died and God raised to life, is at God's right hand interceding for us.*Ro 8:34* Be anxious about nothing.*Php 4:6* Have no needs, but instead learn contentment whatever your circumstances.*Php 4:11* While you have known both need and plenty, learn contentment's secret for every situation, whether you are fed or hungry, or living in plenty or in want.*Php 4:12* You can do all things through Christ who strengthens you.*Php 4:13* God meets all your needs with the riches of his glory in Christ Jesus.*Php 4:19* If you were bound when God called, then don't let it trouble you, although gain your freedom if you can.*1Co 7:21* The slave called to faith in the Lord is free in the Lord, while the person free when called is Christ's slave.*1Co 7:22* Do not make yourself a slave to another person, recognizing instead that God bought you at a price.*1Co 7:23*

Inheritance

The letters point us forward toward our promised inheritance as free children of God. Idolaters do not inherit from our properly jealous God. Inheritance requires a beloved one's death, which the free children of God receive only through Jesus Christ. See how the letters describe the inheritance that God guarantees us in Christ. Are you pursuing your inheritance as you should?

Promise. God has a glorious inheritance in his holy people._{Eph 1:18-19} God keeps in heaven for us an inheritance that can never perish, spoil or fade._{1Pe 1:4} Abraham and his offspring received God's promise that they would inherit the world through righteousness from faith._{Ro 4:13} Faith invokes the promise of inheritance. _{Ro 4:14-15} The poor who are rich in faith and love God inherit his promised kingdom._{Jas 2:5} Our inheritance is as free children of God rather than slave children who do not inherit._{Gal 4:30-31} Only free children, not slave children, share our inheritance from God._{Gal 4:30-31} Sin keeps one from inheriting God's kingdom._{Gal 5:19-21} Wrongdoers, the sexually immoral, idolaters, adulterers, men who have sex with men, thieves, the greedy, drunkards, slanderers, and swindlers do not inherit God's kingdom._{1Co 6:9-10} Inherit blessing by repaying evil with good._{1Pe 3:9} Imitate those who through faith and patience inherit the promised reward._{Heb 6:12} Do not relinquish your inheritance like the godless Esau who for a single meal sold his right to a blessing, wanted it back, but despite tears could not change what he had done._{Heb 12:17} Thank the Father, who has qualified you to share in the inheritance of his holy people._{Col 1:12}

Death. A beneficiary must prove the death of the one who makes a will because a will takes effect only when the testator dies, not while the testator still lives.*Heb 9:16-17* Even the first covenant required animal blood for the covenant that God commanded them to keep.*Heb 9:18-21* The law required that nearly everything be cleansed with blood, without which God would not forgive.*Heb 9:22* If the copies of the heavenly things required animal blood, then the heavenly things would require better sacrifices.*Heb 9:23* The Spirit testifies with our spirit that we are God's children who, if we suffer with Christ, inherit Christ's glory with him.*Ro 8:16-17* Christ mediates a new covenant, that those whom God calls may receive the promised eternal inheritance, now that Christ has died as a ransom to set us free from the sins committed under the first covenant.*Heb 9:15* Angels are ministering spirits sent to serve those who inherit salvation.*Heb 1:14* The pure inherit the kingdom of Christ and God.*Eph 5:5* Idolaters do not inherit the kingdom of Christ and God.*Eph 5:5* As a hardworking farmer, expect to be first to receive a share of the crops.*2Ti 2:6* You receive an inheritance from the Lord to reward you for sound earthly work, as working for the Lord Christ.*Col 3:24*

Sanctification

The letters treat at length our sanctification into God's righteousness through faith in the righteousness of Jesus Christ. We do not sanctify ourselves through law-keeping or other works. Rather, God sanctifies us as we believe and trust in the perfect work and sacrifice of Jesus Christ. Faith leads us to pursue holiness, conducting ourselves freed by Christ from sin. See how the letters address sanctification. Do you see and pursue your sanctification in the image and righteousness of Christ?

God. God's will is that he sanctify you.$_{1Th\ 4:3}$ The law and prophets testify to God's righteousness.$_{Ro\ 2:21}$ God called us to holy life.$_{1Th\ 4:7}$ May the God of peace sanctify you through and through.$_{1Th\ 5:23}$ God is faithful and will sanctify you.$_{1Th\ 5:24}$ The Spirit's sanctifying work saved believing brothers and sisters.$_{2Th\ 2:13}$ True godliness springs from the great mystery that Christ appeared in the flesh, received the Spirit's vindication, had angels see him, had persons preach him among the nations, had people believe in him, and ascended in glory.$_{1Ti\ 3:16}$ Godliness with contentment in food and clothing is great gain because we brought nothing into the world and take nothing out of it.$_{1Ti\ 6:6-8}$ Believers in God should pursue righteousness and godliness.$_{1Ti\ 6:11}$ God called us to a holy life out of his own purpose and grace.$_{2Ti\ 1:9}$

Faith. Abraham, our ancestor, got God's credit for righteousness because Abraham believed God.$_{Ro\ 4:1-3}$ Abraham and his offspring received God's promise through righteousness from faith.$_{Ro\ 4:13}$ Because of what Abraham did, God credited Abraham with righteousness and called him his friend, proving that righteousness comes from faith and action together.$_{Jas\ 2:23-24}$ God even treated the prostitute Rahab as righteous for hiding and saving the Israelite spies.*Jas 2:25* God credits our faith as righteousness when we, the ungodly, trust him.*Ro 4:4-5* God credits to us as righteouness our belief that he raised Jesus from the dead.*Ro 4:22-24* God forgives our sins and blesses us with righteousness apart from our works.*Ro 4:6-7* When we believe God, he credits our belief to us as righteousness.*Gal 3:6* Eagerly await your hoped-for righteousness from faith.*Gal 5:2-5*

Works. Those who did not pursue righteousness by law obtained it by faith, while those who pursued righteousness by law did not obtain it because they pursued it by works.*Ro 9:30-32* For God to judge us righteous, we must live by faith rather than under law, which justifies no one.*Gal 3:11* Our righteousness is not our own from the law but comes from God based on faith in Christ.*Php 3:9* Zealousness for God is not enough when one pursues one's own righteousness rather than submitting to God's righteousness.*Ro 10:2-3* Animal blood and ashes on the ceremonially unclean sanctify only outwardly.*Heb 9:13*

Christ. God gives righteousness to all who believe through faith in Jesus Christ.*Ro 2:22* God sanctifies those who call on the Lord Jesus Christ as his holy people in Christ Jesus.*1Co 1:2* Christ Jesus is our righteousness.*1Co 1:30* By sacrificing Christ, God demonstrated his righteousness after having left unpunished prior sins.*Ro 2:25-26* The blood of Christ, who through the eternal Spirit offered himself unblemished to God, cleanses inwardly, clearing our consciences from acts leading to death, so that we serve the living God.*Heb 9:14* The covenant's blood sanctified us.*Heb 10:29* God's righteousness reigns in life through one man Jesus Christ, whose one righteous act resulted in justification and life for all.*Ro 5:17-18* One man's obedience made many righteous.*Ro 5:19* Grace reigns through righteousness, bringing eternal life through Jesus Christ our Lord.*Ro 5:21* We received so precious of a faith through our God and Savior Jesus Christ's righteousness.*2Pe 1:1-2* May God fill you with righteousness's fruit that comes through Jesus Christ, to God's glory and praise.*Php 1:11* May your whole spirit, soul, and body be blameless at our Lord Jesus Christ's return.*1Th 5:23*

Pursuit. Pursue righteousness with those who call on the Lord out of a pure heart.*2Ti 2:22* Be an example in purity for believers.*1Ti 4:11* Offer yourselves to God as those whom he brought from death to life, making every part of yourself an instrument of righteousness.*Ro 6:13* You are slaves of the one you obey, if to obedience, then leading to righteousness.*Ro 6:16* God made you a slave of righteousness.*Ro 6:18* Because we know his glory and goodness, God by his great and precious promises and power gives us everything for a godly life, to participate in his divine nature and escape the world's corruption that evil desires cause.*2Pe 1:3-4* Because God so favors us, we should be good, knowledgeable, self-controlled, persevering, godly, affectionate, and loving, one after another.*2Pe 1:5-7* Have in store for you the crown of righteousness, which the Lord will on that day award to all who have longed for his appearing.*2Ti 4:8* My believing brothers and sisters are full of goodness.*Ro 15:14*

Sin. Rid yourself of all moral filth and the prevalent evil, instead humbly accepting the word that God planted in you that saves you.*Jas 1:21* Have nothing to do with people who love themselves, money, and pleasure rather than God, and are boastful, proud, abusive, disobedient to parents, ungrateful, unholy, without love, unforgiving, slanderous, without self-control, brutal, not lovers of the good but instead treacherous, rash, and conceited, and while having a form of godliness yet denying its power.*2Ti 3:2-5* Some of you were sexually immoral, idolaters, adulterers, thieves, greedy, drunkards, slanderers, and swindlers, but the name of the Lord Jesus Christ and Spirit of our God sanctified you.*1Co 6:9-11* Our unrighteousness brings out God's righteousness more clearly.*Ro 2:5* To be righteous is to do the right things that Christ does, while to be sinful is to do the opposite as the devil does, that which Christ came to destroy.*1Jn 3:7-8* Imitate only what is good, not what is evil, because those who do good are from God, while those who do evil have not seen God.*3Jn 11* Be ready to suffer bodily as Christ suffered, because you do not pursue evil desires in sin when suffering, but instead seek God's will.*1Pe 4:1-2* Offer yourself as a slave to righteousness leading to holiness, as you once offered yourself to wickedness.*Ro 6:19*

Conduct. Conduct yourselves appropriately in purity, understanding, patience, and kindness, in the Holy Spirit and sincere love, in truthful speech and God's power, and with weapons of righteousness in both hands.*2Co 6:6-7* Conduct yourselves appropriately through glory and dishonor, bad and good report, while genuine but regarded as impostors, known but regarded as unknown, dying and yet living on, beaten but not killed, sorrowful yet always rejoicing, poor yet making many rich, and having nothing and yet possessing everything.*2Co 6:8-10* Keep yourself from anything contaminating body or spirit, perfecting holiness.*2Co 7:1* Scripture teaches, rebukes, corrects, and trains in righteousness.*2Ti 3:16-17* The Holy Spirit sanctifies hearers of the proclaimed gospel.*Ro 15:16* Pray to God not to do anything wrong, not so people see your faith but so you do right even though others believe you failed.*2Co 13:7* Make every effort to be holy because without holiness no one will see the Lord.*Heb 12:14*

Return

The letters address at length Christ's anticipated return. Every believer should celebrate Christ's second coming in which God fulfills all. We do not know the timing of Christ's return other than that his return is near, keeping us alert and sober. Yet Christ's return is not simply for eager believers. On his return, Christ will redeem everything, raising the dead and bringing a new heaven and earth. See how the letters address Christ's return. Are you longing as you should for his glorious coming?

Fulfillment. With all wisdom, God made known to us his will's mystery, as was his good pleasure in Christ when times reach fulfillment, to unify everything in heaven and on earth under Christ.*Eph 1:8-10* We indeed look forward to the Lord's promised righteous new heaven and new earth after Christ's return.*2Pe 3:13* God will reveal the Lord Jesus from heaven in blazing fire with his powerful angels.*2Th 1:7* The Lord Jesus in the splendor of his return will overthrow and destroy the lawless one.*2Th 2:7-8* After Christ sacrificed himself once to take away the sins of many, his second appearance will not be to bear sin but to bring salvation to those awaiting him.*Heb 9:27-28* Fellow believers will be your glory when our Lord Jesus returns.*1Th 2:20* Encourage one another with how God treats believers on Christ's return.*1Th 4:18* The Lord will on that day award righteousness's crown to all who have longed for his appearing.*2Ti 4:8*

Timing. Time differs to the Lord to whom a day is like a thousand years and thousand years like a day.*2Pe 3:8* The Lord will indeed return but in waiting is just being patient, wanting everyone to repent rather than any to perish.*2Pe 3:9* The last days will be terrible times.*2Ti 3:1* But the Lord's return will come sneaking up when fire destroys the elements and the Lord lays everything bare.*2Pe 3:10* Be alert and aware, ready to pray because all things are about to end.*1Pe 4:7* The Lord is near.*Php 4:5* Wait for God's Son Jesus, who rescues us from the coming wrath.*1Th 1:10* Don't look for times and dates because the Lord's return will come unexpectedly.*1Th 5:1-2* Do not worry as some say that our Lord Jesus Christ's return has already come because it hasn't.*2Th 2:2-3* Jesus will not return until the rebellion occurs and the man of lawlessness appears.*2Th 2:3-6* God will bring about our Lord Jesus Christ's return in his own time, until which you should keep God's commands without spot or blame.*1Ti 6:14-15* The Lord's return will not surprise believers, who know the truth.*1Th 5:4* Now is the time to wake up from your slumber because salvation is nearer now than when you first believed.*Ro 13:11* Judge nothing before the appointed time, but wait until the Lord comes.*1Co 4:5* Then each will receive their praise from God.*1Co 4:5*

You. When Christ appears, you will appear with him in glory.*Col 3:4* The Lord's holy people who believed in Jesus, including you, will glorify Jesus and marvel at him on his return.*2Th 1:10-11* When Christ returns, dear children of God, we do not yet know what we will be, but we know we will be like him, seeing him as he is.*1Jn 3:2* Our expectation of his return keeps us trying to stay pure, just as he is pure.*1Jn 3:3* We should patiently await the Lord's near coming like the farmer waits patiently for rains to bring a valuable crop and like the prophets suffered while speaking in the Lord's name.*Jas 5:7-8,10* God's power shields us in our faith until the salvation comes that he will reveal in the last time.*1Pe 1:5* Keep alert and sober for the grace that Jesus Christ's coming revelation will bring to you.*1Pe 1:13* Be able to boast at Christ's return that you did not run or labor in vain.*Php 2:16* We know that God who began a good work in us will continue until the day Christ Jesus returns.*Php 1:6* We lack no spiritual gift as we eagerly wait for God to reveal our Lord Jesus Christ.*1Co 1:7* God will keep you firm to the end, so that no one blames you on the day of our Lord Jesus Christ.*1Co 1:8*

Pursuit. Because the end exposes everything, you should live holy and godly, looking forward to the Lord's speedy coming when all ends.*2Pe 3:11-12* When Jesus returns, God will punish with permanent destruction those who do not know God and do not obey the Lord Jesus's gospel, shutting them out from the Lord's presence and glory of his might.*2Th 1:8-10* Make every effort to be spotless, blameless and at peace with the patient God of salvation, as you await the end of all things as scripture accurately foretells but ignorant and unstable people distort to their own destruction.*2Pe 3:14-16* Forewarned, be on guard so that lawlessness's error does not cause you to fall from your secure position, but instead learn more of the grace of our Lord and Savior Jesus Christ to whom we give glory now and forever.*2Pe 3:17-18* May deep insight abound in your growing love, so that you are discerning, pure, and blameless for Christ's return.*Php 1:9-10* Be blameless and holy in the presence of our God and Father when our Lord Jesus returns with all his holy ones.*1Th 3:13* Be blameless at our Lord Jesus Christ's return.*1Th 5:23*

Dead. The resurrection of the dead has not yet taken place.*2Ti 2:18* Know how God treats those who died as Christ followers, so that you do not grieve like non-believers who have no hope.*1Th 4:13* Believe that Jesus died and rose again, so that God brings with Jesus those who died in him.*1Th 4:14* The Lord's word is that we who are alive when the Lord returns will certainly not go with him before believers who have already died go with him.*1Th 4:15* Instead, when the Lord comes down from heaven, with a loud command, with the voice of the archangel and with the trumpet call of God, those who died in Christ will rise first.*1Th 4:16* Then, God will catch up in the clouds together with the rising dead, the living who remain, to meet the Lord in the air to be with him forever.*1Th 4:17* God saves a person's spirit on the Lord's day.*1Co 5:4-5*

Christ. Christ comes first, then when he comes, those who belong to him.*1Co 15:23* Then the end will come when he hands God's kingdom to the Father after destroying all dominion, authority, and power.*1Co 15:24* Christ must reign until all enemies are under his feet.*1Co 15:25* The last enemy Christ destroys is death.*1Co 15:26* God has put everything under Christ's feet other than God himself.*1Co 15:27* When the Son finishes, the Son will subject himself to the Father who put everything under him, so that God is everything in all.*1Co 15:28* Come, Lord.*1Co 16:22* Boast of one another as you will boast in the day of the Lord Jesus.*2Co 1:14* When Christ ascended, he took many captives while giving gifts to his people.*Eph 4:8* Christ, who also descended to the lower, earthly regions, ascended higher than heaven, so high as to fill the whole universe.*Eph 4:9-10* Christ ascended in glory.*1Ti 3:16* Keep meeting together, all the more as the last day approaches.*Heb 10:25* Christ will return in just a little while and will not delay.*Heb 10:37*

Eternity

The letters recognize that God's promise in Jesus Christ is not temporary but instead eternal. Everything will perish, but the Lord will remain. And those who fight the good fight of faith, holding to Jesus until the end, will live with him forever. See how the letters address eternity. No matter how tired and vexed you may be here, or how near and seemingly bitter may be your end, do you grasp and endure for your eternal victory?

Christ. Our Savior Christ Jesus brought immortality to light.$_{2Ti\ 1:10}$ The King eternal, immortal, invisible, the only God, has honor and glory forever.$_{1Ti\ 1:17}$ Everyone is like grass withering or flowers falling, but the Lord's word endures forever, just as you have heard.$_{1Pe\ 1:24-25}$ The covenant under which God raised our Lord Jesus from the dead is eternal.$_{Heb\ 13:20}$ While sin reigned in death, grace reigns through righteousness, bringing eternal life through Jesus Christ our Lord.$_{Ro\ 5:21}$ Fix your eyes on the unseen rather than what you see because what you see is temporary, while the unseen is eternal.$_{2Co\ 4:18}$ The Son's throne, as God, will last forever.$_{Heb\ 1:8}$ The earth and heavens will perish, wearing out like garments, but the Lord will remain.$_{Heb\ 1:11}$ The Lord will roll up earth and heavens like a robe, changing them like a garment, but the Lord will remain the same, for never-ending years.$_{Heb\ 1:12}$

You. Justified by God's grace, we are heirs to eternal life.$_{Tit\ 3:7}$ We receive the promised eternal inheritance, now that Christ has died as a ransom to set us free from the sins committed under the first covenant.$_{Heb\ 9:15}$ Our Lord Jesus Christ and God our Father gave us good hope of eternity.$_{2Th\ 2:16-17}$ Those who believe in Christ Jesus receive eternal life.$_{1Ti\ 1:16}$ The living and enduring word of God has given you rebirth, not perishable but imperishable.$_{1Pe\ 1:23}$ Christ's one sacrifice made you, whom God is making holy, perfect forever.*Heb 10:14* When you build yourself up in your most holy faith and pray in the Holy Spirit, you keep yourself in God's love, waiting for the mercy of our Lord Jesus Christ to bring you to eternal life.*Jude 20-21* Fight faith's good fight to take hold of eternal life.*1Ti 6:12* The elect obtaining salvation in Christ Jesus receive eternal glory.*2Ti 2:10* God gives eternal life to those who by persistence in doing good seek glory, honor, and immortality.*Ro 2:7* One reaps no benefit from sin, only shame and death, but one reaps holiness and eternal life as a slave to God, because sin's wage is death, but God's gift is eternal life in Christ Jesus our Lord.*Ro 6:21-22* Everyone in competition has strict training to get a temporary crown, but you train to get a crown that lasts forever.*1Co 9:25* Our eternal glory far outweighs the light and momentary troubles achieving that glory for us.*2Co 4:17*

Part II: Darkness

Satan. Sin. Death. Law. Circumcision. Deceivers. Desertion. Idols. Persecution. Traditions. Quarrels. Slavery. World. Riches. Flesh. Curse. Spirits. Doubt. Favoritism. Judgment.

While the Bible tells the great story of light coming into the world as the life of humankind, giving us ultimate victory over death through Christ's resurrection, the Bible also tells that spiritual warfare will continue until Christ's return. Darkness retreats but is not yet banished. Legalism still tempts us to give up our freedom for law's custody. We seek outward adornment, deserting the faith in favor of idols, confused over faith's meaning. Opponents still persecute us, while we also fall prey to our own traditions, temptation, and pride. We unwisely accept a slavery of the flesh, falling under the curse of evil spirits that we should know better to resist. See how the letters address the darkness around us. Do you see and resist the darkness?

Satan

The letters address the adversary Satan, the devil and his demons. We must know the opponent in order that we can resist him, keeping our minds focused on Christ. Christ triumphed over Satan, for us to share in that triumph. See how the letters address our formidable adversary, made weak and subject in Christ. Can you identify the devil, so that you may resist in the name and power of Christ?

Enemy. Watch out because your enemy the devil prowls like a roaring lion looking to devour someone.$_{1Pe\ 5:8}$ Simply believing in God is not enough because even shuddering demons know he exists.$_{Jas\ 2:19}$ The devil traps gospel opponents who don't know truth, so that they are captive to do the devil's will.$_{2Ti\ 2:25\text{-}2}$ The tempter does his tempting work to destroy your faith.$_{1Th\ 3:5}$ Satan blocks your way from seeing fellow believers.$_{1Th\ 2:17}$ The lawless one will come in the wicked way that Satan works, using all sorts of powerfully deceiving displays, signs, and wonders serving the deadly lie.$_{2Th\ 2:9}$ The difference between God's children and children of the devil is that God's children love one another and stop sinning, while the devil's children do not.$_{1Jn\ 3:9}$ Satan masquerades as an angel of light.$_{2Co\ 11:14}$ No surprise, then, that Satan's servants masquerade as if serving righteousness, but they will end as they deserve.$_{2Co\ 11:15}$ Bitter envy and selfish ambition are earthly and demonic, sowing disorder and evil.$_{Jas\ 3:14\text{-}16}$ Satan can send a thorn in the flesh to torment.$_{2Co\ 12:7}$ The Spirit warns against following deceiving spirits and demons.$_{1Ti\ 4:1}$ Do not in sensual desire turn away to follow Satan.$_{1Ti\ 5:14\text{-}15}$ The faithful may hand over to Satan those who reject faith and a good conscience, to learn not to blaspheme.$_{1Ti\ 1:20}$ An overseer must not become conceited and fall under the same judgment as the devil.$_{1Ti\ 3:6}$ An overseer must also have a good reputation with outsiders, so that he will not fall into disgrace and into the devil's trap.*1Ti 3:7* Non-believers offer sacrifices to demons, not to God, so do not participate with demons.*1Co 10:20*

Resistance. We struggle not against flesh and blood but against rulers, authorities, and powers of this dark world and spiritual forces of evil in the heavenly realms.*Eph 6:12* The devil flees us when we resist him.*Jas 4:7-8* God rescues us from the dominion of darkness.*Col 1:13* The archangel Michael did not dare condemn the devil's slander but said instead that the Lord would rebuke him.*Jude 8-10* Wear God's full armor so that you withstand the devil's schemes.*Eph 6:11* Resist him, standing firm in the faith, because you know that followers everywhere face the same sufferings.*1Pe 5:9* Wear God's full armor so that when evil's day comes, you can stand your ground and remain standing.*Eph 6:13* Do not give the devil a foothold by remaining angry.*Eph 4:27* Be very careful that you live wisely, making the most of every opportunity, because the days are evil.*Eph 5:15-16* Use the shield of faith to extinguish the evil one's flaming arrows.*Eph 6:16* The Lord delivers from the lion's mouth.*2Ti 4:17* The God of peace will soon crush Satan under your feet.*Ro 16:20*

Christ. Christ disarmed and triumphed over evil powers and authorities, making a public spectacle of them.*Col 2:15* No harmony exists between Christ and Satan.*2Co 6:15* You cannot drink the Lord's cup and the demons' cup, too, taking part in both the Lord's table and demons' table.*1Co 10:21* Don't let the serpent's cunning lead your minds astray from Christ.*2Co 11:3* Jesus shared in our humanity because we are human, so that by his death he would break the devil's power of death.*Heb 2:14* The Lord protects you from the evil one.*2Th 3:3* Assemble with the Lord Jesus's power present, to hand wrongdoers among you, who practice sexual immorality that not even non-believers practice, over to Satan to destroy the flesh, so that God may save the disobedient one's spirit on the Lord's day.*1Co 5:4-5* If you forgive, then others will also forgive, all in Christ's sight for your sake, so that Satan, of whose schemes we know, does not outwit us.*2Co 2:10-11* To be righteous is to do the right things that Christ does, while to be sinful is to do the opposite as the devil does, that which Christ came to destroy.*1Jn 3:7-8* Neither death nor life, angels nor demons, nor any powers, nor anything else in all creation, can separate us from God's love in Christ Jesus our Lord.*Ro 8:38-39*

Sin

The letters address sin at considerable length, as indeed they should, given our sinful nature. Disobedience brought sin into the world and made sin our nature. Those who sin fall under sin's curse, which is death. Although sin came before the law, the law accentuated and increased our sin. The law's violation also brought God's judgment. You, though, have died to sin, giving you freedom and eternal life in Christ Jesus. You must flee sin, avoiding temptation and ridding yourself of anger, while pursuing God's holiness, anticipating the day when Christ will transform your sinful body. See how extensively the letters address sin. Do you know your former corrupt condition and continuing need for the righteousness of Christ?

Disobedience. Sin entered the world through one man, death following for all because all sinned.$_{Ro\ 5:12}$ All turn away from God to become worthless, without any doing good, not even one.$_{Ro\ 2:12}$ All sin, falling short of God's glory.$_{Ro\ 2:23}$ Adam, the first to sin, was a pattern of the one to come, the sinless Jesus.$_{Ro\ 5:14}$ Jesus, though, is different from Adam, in that many died from Adam's trespass, but many lived from the gift of God's grace in Jesus Christ$_{Ro\ 5:15}$ The penalty of Adam's sin differs from God's gift of grace, in that judgment's condemnation followed sin, but grace's justification followed many sins.$_{Ro\ 5:16}$ Death reigned by one man's sin, but God's abundant grace and righteousness reign in life through one man Jesus Christ's gift.$_{Ro\ 5:17}$ One sin resulted in condemnation for all, while one righteous act resulted in justification and life for all.$_{Ro\ 5:18}$ One man's disobedience made many sinners, yet another man's obedience made many righteous.$_{Ro\ 5:19}$ All wrongdoing is sin.$_{1Jn\ 5:17}$ All are under sin's power.$_{Ro\ 2:8-11}$

Nature. We are unspiritual, slaves to sin.~Ro 7:14~ We don't understand the bad that we do or why we do it, when we want instead to do good, except that we know sin lives in our sinful nature.~Ro 7:15-20~ Whenever we want to do good, evil is right there with us.~Ro 7:21~ Sin wages war against our minds, imprisoning us in sin.~Ro 7:23~ We are wretched indeed, with minds devoted to God while trapped in bodies with sinful natures subject to death, but we thank God for delivering us through Jesus Christ our Lord.~Ro 7:24-25~ Before our salvation, we were foolish, disobedient, deceived and enslaved by passions and pleasures, living in malice and envy, hated and hating others.~Tit 3:3-4~ We were once dead in our transgressions and sins, in which we used to live when we followed the world's ways and ways of the evil spirit still at work in the disobedient.~Eph 2:1-2~ You once lived debauched as pagans live in lust, drunkenness, and detestable idolatry, and so now they heap abuse on you for not joining them in their reckless living.~1Pe 4:3-4~

Cursed. Whoever does not have godly qualities is nearsighted and blind, forgetting that they have been cleansed from their past sins.~2Pe 1:9~ Those accursed experts in greed whose eyes fill with adultery, they never stop sinning, seducing the unstable while wandering after the wages of wickedness, so stupid as to suffer rebuke and restraint by an ordinarily speechless animal.~1Pe 2:14-16~ Sinners are springs without water and mists driven by a storm, for whom God reserves blackest darkness.~1Pe 2:17~ Allow among God's holy people not even a hint of sexual immorality, any impurity, or greed.~Eph 5:3~ Banish obscenity, foolish talk, and coarse joking, in favor of thanksgiving.~Eph 5:4~ No immoral, impure, or greedy person inherits the kingdom of Christ and God.~Eph 5:5~ Immorality is disobedience bringing God's wrath.~Eph 5:6~ Do not partner with the immoral.~Eph 5:7~ One reaps no benefit from sin, only shame and death, because sin's wage is death.~Ro 6:21-22~

Law. Sin and death were in the world before God gave the law, although God charges sin against no one without breaking a command of the law.~Ro 5:13-14~ God gave the law to increase sin so that grace would increase even more.~Ro 5:20~ The law defines sin for us, such as when the law says not to covet, showing us that coveting is sin.~Ro 7:7~ The law makes us conscious of our sin.~Ro 2:20~ Yet commands make us want to break them.~Ro 7:8~ Apart from the law, sin was dead, and we were alive, but with the commandment, sin sprang to life and we died.~Ro 7:8-9~ The commandment that should bring life instead brought death because sin deceived, through the commandment putting us to death.*Ro 7:10-11* The good law did not become death, but sin used the good law to bring death, showing sin's utter sinfulness.*Ro 7:13* Before Jesus returns, the lawless man's rebellion will occur, in which the lawless man, doomed to destruction, will oppose and exalt himself over everything connected with God trying to take God's place and proclaim himself God.*2Th 2:3-4* Lawlessness's secret power already works, even though the Lord Jesus will overthrow and destroy the lawless one.*2Th 2:7-8*

Judgment. All who sin apart from the law perish, while all who sin under the law face law's judgment.*Ro 2:12* God's wrath is coming for sin.*Col 3:6* God got angry with our ancestors who sinned, leaving them to perish in the wilderness, while swearing that those who disobeyed in unbelief would never enter his rest.*Heb 3:17-19* The Lord punishes all who commit sins, as others have warned you.*1Th 4:6* Anyone who does wrong will be repaid for their wrongs.*Col 3:25* Your evil behavior once alienated you from God, making you enemies in your minds.*Col 1:21* Don't worry about those with whom you once sinned and who now persecute you for abandoning them to their sin because they must account to God who judges both the living and dead.*1Pe 4:5* The sins of some are obvious, reaching the place of judgment ahead of them, while the sins of others trail behind them.*1Ti 5:24* Establish accusations by the testimony of two or three witnesses, but do not spare those who sin because Christ is not weak but powerful in dealing with you.*2Co 13:1-3*

You. You have died to sin and can no longer live in it, so don't sin simply expecting more grace.*Ro 6:1-2* Our old self's crucifixion with Jesus killed the sinful body, setting us free from sin and making us no longer slaves to sin.*Ro 6:6-7* Christ died to sin once for all.*Ro 6:10* Like Christ, count yourselves dead to sin but alive to God in Christ Jesus.*Ro 6:11* Do not let sin reign in your body, obeying its evil desires.*Ro 6:12* Do not offer any part of yourself as an instrument of wickedness.*Ro 6:13* Sin is not your master because you are under grace, not law.*Ro 6:14* Do not sin simply because you are under grace rather than law.*Ro 6:15* You are slaves of the one you obey, if of sin, then leading to death.*Ro 6:16* You may have the right to do anything, but not everything is beneficial, and you should not let anything master you.*1Co 6:12* Come back to your senses as you should, stop sinning, and don't be ignorant of God, otherwise shame on you.*1Co*

15:34 Men crucified Christ in weakness, but Christ lives by God's power, just as you are weak in him but live by God's power in dealing with the sin of one another.*2Co 13:4*

Freedom. Thank God that although you were once slave to sin, you now obey the teaching from your heart.*Ro 6:17* God set you free from sin.*Ro 6:18* While sin reigned in death, grace reigns through righteousness, bringing eternal life through Jesus Christ our Lord.*Ro 5:21* Because a great cloud of witnesses surrounds you, throw off anything hindering you, especially the sin that so easily entangles, so that you can run the right race with perseverance.*Heb 12:1* Resist to the point of bleeding, if you must, when struggling against sin.*Heb 12:4* Do not be overcome by evil, but overcome evil with good.*Ro 12:21* You once offered yourselves as slaves to increasing wickedness, and so now offer yourselves as slaves to righteousness.*Ro 6:19* Righteousness cannot influence a slave to sin.*Ro 6:20* Do not yoke yourself to unbelievers, because righteousness and wickedness, and light and darkness, have nothing in common.*2Co 6:14* The Lord says to separate ourselves, staying clean, so that he may receive us.*2Co 6:17*

Temptation. Restore gently the one whom you catch in a sin, while guarding yourself against temptation.*Gal 6:1* Just as evil cannot tempt God, so, too, God does not tempt with evil, which instead comes from our own evil desire inducing sin that leads to death.*Jas 1:13-15* Rather than think you stand firm, be careful that you don't fall.*1Co 10:12* Only common temptations overtake you, but when they do, God is faithful in not letting them tempt you beyond what you can bear, instead providing a way out so that you endure.*1Co 10:13* Believers in God should flee from sin.*1Ti 6:11* Never unite your body, which is a member of Christ, with a prostitute because the two then become one flesh.*1Co 6:15-16* Flee sexual immorality because while all other sins are outside the body, sexual sin is against one's own body.*1Co 6:18* Do not sin, and repent of impurity, sexual sin, and debauchery in which others indulge.*2Co 12:21* Let no one be sexually immoral.*Heb 12:17* God did not mean the body for sexual immorality but for the Lord, and the Lord for the body.*1Co 6:13* Foolish and harmful desires for riches tempt, trap, and plunge people into ruin and destruction.*1Ti 6:9* Loving money is an evil root, causing some to wander from the faith while piercing themselves with many griefs.*1Ti 6:10*

Anger. Don't get angry quickly because anger does not produce God's desired righteousness.*Jas 1:20* Evil hates and murders a righteous one.*1Jn 3:12* You either love or hate, and those who hate die, while those who love in Christ gain eternal life.*1Jn 3:14-15* Get rid of all malice, deceit, hypocrisy, envy, and slander of every kind.*1Pe 2:1* In your anger do not sin, nor let the sun go down while you are still angry.*Eph 4:26* Get rid of all bitterness, rage, anger, brawling, slander, and other form of malice.*Eph 4:31* While you used to be sinful in your former life, you must now rid yourself of all sin including anger, rage, malice, slander, and bad language.*Col 3:7-8* Men should pray and lift holy hands without anger.*1Ti 2:8* Love does not easily anger.*1Co 13:5*

Holiness. God's will is that he sanctify you, that you avoid sexual immorality, control your own body to be holy and honorable, avoid passionate lust like those who do not know God, and not wrong or take advantage of a brother or sister.*1Th 4:3-6* God called us not to impurity but to holy life.*1Th 4:7* Do not lie to each other, because you have taken off your old self with its practices.*Col 3:9* Do not slumber and get drunk like non-believers but instead be awake and sober.*1Th 5:6-7* Hold on to what is good while rejecting every kind of evil.*1Th 3:19-22* Ask God to deliver you from wicked and evil people.*2Th 3:2* Do not in idleness go from house to house as a busybody talking nonsense you should not say.*1Ti 5:13* Do not share in the sins of others, but keep yourself pure.*1Ti 5:22* Behave decently, as in daytime, not in carousing and drunkenness, sexual immorality and debauchery, or in dissension and jealousy.*Ro 13:13* Celebrate not with malice and wickedness but with sincerity and truth.*1Co 5:8* Our Savior the Lord Jesus Christ will by his complete power transform our lowly bodies to be like his glorious body.*Php 3:20-21*

Death

The letters address at length the topic of death. Sin in pursuit of the flesh's desires brings death. Death to the flesh in pursuit of Christ's Spirit brings life. Jesus died that all who embrace him may live. Jesus's resurrection defeated death. Gospel preachers face persecution even to the point of death, that you may have life in hearing and accepting the gospel. God indeed gives life to the dead. See how earnestly the letters address death. Have you renounced death's fear in full embrace of your salvation and resurrection in Christ?

Sin. When we were in the flesh's realm, law aroused sinful passions that led to death.$_{Ro\ 7:5}$ Apart from the law, sin was dead, and we were alive, but with the commandment, sin sprang to life, and we died.$_{Ro\ 7:8-9}$ The good did not become death, but sin used the good to bring death, showing its utter sinfulness.$_{Ro\ 7:13}$ The commandment that should bring life instead brought death because sin deceived, through the commandment putting us to death.$_{Ro\ 7:10-11}$ All who sin apart from the law perish, while all who sin under the law face law's judgment.$_{Ro\ 2:12}$ Law just helped us die to the law so that we could live for God.$_{Gal\ 2:19}$ The law has authority over someone only as long as that person lives.$_{Ro\ 7:1}$ For example, a husband's death releases a married woman from the law binding her to him, so that she may marry another man without committing adultery.$_{Ro\ 7:2-3}$ Likewise, you died to the law through the body of Christ so that you could belong to Christ raised from the dead, bearing fruit for God.$_{Ro\ 7:4}$ Death to the flesh released us from the law so that we serve in the Spirit's new way rather than the written code's old way.$_{Ro\ 7:6}$ The godless know God's righteous decree that those who do wrong things deserve death, but they continue to do those things.$_{Ro\ 1:32}$ One reaps no benefit from sin, only shame and death, because sin's only wage is death.~Ro 6:21-22~ We must put to death the body's misdeeds to live, rather than live for the flesh, in which case we die.~Ro 8:12-13~

Jesus. God delivered Jesus over to death for our sins and raised him to life for our justification.~Ro 4:25~ When living on earth, Jesus prayed and petitioned fervently to God who could save him from death, and God heard Jesus because of his reverent submission.~Heb 5:7~ Christ Jesus made himself nothing in the very nature of a servant, humbly obedient even to death on a cross.~Php 2:6-8~ The last enemy Christ destroys is death.~1Co 15:26~ While Christ died for our sins as the Scriptures say, he rose on the third day after burial, as the Scriptures also say.~1Co 15:3~ The God of peace, through the blood of the eternal covenant, raised from the dead our Lord Jesus, the great Shepherd of the sheep.~Heb 13:20~ Christ's purpose on the cross was to reconcile in him one new peaceful humanity out of the divided two sides, putting to death their hostility.~Eph 2:15-16~ Jesus shared in our humanity because we are human, so that by his death he would break the devil's power of death.~Heb 2:14~ Christ redeemed us from law's curse when crucifixion cursed Christ who died for us.~Gal 3:13~ All those baptized into Christ Jesus were buried with him through baptism into death so that just as the glory of the Father raised Christ from the dead, we also live a new life.~Ro 6:3-4~ Through Christ Jesus, the law of the Spirit who gives life freed us from the law of sin and death.~Ro 8:2~ Godly sorrow brings repentance leading to salvation without regret, while worldly sorrow brings only death.~2Co 7:10~ Foundational teaching in Christ includes repenting from acts leading to death.~Heb 6:1-2~

Resurrection. Desire to know the power of Christ's resurrection and participation in his sufferings, becoming like him in his death and so attaining to resurrection from death.~Php 3:10-11~ We should thank God the Father of our Lord Jesus Christ for his great mercy, giving us new birth into living hope through Jesus's resurrection from the dead.~1Pe 1:3~ Through Christ you believe in God and place your hope in God, for raising Christ from the dead and glorifying him.~1Pe 1:21~ Jesus Christ's resurrection saves you because he is in heaven at God's right hand with angels, authorities, and powers submitting to him.~1Pe 3:21-22~ We neither live nor die for ourselves alone but live and die for the Lord, either way belonging to the Lord.~Ro 14:7-8~ Because death came through a man, resurrection also comes through a man.~1Co 15:21~ In Adam all died so that in Christ all could live.~1Co 15:22~

Teachers. Some are exposed to death repeatedly for sharing the gospel.*2Co 11:24-26* Some face death daily for Christ Jesus our Lord.*1Co 15:31* Some feel they have received a death sentence, making them rely on God, who raises the dead.*2Co 1:9* Death works against our teachers so that life works in us.*2Co 4:12* To sinners, gospel teachers are an aroma bringing death, while to believers an aroma bringing life.*2Co 2:16* Persecuted preachers always carry around in their body Jesus's death, so that their body may also reveal Jesus's life.*2Co 4:10* They face death for Jesus's sake, so that their mortal body may reveal his life.*2Co 4:11*

You. Those who die with Christ will also live with him.*2Ti 2:11* The death of God's Son reconciled us to God while we were still God's enemies, just as Christ now saves us through his life.*Ro 5:10* God reconciles us by Christ's physical body through death to present you holy, without blemish, and free from accusation, in his sight.*Col 1:22* Jesus frees those held in slavery by their fear of death.*Heb 2:15* Because you joined him in a death like his, you will certainly also join with him in a resurrection like his.*Ro 6:5* Because you died with Christ, you believe that you will also live with him.*Ro 6:8* If Christ is in you, then even though your body dies because of sin, the Spirit gives life because of righteousness.*Ro 8:10* If the Spirit of God who raised Jesus from the dead lives in you, then God who raised Christ from the dead will also give your body life because of his Spirit who lives in you.*Ro 8:11* You died to the law so that you could belong to Christ raised from the dead, bearing fruit for God.*Ro 7:4* Everything is yours, whether that of the world, life or death, or present or future, because you are of Christ, and Christ is of God.*1Co 3:21-23* You've heard from the start: love one another, and you will go from death to life.*1Jn 3:11-14* In our earthly tent, we groan with burden, fearing deadly exposure while wanting heaven's protection from death.*2Co 5:4* Know with confidence that to be at home in the body is to be away from the Lord.*2Co 5:6* Prefer to be away from the body and at home with the Lord.*2Co 5:8*

Life. God gives life to the dead.*Ro 4:17* Because God raised Christ from the dead, he cannot die again, and death no longer has mastery over him.*Ro 6:9* Christ died once for all and so lives to God.*Ro 6:10* The Lord Jesus died for us so that, whether we are alive or dead, we may live together with him.*1Th 5:10* Those who die with Christ will also live with him.*2Ti 2:11* Christ died and returned to life so that he might be the Lord of both the dead and the living.*Ro 14:9* Our Savior Christ Jesus destroyed death and brought immortality.*2Ti 1:10* When the perishable puts on the imperishable, and the mortal immortality, then the Scriptures' saying that victory swallowed up death will be true.*1Co 15:54* Death has no victory or sting when death's sting is sin and sin's power is the law.*1Co 15:55-56* Enoch's faith pleased God so much that God took him away before death.*Heb 11:5* Abraham had faith that God could raise the dead, as in a way God brought Isaac back from death.*Heb 11:19* Faith enabled others to face death by sword, stoning, or sawing in two, and others to go about in sheepskins and goatskins, destitute, persecuted, and mistreated.*Heb 11:37*

Law

The letters address the law and commandments, under which all lived and died, before God sent his Son with a new commandment. The law is for lawbreakers, highlighting our sin. The law thus brings not life but death. The law's zealous pursuit leads only to deadly legalism. The law was a shadow of Christ's coming righteousness, which freed us from law's judgment of death. The Spirit of Christ keeps the law on our hearts so that we obey the law as our conscience guides us. See how the letters address law. Has the Spirit written the law on your heart, even as you avoid legalism's perils?

Sin. The law is for lawbreakers and rebels, the ungodly and sinful, the unholy and irreligious, those who kill their fathers or mothers, murderers, the sexually immoral, those practicing homosexuality, slave traders, and liars and perjurers.*1Ti 1:8-10* The law makes us conscious of our sin.*Ro 2:20* The law, while not in itself sinful, defines sin for us, such as when the law says not to covet, showing us that coveting is sin.*Ro 7:7* When we were in the flesh's realm, law aroused sinful passions that led to death.*Ro 7:5* Commands make us want to break them.*Ro 7:8* The law brings wrath because the law brings trangression. *Ro 4:14-15* The law and commandment are nonetheless holy, righteous, and good.*Ro 7:12* The law is spiritual, but we are unspiritual, slaves to sin.*Ro 7:14* Inside, we delight in God's law, but sin wages war against our minds, imprisoning us in sin.*Ro 7:23*

Death. Apart from the law, sin was dead, and we were alive, but with the commandment, sin sprang to life and we died.*Ro 7:8-9* The good did not become death, but sin used the good to bring death, showing its utter sinfulness.*Ro 7:13* The commandment that should bring life instead brought death because sin deceived, through the commandment putting us to death.$_{Ro\ 7:10\text{-}11}$ All who sin apart from the law perish, while all who sin under the law face law's judgment.$_{Ro\ 2:12}$ The law, addressing those under the law, silences every mouth holding the whole world accountable to God.$_{Ro\ 2:19}$ Law just helped us die to the law so that we could live for God.$_{Gal\ 2:19}$ The law has authority over someone only as long as that person lives.$_{Ro\ 7:1}$ For example, a husband's death releases a married woman from the law binding her to him, so that she may marry another man without committing adultery.$_{Ro\ 7:2\text{-}3}$ Likewise, you died to the law through the body of Christ so that you could belong to Christ raised from the dead, bearing fruit for God.$_{Ro\ 7:4}$ Death to the flesh released us from the law so that we serve in the Spirit's new way rather than the written code's old way.$_{Ro\ 7:6}$

Shadow. The law is only a shadow of good things coming, not the reality, and so can never by endless sacrifices make perfect those who draw near to worship.$_{Heb\ 10:1}$ Those of you who want to be under the law had better beware of what the law says.$_{Gal\ 4:21}$ The law contradicts faith, saying that we live by doing certain things.$_{Gal\ 3:12}$ God set aside the former regulation as weak and useless, the law making nothing perfect, to offer us a better hope to draw near to God.$_{Heb\ 7:18\text{-}19}$ The law's priests serve at a copy and shadow sanctuary of heaven's sanctuary, which is why God mandated the shadow sanctuary's pattern.$_{Heb\ 8:5}$ Christ said that God had not desired sacrifices and offerings, which did not please God, even though our ancestors offered according to the law.$_{Heb\ 10:8}$

Legalism. Works of the law declare no one righteous in God's sight.$_{Ro\ 2:20}$ For example, some will forbid people to marry and order them to abstain from certain foods that God created for believers who know the truth to receive with thanksgiving.$_{1Ti\ 4:3}$ God elects us before we do anything good or bad, and not by right but by grace, to show that his call, not our works, makes the difference.$_{Ro\ 9:10\text{-}12}$ Salvation depends on God's mercy, not human desire or effort.$_{Ro\ 9:16}$ Legalistic works never justify a person, but faith in Jesus Christ justifies.$_{Gal\ 2:16}$ Christ in no way promotes sin by justifying us outside of the old legalism.$_{Gal\ 2:17}$ We would become lawbreakers all over again if we resumed the legalism that Christ's justification helped us destroy.$_{Gal\ 2:18}$ We first received the Spirit by believing the gospel message, not by works under law, and so we must continue under the Spirit rather than foolishly trying to finish with legalistic works of the flesh, which would only make our belief in vain.*Gal 3:2-4*

Christ. God gives us his Spirit and works miracles among us not by works of the law but by our believing what we heard of the gospel.*Gal 3:5* Through Christ Jesus, the law of the Spirit, who gives life, freed us from the law of sin and death.*Ro 8:2* Christ culminates the law so that everyone who believes has God's righteousness.*Ro 10:4* God gave the law because of transgressions but only until Christ had come.*Gal 3:19* The law, which does not impart righteousness and life, in no way opposes God's promises but instead shows everything under the control of sin aside from the righteousness and life that comes through faith in Jesus Christ.*Gal 3:21-22* The law held us in custody like a guardian, until God revealed faith in Christ as our justification, after which we no longer needed law's guardianship.*Gal 3:23-23* The law had no power to free us from sin because the flesh weakened us, but God sent his own Son in the likeness of sinful flesh to condemn sin in the flesh, to meet the law's righteous requirement in those of us who live by the Spirit rather than the flesh.*Ro 8:3-4*

Faith. Our righteousness is not our own from the law but that which is through faith in Christ.*Php 3:9* One must not boast about keeping the law because of the law that requires faith.*Ro 2:27* Faith justifies a person apart from works of the law.*Ro 2:28* Faith upholds the law.*Ro 2:31* While wages are due for working, when we instead fail to keep the law, God still credits our faith as righteousness when we, the ungodly, trust him.*Ro 4:4-5* God forgives our sins and blesses us with righteousness apart from works of the law.*Ro 4:6-7* The law and prophets testify to God's righteousness.*Ro 2:21* When the Spirit leads us, we are not under the law.*Gal 5:18*

Obedience. Obeying the law, not just hearing the law, makes one righteous in God's sight.*Ro 2:13* When those who do not have the law do what law requires, they are a law for themselves, because even though they do not have the law, they show the law is on their hearts, their consciences guiding them.*Ro 2:14-15* When you rely on the law, you know his will and approve the better, but then when you convince yourself that you guide the blind, light the dark, instruct the foolish, and teach children because law embodies knowledge and truth, you fail to teach yourself because you still steal, commit adultery, rob temples, and, though boasting in the law, dishonor God by breaking the law.$_{Ro\ 2:17-24}$ The law still provides an advantage in having the very words of God.$_{Ro\ 2:2}$

Circumcision

The letters address circumcision as both a literal tradition and spiritual condition. The literal tradition has no value because its source is in the law and keeping the tradition for righteousness is legalistic. The spiritual condition, though, is essential, to let Christ put off our old self. See how the letters address circumcision. Have you let God circumcise your heart?

Traditional. Watch out for evildoers who would mutilate the flesh with circumcision.*Php 3:2* While some could claim reason for confidence in the flesh, out of zeal for the law, better to consider any gains from such things to be loss for the sake of Christ.*Php 3:4-7* You were once called uncircumcised by those who call themselves the circumcision, which is only done in the body by human hands.*Eph 2:11* Now listen, if you let yourself be circumcised, Christ has no value to you, none, because then you must obey the whole law, alienating you from Christ and his grace.*Gal 5:2-5* Those who agitate against the cross, and for circumcision, should just go ahead and emasculate themselves.*Gal 5:11-12* People who impress others in the flesh, trying to compel your circumcision, do so to avoid being associated with the cross of Christ.*Gal 6:12* The circumcised do not even keep the law but only want you circumcised to boast about your circumcision.*Gal 6:13* Circumcision has value only if you observe the law, but when you break the law, you are as if uncircumcised.*Ro 2:25* Rather than let yourself be circumcised by others, you should instead through the Spirit eagerly await your hoped-for righteousness from faith.*Gal 5:2-5*

Spiritual. Genuine circumcision is to serve God by his Spirit and boast in Christ Jesus while putting no confidence in the flesh.*Php 3:3* God is the God of both the circumcised and uncircumcised because only one

God exists, who justifies all through the same faith.$_{Ro\ 2:29-30}$ Christ circumcised us with a circumcision not performed by human hands, putting off our whole self ruled by the flesh.$_{Col\ 2:11-12}$ Uncircumcision of our flesh makes us dead in sin.$_{Col\ 2:13}$ Whether you are circumcised means nothing in Christ Jesus, in whom only faith expressing itself through love counts.$_{Gal\ 5:6}$ Circumcision and uncircumcision mean nothing, while new creation means everything.$_{Gal\ 6:15}$ Among believers, we do not distinguish between circumcised or uncircumcised because Christ is everything.$_{Col\ 3:11}$ When those who are not circumcised keep the law, one may as well regard them as circumcised.$_{Ro\ 2:26}$ The uncircumcised who keep the law condemn the circumcised who break the law.$_{Ro\ 2:27}$ Circumcision is not merely outward and physical but is instead of the heart, by the Spirit rather than the written code, the Spirit whom God rather than people praise.$_{Ro\ 2:28-29}$ God's blessing is for the circumcised and uncircumcised, a righteousness credited to us by faith.$_{Ro\ 4:9-10}$ Abraham's circumcision was a seal of the righteousness that he already had by faith while he was still uncircumcised, just as will be so for all who believe.$_{Ro\ 4:11-12}$ Don't circumcise or uncircumcise yourself, because both are nothing, when keeping God's commands is what counts.$_{1Co\ 7:18-19}$

Deceivers

The letters address deceivers at length. Unfortunately, we face deceivers, making critical that we resist deception and not let others deceive. We must know and adhere to the truth, especially the gospel about our Lord and Savior Jesus Christ. We must also avoid, ignore, and oppose false teachers, while ensuring that we learn God's truth. God brings judgment on false teachers. See how frequently, consistently, and strongly the letters condemn deceivers. Are you identifying, resisting, and opposing those who deceive?

Deception. The Spirit warns against following deceiving spirits and things taught by demons.*1Ti 4:1* Some people will confuse you with a perverted gospel.*Gal 1:7* False teachers among you will secretly introduce destructive heresies, denying the Lord's salvation while destroying themselves.*1Pe 2:1* Greedy teachers will exploit you with stories they make up, leaving sure condemnation hanging over them.*1Pe 2:3* Some have an unhealthy interest in controversies and quarrels about words that result in envy, strife, malicious talk, and evil suspicions, producing constant friction between people of corrupt mind, robbed of the truth, thinking that godliness means financial gain.*1Ti 6:4-5* Those whom sin loads down and evil desires sway worm their way into homes and gain control over the gullible.*2Ti 3:6* Evildoers and impostors go from bad to worse, deceiving and being deceived.*2Ti 3:13* Those who turn from God are open graves swift to shed blood, speaking deceit, poison, curses, and bitterness, with ruin and misery marking their way.*Ro 2:13-16* If you want to enjoy life with good days, then don't speak evil or lies because the Lord watches and responds.*1Pe 3:10-11*

Resisting. Don't let others deceive you, friends.*Jas 1:16* Do not let another speak evil about what you know is good.*Ro 14:16* Don't be foolish, letting others bewitch you into abandoning the crucifixion's truth.*Gal 3:1* They may be zealous to win you over, but for no good, to alienate you from those who know the truth, so that you have zeal instead for them.*Gal 4:17* Mature believers should no longer be infants, tossed by the cunning and craftiness of deceitful schemers.*Eph 4:14* Let no one deceive you with empty words, especially when saying that disobedience does anything other than bring God's wrath.*Eph 5:6* Let no one deceive you by fine-sounding arguments.*Col 2:4* Let no one capture you through hollow and deceptive philosophy that depends on tradition and this world's elemental spiritual forces rather than on Christ.*Col 2:8* Do not listen to anyone who, unspiritual mind puffed up with idle notions, delights in false humility and goes into great detail about seeing worshiping angels.*Col 2:18* Do not appeal to others in error, from impure motives, or with tricks.*1Th 2:3* Never use flattery, nor a mask to cover up greed.*1Th 2:5* Have nothing to do with godless myths and old wives' tales.*1Ti 4:7* Don't listen to godless chatter and false so-called knowledge that those who have departed from the faith profess.*1Ti 6:20* Don't let anyone deceive because, in fact, bad company corrupts good character.*1Co 15:33*

Truth. Be zealous only for the good, and be so always, not just when around those who know the truth, and make no enemy among those who tell you the truth.*Gal 4:16* Do not perplex those who labor strenuously to see Christ formed in you.*Gal 4:19-20* Act in line with the truth of the gospel, lest someone who does live out that truth calls out your hypocrisy.*Gal 2:14* Many who follow their depraved doctrine will bring disrepute on the way of truth.*1Pe 2:2* A little confusion destroys the whole truth.*Gal 5:9* We renounce secret and shameful ways, not using deception nor distorting God's word.*2Co 4:2* Keep working to cut the ground from under false apostles and deceitful workers masquerading as Christ's apostles.*2Co 11:12-13* The God and Father of the Lord Jesus, praised forever, knows whether we lie.*2Co 11:31*

Christ. The world has many deceivers, antichrists really, who do not acknowledge Jesus Christ as having come from God.*2Jn 7* Certain individuals, long-condemned ungodly people who deny Jesus Christ our only Sovereign Lord and pervert God's grace as a license for immorality, may secretly slip in among us.*Jude 4* Some will try to deceive you into believing that our Lord Jesus Christ has already returned.~2Th 2:2-3~ Those who say that the resurrection of the dead has already taken place, depart from the truth and destroy the faith of some.~2Ti 2:18~ Those who teach other than the sound and godly instruction of our Lord Jesus Christ are conceited and understand nothing.~1Ti 6:3-4~ Guard against those who strongly oppose the message.~2Ti 4:15~ Don't let the serpent's cunning lead your minds astray from sincere and pure devotion to Christ.~2Co 11:3~ Stop putting up so easily with those who preach to you a Jesus other than the Jesus you learned, a different spirit from the Spirit you received, or a different gospel from the one you accepted.~2Co 11:4~

Teaching. When appointed to lead, command others not to teach false doctrines or to devote themselves to myths and long genealogies that promote divisive speculation rather than advancing God's faithful work.~1Ti 1:3-5~ Those who want to teach but don't know what they talk about and confidently affirm, turn away from purity, sincerity, and conscience, to meaningless talk.~1Ti 1:6-7~ Avoid deceiving teachings from hypocritical liars whose consciences a hot iron has seared.~1Ti 4:2~ Ignore strange teachings, such as about eating ceremonial foods, which helps no one, but instead let grace strengthen your heart.~Heb 13:9~ The faith rejects teachers who oppose the truth with depraved minds.~2Ti 3:8~ People who teach contrarily are not serving our Lord Christ but their own appetites, deceiving naïve people's minds by smooth talk and flattery.~Ro 16:18~

Learning. Some are always learning but never able to come to a knowledge of the truth.~2Ti 3:7~ Watch out for and keep away from those who put obstacles in your way that are contrary to the teaching that you learned.~Ro 16:17~ Do not deceive yourselves, but instead, if anyone claims to be wise by this age's standards, then you should become fools for God so that you may become wise.~1Co 3:18~ The world's wisdom is foolishness in God's sight because he catches the wise in their craftiness.~1Co 3:19~ The Lord knows that the thoughts of the wise are futile.~1Co 3:20~ Come back to your senses as you should, stop sinning, and don't be ignorant of God, otherwise shame on you.~1Co 15:34~ Don't gladly put up with fools or those who enslave or exploit you, take advantage of you, put on airs, or slap you in the face.~2Co 11:19-20~ Encourage one another so that sin's deceitfulness hardens none of you.~Heb 3:13~

Judgment. Those who accept deception will perish because they refused to love the saving truth.~2Th 2:10~ God permits those who reject the truth and instead delight in wickedness, to suffer the powerful delusion that condemns them as they believe the lie.*2Th 2:11-12* Those who indulge in godless chatter become more and more ungodly, their teaching spreading like gangrene.*2Ti 2:17* Opponents of the truth do not get very far because their folly is clear to everyone.*2Ti 3:9* The Lord repays those who do teachers a great deal of harm.*2Ti 4:14* The one who confuses you will pay.*Gal 5:9-10* Don't be deceived because we know that wrongdoers do not inherit God's kingdom.*1Co 6:9-10* Satan's servants masquerade as if serving righteousness, but they will end as they deserve.*2Co 11:15*

Desertion

The letters also address those whom deceivers tempt to desert the truth once they have already come to know it. God made examples of our disobedient ancestors who deserted faith's way. Those who turn away from God to pursue sensual desires become hard and corrupt. Christ disowns those who disown him. See how the letters address desertion. Are you holding fast to the truth that you learned?

Ancestors. God was displeased with most of our ancestors and scattered their bodies in the wilderness as examples to keep us from setting our hearts on evil things as they did.*1Co 10:5-6* Do not be idolaters, as some of our ancestors were when they ate, drank, and indulged in revelry.*1Co 10:7* We should not commit sexual immorality, as some of our ancestors did, so that in one day twenty-three thousand of them died.*1Co 10:8* We should not test Christ, as some of our ancestors did, and were killed by snakes.*1Co 10:9* We should not grumble, as some of our ancestors did, and were killed by the destroying angel.*1Co 10:10* These things happened to them as examples, recorded as warnings for us, on whom the culmination of the ages has come.*1Co 10:11* God was angry with your ancestors whose hearts were always going astray, while not knowing God's ways, so that God declared in anger that they would never enter his rest.*Heb 3:10-11*

Corruption. All things are pure to the holy, but nothing is pure to the non-believer who is corrupt in mind and conscience.*Tit 1:15* Those who claim to know God but by their actions deny him are detestable, disobedient, and unfit for anything good.*Tit 1:16* The Lord insists that you must no longer live as non-believers do in their futile thinking.*Eph 4:17* Their misunderstanding and ignorance darken them and separate them from God's life because they harden their hearts._{Eph 4:18} No longer sensitive, they pursue sensuality, indulging in every impurity, full of greed._{Eph 4:19} Some people do not put up with sound doctrine but to suit their own desires gather many teachers to say what their itching ears want to hear._{2Ti 4:3} They turn away from the truth to myths._{2Ti 4:4} Land that drinks rain, producing a useful crop for the farmer, receives God's blessing, not cursed and burned land that produces only worthless thorns and thistles._{Heb 6:8} Those who love the world desert their teachers._{2Ti 4:10}

Godless. Some are yet to enter God's rest, while others who heard the good news rejected God's rest out of disobedience._{Heb 4:6} No one repents again whom the Holy Spirit has already enlightened and has tasted the heavenly gift, goodness of God's word, and coming age's power, but has nonetheless fallen away._{Heb 6:4-6} God gives those who turn away from him a spirit of stupor, eyes that cannot see, and ears that cannot hear._{Ro 11:8} The godless are full of envy, murder, strife, deceit and malice._{Ro 1:29} The godless are gossips, slanderers, God-haters, insolent, arrogant, and boastful, inventing ways of doing evil, and disobeying their parents._{Ro 1:30} The godless have no understanding, fidelity, love, or mercy._{Ro 1:31} The godless know God's righteous decree that those who do wrong things deserve death, but they not only continue to do those things but also approve of those who practice them._{Ro 1:32} All turn away from God to become worthless, without any doing good, not even one._{Ro 2:12} Do not have a sinful, unbelieving heart that turns away from the living God._{Heb 3:12} When you hear God, do not rebel._{Heb 3:15} God takes no pleasure in those who shrink back._{Heb 10:38} Do not belong to those who shrink back to their destruction._{Heb 10:39}

Christ. Those who disown Christ, he will also disown._{2Ti 2:12} If we claim to follow Jesus but instead walk in the darkness, we lie and do not live out the truth._{1Jn 1:6} Why would you so quickly desert the one who called you to live in the grace of Christ and turn to a different gospel, which is really no gospel at all?_{Gal 1:6-7} If we say we are without sin, then we lie and deceive, while suggesting Christ lies and while rejecting his word, but if we admit sin, the faithful and just Christ forgives and purifies us._{1Jn 1:8-10} Some who should accept the good news do not do so._{Ro 10:16} Insiders who should accept Christ but do not will envy and be angry about those who do accept Christ._{Ro 10:19} They mean to crucify God's Son all over again, subjecting him to public disgrace._{Heb 6:6} Those who reject the precious stone Jesus find that he is nonetheless the cornerstone over which they stumble and fall in disobeying his message, as is their destiny.*1Pe 2:7-8* Keep running the good race rather than letting someone cut you off, someone who persuades apart from God who calls you.*Gal 5:7-8*

Idols

The letters address idols, idolatry, and idolaters, those who believe and pursue lies. We must continually turn, and help our faithful brothers and sisters turn, from the world's many dead and destructive idols, to live instead for our loving and saving God. See how the letters address idols. Do you recognize and reject idols as they try to capture your attention and destroy your life in Christ?

Lies. Non-believers exchange the immortal God's glory for images made to look like a mortal human, birds, animals, and reptiles._{Ro 1:23} They exchange the truth about God for a lie, worshiping and serving created things rather than the Creator whom we forever praise._{Ro 1:25} They destine themselves for destruction when they make their god their stomach and their glory their shame, setting their desire on earthly things._{Php 3:19} Some with weak consciences don't know God but are instead so accustomed to idols that they think the defiled sacrificial food they eat was for a god._{1Co 8:7} But food does not bring us near to God, when to the contrary we are no worse if we do not eat or better if we do eat._{1Co 8:8} Weep that many live as enemies of Christ's cross._{Php 3:18}

Turn. Turn from idols to serve the living and true God._{1Th 1:9} An idol is nothing at all in the world because we have only one God._{1Co 8:4} Others claim many so-called gods in heaven and on earth, and many lords._{1Co 8:5} We have only one God, the Father, from whom all things came and for whom we live, and we have only one Lord, Jesus Christ, through whom all things came and through whom we live._{1Co 8:6} Flee from idolatry._{1Co 10:14} Keep yourselves from idols, from putting other things above God._{1Jn 5:20} Do not partner with the idolater._{Eph 5:7} Put to death idolatrous things belonging to your earthly nature._{Col 3:5} An idol, or food sacrificed to an idol, are nothing.*1Co 10:19-20* The temple of God and idols do not agree.*2Co 6:16*

Others. Before you believed, others influenced and led you astray to mute idols.*1Co 12:2* Be careful to exercise your rights without being a stumbling block to the weak.*1Co 8:9* You embolden a person with weak conscience, to eat food sacrificed to idols, when they see you eat in an idol's temple, even though you know better.*1Co 8:10* Your knowing better can destroy a weak brother or sister for whom Christ died.*1Co 8:11* You sin against Christ when you sin against another by wounding their weak conscience.*1Co 8:12* Better not to eat that food again if what you eat causes your brother or sister to fall into sin.*1Co 8:13* Do not arouse the Lord's jealousy because you are not stronger than he.*1Co 10:22* No idolater inherits the kingdom of Christ and God.*Eph 5:5* Idolatry brings God's wrath.*Eph 5:6*

Persecution

The letters address the persecution of both apostles and believers. God lets the apostles' perseverance through persecution be a spectacle of faith. The Spirit of Christ delivers believers from persecution. We should act of worthy of Christ, loving and blessing him and others even through persecution. See how the letters address persecution. What power do your persecutors hold against Christ's grasp and deliverance?

Apostles. Apostles become earth's scum, the world's garbage.₁Co 4:13 God puts apostles on display at the end of the procession, like those condemned to die in the arena.₁Co 4:9 God makes apostles a spectacle to the whole universe, to angels as well as to humans.₁Co 4:9 Apostles are weak, dishonored, fools for Christ, while others who are not apostles appear so wise, strong, and honored in Christ.₁Co 4:10 Apostles go hungry and thirsty, in rags, brutally treated, and homeless, while working hard with their own hands.₁Co 4:11-12 Some apostles work harder and are imprisoned more frequently, flogged more severely, and exposed to death repeatedly, while facing many other hardships.₂Co 11:24-26 The apostle Paul felt he was the least of the apostles and did not deserve to be called one because he persecuted God's church.₁Co 15:9 Paul was by God's grace what he was, and God's grace had good effect, making him work harder than the other apostles.₁Co 15:10

Believers. Some face death daily, even those who boast about you in Christ Jesus our Lord.₁Co 15:31 Know that persecution of a leading believer may serve to advance the gospel.Php 1:12 Those who participate in and witness persecution will know that the believer wears chains for Christ.Php 1:13 The chains of a leading believer make brothers and sisters so confident in the Lord as to proclaim the gospel without fear.Php 1:14

God's provision of Jesus Christ's Spirit, together with prayer, deliver believers who face persecution.*Php 1:19* Know the troubles fellow believers experience under great pressure, beyond their ability to endure, despairing of life.*2Co 1:8* Some will feel they have received a death sentence, but this happens that we rely not on ourselves but on God, who raises the dead.*2Co 1:9* Some will intensely persecute the church, trying to destroy it.*Gal 1:13* Yet those who persecute the church initially, may soon preach the faith that they formerly tried to destroy.*Gal 1:23* Turnabouts of that kind will cause believers to praise God.*Gal 1:24* God will show mercy to a violent persecutor who acts in ignorance and unbelief.*1Ti 1:13* Remember one another's chains.*Col 4:18*

Attitude. Whatever happens, act worthy of Christ's gospel.*Php 1:27* Delight in persecutions for Christ's sake.*2Co 12:10* When others curse you, you should bless, while when others persecute you, you should endure it.*1Co 4:12* Bless rather than curse those who persecute you.*Ro 12:14* When others slander, you should answer kindly.*1Co 4:13* When those who oppose you fail to frighten you, you should show them a sign that God will save you but destroy them.*Php 1:28* You may at times find no rest, harassed at every turn, conflicts on the outside, fears within.*2Co 7:5* God grants for Christ that you not only believe in him but also suffer for him, struggling as other believers struggle.*Php 1:29-30* Wear salvation's helmet against spiritual attack.*Eph 6:17* Non-believers killed the Lord Jesus and the prophets, and so they may also drive you out, even though they displease God and are hostile to all while trying to keep you from saving others.*1Th 2:15-16* Persevere in faith through persecutions.*2Th 1:4* Warn one another of persecution.*1Co 4:14* God repeatedly delivers us from deadly peril and, we trust, will continue to deliver us.*2Co 1:10* Prayers for one another help defeat persecution, a gracious favor for which many give thanks.*2Co 1:11*

Traditions

The letters address how traditions become an obstacle to faith. Before Jesus entered the Most Holy Place, our ancestors kept the tabernacle with all its regulations. Christ's crucifixion for our sins made unnecessary the priests' endless sacrifices. We should oppose those who show great zeal for their traditions while rejecting Christ. Faith in Christ frees us from traditions, although we should not exercise our freedom as an obstacle to other believers. See how the letters address traditions. Are you preserving your living faith against the pull of dead traditions?

Tabernacle. The first covenant had regulations for worship and also an earthly sanctuary with a tabernacle and Holy Place.*Heb 9:1-2* The tabernacle also had a Most Holy Place with a golden altar of incense and gold-covered ark of the covenant containing a gold jar of manna, Aaron's staff that had budded, and the stone tablets of the covenant.*Heb 9:3-4* Above the ark were the cherubim of the Glory, overshadowing the atonement cover, with other detail.*Heb 9:5* The priests entered regularly into the outer room to carry on their ministry.*Heb 9:6* But only the high priest entered the inner room, and that only once a year, and never without blood, which he offered for himself and for the people's sins committed in ignorance.*Heb 9:7* The Holy Spirit was showing that God had not yet disclosed the way into the Most Holy Place while the first tabernacle still functioned.*Heb 9:8* The gifts and sacrifices did not clear the worshiper's conscience but were only external regulations applying until the new order.*Heb 9:10* Those who minister at the old tabernacle have no right to eat at our new altar.*Heb 13:10*

Sacrifices. Endless sacrifices can never make perfect those who draw near to worship.*Heb 10:1* The sacrifices would have stopped if they had cleansed the worshipers once for all.*Heb 10:2* Repeated sacrifices only remind of sin.*Heb 10:3* Animal blood cannot take away sins.*Heb 10:4* Priests perform religious duties daily, repeatedly offering the same sacrifices that can never take away sins.*Heb 10:11* Christ did not enter heaven to offer himself repeatedly, the way a human high priest entered the Most Holy Place every year with animal blood.*Heb 9:25* Otherwise, Christ would have had to suffer many times since the world's creation, but he appeared once for all, at the ages' culmination, to do away with sin by his own sacrifice.*Heb 9:26* When Christ as high priest offered for all time one sacrifice for sins, his one sacrifice made perfect forever those whom God is making holy.*Heb 10:12-14* Sacrifice for sin is no longer necessary, where God has forgiven.*Heb 10:18*

Priests. God calls high priests, as he did Aaron.*Heb 5:4* The people select a high priest to represent them before God, to offer gifts and sacrifices for their sins.*Heb 5:1* High priests should deal gently with the ignorant and straying because the high priest is likewise weak and must also sacrifice for his own sins.*Heb 5:2-3* Priests die, ending their office.*Heb 7:23* The law appoints weak men as high priests, but God's oath, which came after the law, appointed the Son, whom God made perfect forever.*Heb 7:28* Every high priest offers gifts and sacrifices, and so Jesus also offered, but not as a priest serving the law would offer.*Heb 8:3-4* Unlike the other high priests, Jesus needs no daily sacrifices for his own sins or the people's sins because he sacrificed once for all, offering himself.*Heb 7:27* We have a high priest who sat down at the right hand of the Majesty's throne in heaven, who serves in the Lord's own inner sanctuary, and not as a mere human.*Heb 8:2*

Christ. Jesus our Lord is an indestructible priest forever rather than from the Levitical priesthood that administered the law.*Heb 7:1-17* Jesus lives forever in permanent priesthood.*Heb 7:24* The high priest Jesus truly meets our need, as holy, blameless, pure, set apart from sinners, and exalted above the heavens.*Heb 7:26* Do not compel anyone who wishes to follow the gospel to first give in to tradition.*Gal 2:3* Christ came as high priest of the good things that are now here, the greater and more perfect divine tabernacle, not part of creation.*Heb 9:11* Christ entered the Most Holy Place not by animal blood but once for all by his own blood, for eternal redemption.*Heb 9:12* Animal blood and ashes on the ceremonially unclean sanctify only outwardly.*Heb 9:13* The blood of Christ, who through the eternal Spirit offered himself unblemished to God, cleanse inwardly, clearing our consciences from acts leading to death, so that we serve the living God._{Heb 9:14}

Freedom. False believers who see how free we are in Christ Jesus will infiltrate us, trying to use tradition to make us slaves again._{Gal 2:4} Some will forbid people to marry and will order them to abstain from certain foods that God created for believers, who know the truth to receive with thanksgiving._{1Ti 4:3} Don't give in to them for a moment, but instead preserve the gospel's truth._{Gal 2:5} Useless rules like those not to handle, taste, or touch certain things are merely human commands and teachings having only a false appearance of wisdom based on self-imposed worship, false humility, and the body's harsh treatment._{Col 2:21-23} Do not let anyone judge you by what you eat or drink, or by a religious festival, celebration, or Sabbath day, which are only shadows of things that were to come, when we find the reality of those things in Christ._{Col 2:16} Whether you consider one day more sacred than another or not doesn't matter, if you convinced your mind and you do so for the Lord._{Ro 14:5-6} Whether you eat meat or abstain doesn't matter if you thank God and do so for the Lord._{Ro 14:6} Eat anything sold in the meat market without raising questions of conscience because the earth and everything in it belong to the Lord._{1Co 10:25-26} God's kingdom is not about eating and drinking._{Ro 14:17}

Opposition. Some show extreme zeal for their own traditions, advancing them among their own kind._{Gal 1:14} Oppose to the face those who condemn themselves by drawing apart, in fear that others would exclude them from religious traditions._{Gal 2:11-12} Abandoning the gospel for tradition is hypocrisy that will lead others astray._{Gal 2:13} You should silence the many rebellious people who are full of meaningless talk and deception, and would have believers return to the old traditions, because they disrupt households and teach falsely for dishonest gain._{Tit 1:10-11} False teachers are liars, evil brutes, and lazy gluttons whom you must rebuke sharply, until they become sound in faith and give up their old myths and useless traditions._{Tit 1:12-14}

Others. Do not cause anyone to stumble, whether insiders, outsiders, or God's church._{1Co 10:32} Put no stumbling block or obstacle in the way of a brother or sister._{Ro 14:13} The Lord Jesus persuades us that nothing is unclean in itself, but if someone regards something as unclean, then for that person it is unclean.*Ro 14:14* Do not distress your brother or sister because of what you eat, because doing so is not love and instead destroys someone for whom Christ died.*Ro 14:15* If a non-believer offers you a meal you like, then eat it without raising questions of conscience.*1Co 10:27* But don't eat food offered in sacrifice, for the conscience of the one who offered it.*1Co 10:28-30* Do not destroy God's work for the sake of food because while all food is clean, a person is wrong to eat anything that causes someone else to stumble.*Ro 14:20* Better not to eat meat or drink wine or to do anything else that will cause your brother or sister to fall.*Ro 14:21* Whatever you believe about these things, keep them between yourself and God because God blesses the one who does not condemn himself by what he approves.*Ro 14:22*

Quarrels

The letters warn against quarrels, for the division and discouragement that they engender. Believers should remain harmonious and united in Christ, trying not to provoke one another, while keeping away from the disruptive. See how the letters address quarrels. Are you preserving the unity among believers in Christ?

Disputes. Men should pray and lift holy hands without disputing.$_{1Ti\ 2:8}$ Remind and warn God's people against quarreling about words, which is of no value and only ruins those who listen.$_{2Ti\ 2:14}$ Avoid foolish, unprofitable, indeed useless controversies and arguments about the law.$_{Tit\ 3:9}$ Your desires battling within you, for things that you do not have, cause fights and quarrels among you.$_{Jas\ 4:1-2}$ You do not have things that you desire because you either do not ask God or, when you ask, you ask with wrong motives to spend what you get on your pleasures.$_{Jas\ 4:2-3}$ Do everything without grumbling or arguing.$_{Php\ 2:14}$ Have nothing to do with foolish and stupid arguments that only produce quarrels.$_{2Ti\ 2:23}$ If jealousy and quarreling are among you, then you are acting worldly like mere humans.$_{1Co\ 3:3}$ When you argue over whom you follow, one teacher or another through whom you came to believe, you are mere humans.$_{1Co\ 3:4-5}$ The Lord's servant must not be quarrelsome or resentful.$_{2Ti\ 2:24}$

Others. We must avoid provoking and envying others in our conceit.$_{Gal\ 5:26}$ Don't grumble against one another, or God, who stands at the door, will judge you.$_{Jas\ 5:9}$ Accept the one with weak faith, without quarreling over disputable matters.$_{Ro\ 14:1}$ If instead we bite and devour each other, then we will destroy each other.$_{Gal\ 5:15}$ Warn a divisive person once and then a second time, but then have nothing to do with them because they are warped, sinful, and self-condemned.*Tit 3:10-11* Take a mature view, but if you think differently, then let God make truth clear to you.*Php 3:15* Warn the disruptive.*1Th 5:14* Keep away from disruptive believers.*2Th 3:6* Watch out for and keep away from those who cause divisions.*Ro 16:17*

Christ. Christ has made the two groups one and has destroyed the barrier, the dividing wall of hostility, setting aside in his flesh the law with its commands and regulations.*Eph 2:14-15* Christ's purpose was to create in him one new peaceful humanity, in one body reconciling both sides to God through the cross, by which he put to death their hostility.*Eph 2:15-16* Christ came preaching peace both to those far away and those near.*Eph 2:17* Through Christ, both sides have access to the Father by one Spirit.*Eph 2:18* Do not quarrel among you by claiming to follow different teachers whom no one crucified and in whose name no one baptized you, when Christ himself is not so divided.*1Co 1:11-15*

Slavery

The letters address the slavery in which the flesh holds us and that the flesh's sin brings. We are all either children of the flesh or God's children who in receiving Christ receive God's promised freedom. See how the letters address slavery. Have you grasped how fully free you are in Christ?

Flesh. Remember that Abraham had a son with a slave woman, born out of flesh, and a son with a free woman, born out of a divine promise.*Gal 4:22-23* Each woman represented a different covenant, one bearing slave children under law and the other bearing free children out of God's promise.*Gal 4:24-28* Slave children persecuted free children then as they do now.*Gal 4:29* Only free children, not slave children, share our inheritance from God.*Gal 4:30-31* Before we knew God, ungodly principles enslaved us.*Gal 4:8* Anyone who, after knowing God and having God know them, turns back to those weak and miserable principles, like observing special days, seasons, and years, is just wishing enslavement all over again.*Gal 4:9-10* Sinners promise others freedom, while they themselves are slaves to sin, which has mastered them.*1Pe 2:19* Strike a blow to your body to make it your slave so that after you preach to others, God will not disqualify you for the prize.*1Co 9:27* One reaps no benefit from sin, only shame and death, because sin's only wage is death.*Ro 6:21-22*

Christ. Christ freed us for freedom, and so we should stand firm rather than let slavery's yoke burden us again.*Gal 5:1* Jesus frees those held in slavery by their fear of death.*Heb 2:15* We are all together in Christ Jesus, not the insider or outsider, slave or free, or male or female.*Gal 3:28* Though free and belonging to no one, make yourself a slave to everyone to win as many as possible.*1Co 9:19* When we do separate from one another for a little while, we do so that we may have one another back forever, no longer as slaves but as dear brothers and sisters in the Lord.*Phm 15-16* Among believers we see no insider or outside, sinner or saint, slave or free, but Christ is everything and in everyone.*Col 3:11* One reaps holiness and eternal life as a slave to God because God's gift is eternal life in Christ Jesus our Lord.*Ro 6:21-22* Our old self's crucifixion with him killed the sinful body, setting us free from sin and making us no longer slaves to sin.*Ro 6:6-7* One Spirit baptized all, whether insider or outsider, slave or free, to form one body, giving each the same Spirit to drink.*1Co 12:13* The Spirit does not make you fearful slaves but makes you God's child who can cry to your Father.*Ro 8:15*

World

The letters address the nature of the world into which we come and out of which we must come, as we comprehend and then hold onto our faith. The world is evil, while the Spirit is divine. See how the letters address the world. Are you too much of this world, or are you pursuing the kingdom through Christ?

Evil. The whole world is under the control of the evil one._{1Jn 5:19} The world hates you._{1Jn 3:13} The world does not know us because it did not know God._{1Jn 3:1} You cheat on God when you pursue the world as friend because worldly pursuits mean hatred toward God, making you his enemy._{Jas 4:4} Live in the world as a foreigner and exile, abstaining from its sinful desires that destroy your soul._{1Pe 2:11} One's earthly nature is idolatrous, immoral, impure, lustful, evil, and greedy._{Col 3:5} Resist the world's elemental spiritual forces._{Col 2:8} Having died with Christ to the world's elemental spiritual forces, do not act any longer as if you still belong to the world, and do not submit to the world's rules._{Col 2:20} Do not look for praise from people, even when in Christ you could claim reason to do so._{1Th 2:6} To love the world is to desert the teaching._{2Ti 4:10} If jealousy and quarreling are among you, then you are acting worldly like mere humans._{1Co 3:3} The world's people are immoral and greedy, swindlers and idolaters._{1Co 5:10}

Overcome. Do not follow the world's patterns but instead let your renewed mind transform you so that you can discern God's good, pleasing, and perfect will._{Ro 12:2} God longs jealously for the spirit he placed within us, giving us ever more grace._{Jas 4:5-6} God comes near to us when we submit and come near to him, just as the devil flees us when we resist him._{Jas 4:7-8} To overcome the world, one must love God, which means keeping his commands while believing that Jesus is God's son._{1Jn}

5:4-5. Be blameless and pure children of God without fault in this warped and crooked generation.*Php 2:15* God judges the world.*Ro 2:5-6* We received God's Spirit, not the world's spirit.*1Co 2:12* Be people who live by the Spirit rather than who are still worldly—mere infants in Christ.*1Co 3:1* Time is so short that the married should live as if not married, mourners as if they do not mourn, the happy as if they were not happy, owners as if their property was not theirs to keep, and those who use the world's things as if not engrossed in them, because this world in its present form is passing away.*1Co 7:29-31* If you can, then avoid the world's affairs, and focus instead on pleasing the Lord, involved in the Lord's affairs.*1Co 7:32-34* Live in the world but not waging war as the world does.*2Co 10:3* Fight instead with weapons not of the world but having divine power to demolish strongholds.*2Co 10:4*

Riches

The letters address the temptation of worldly riches, admonishing us to avoid the greed that comes from a godless and depraved mind. We should instead pursue God who gives us everything. We should also be generous with others. See how the letters address riches. Do you appreciate where your true wealth resides?

Greed. Foolish and harmful desires for riches tempt, trap, and plunge people into ruin and destruction.*1Ti 6:9* Don't love money, but instead let what you have be enough, because God never leaves or forsakes you.*Heb 13:5* Do not let loving money tempt you to wander from the faith.*1Ti 6:10* Have nothing to do with people who love money.*2Ti 3:2-5* The rich who hoard wealth should cry because of their coming misery, the corrosion of their wealth testifying against them and eating their flesh.*Jas 5:5* They should have paid their workers fair wages so that the workers' complaints would not reach the Lord Almighty's ears.*Jas 5:4* Hoarding wealth and cheating workers to live in luxurious self-indulgence just fattens the rich for due slaughter for having condemned and murdered innocents.*Jas 5:5-6* You must inevitably associate with the world's greedy people because otherwise you would have to leave this world.*1Co 5:10* The world's people are greedy swindlers.*1Co 5:10* Those accursed experts in greed never stop sinning.*1Pe 2:14-16*

Schemes. Because we disappear so quickly and have no real idea of tomorrow, we should avoid arrogant and evil money-making schemes and instead simply pursue the Lord's will.*Jas 4:13-16* No swearing that you will do this or that but instead just say one way or the other and then go do likewise, or God will condemn.*Jas 5:12* Woe to those who hate other followers, rush for profit to undermine the fellowship, and rebel against

God's appointed leaders._{Jude 11} They are blemishes among you, feeding only themselves without the slightest qualm, producing nothing, blown here and there like wild waves foaming up their shame, wandering and uprooted, and thus twice dead, reserved for blackest darkness forever._{Jude 12-13} The Lord will come with countless holy ones to judge and convict for the ungodly acts and defiant words of the grumblers and faultfinders who follow their own evil desires, boasting about themselves while flattering others for their own advantage._{Jude 14-15}

God. Some of you were greedy swindlers, but the name of the Lord Jesus Christ and Spirit of our God sanctified you._{1Co 6:9-11} Everything is yours, whether that of the world, life or death, or present or future, because you are of Christ, and Christ is of God._{1Co 3:21-23} Those who are rich materially should not be arrogant nor hope in uncertain wealth but instead in God who richly provides everything for enjoyment._{1Ti 6:17} The rich should be rich in good deeds, generous, and willing to share, laying up treasure for themselves as a firm foundation for the coming age for true life._{1Ti 6:18-19} Avoid arrogant and evil money-making schemes and instead simply pursue the Lord's will._{Jas 4:13-16} God gives a depraved mind to those who do not think knowing him worthwhile, so that they fill with greed._{Ro 1:28-29} Overseers are not to be lovers of money._{1Ti 3:2-3} The greedy do not inherit God's kingdom._{1Co 6:9-10} Allow among God's holy people not even a hint of greed._{Eph 5:3}

Giving. We don't give to God in that he must repay us because everything is from him, through him, and for him._{Ro 11:35-36} Give the poor person just as good a seat and just as much attention in meetings as the rich person, or you will have let evil judge among you._{Jas 2:2-4} God chose the world's poor to be rich in faith._{Jas 2:5} Why should you dishonor the poor when the rich are the ones exploiting you?_{Jas 2:6-7} Let your overflowing joy and extreme poverty well up in rich generosity._{2Co 8:2} Conduct yourselves appropriately, poor yet making many rich, and having nothing and yet possessing everything._{2Co 6:8-10}

Flesh

The letters address the perils of the flesh, springing from the flesh's desires. God sent Christ in the flesh to meet the law and satisfy its judgment. We resist the flesh and avoid its death when Christ's Spirit lives in us and guides us. See how the letters address the flesh's darkness. Are you sufficiently aware of the flesh's desires and how in Christ's Spirit we resist them?

Desire. We all at one time gratified the flesh's cravings, following its desires and thoughts, while deserving of God's wrath._{Eph 2:3} When we were in the flesh's realm, law aroused sinful passions that led to death._{Ro 7:5} The flesh desires sexual immorality and orgies, idolatry and witchcraft, hatred and discord, jealousy and fits of rage, selfish ambition and envy, dissensions and factions, drunkenness, and like things that keep one from inheriting God's kingdom._{Gal 5:19-21} Sinners mouth empty, boastful words appealing to the flesh's lustful desires, enticing people who are just escaping from those who live in error._{1Pe 2:18} They promise them freedom, while they themselves are slaves to sin, which has mastered them._{1Pe 2:19} The flesh makes the mind hostile to God, rejecting God's law and causing disobedience._{Ro 8:7} Uncircumcision of our flesh makes us dead in sin._{Col 2:13} Those who pursue the flesh cannot please God._{Ro 8:8} God gives non-believers over in their hearts' sinful desires to sexual impurity to degrade their bodies with one another._{Ro 1:24} God gives non-believers over to shameful lusts so that, inflamed by lust, both men and women exchange natural sexual relations for unnatural ones, committing shameful acts with the same sex and receiving the due penalty._{Ro 1:26-27} The widow who lives for pleasure is dead even while she lives._{1Ti 5:6} Human rules lack any value in restraining sensual indulgence._{Col 2:23}

Christ. The flesh weakened us, but God sent his own Son in the likeness of sinful flesh to condemn sin in the flesh, to meet the law's righteous requirement in those of us who live by the Spirit rather than the flesh.$_{Ro\ 8:3\text{-}4}$ Clothe yourselves with the Lord Jesus Christ rather than thinking about how to gratify the desires of the flesh.$_{Ro\ 13:14}$ The flesh ruled our whole self until Christ circumcised us.$_{Col\ 2:11\text{-}12}$ We who belong to Christ Jesus have crucified the flesh's passions and desires.$_{Gal\ 5:24}$ If knowing our Lord and Savior Jesus Christ helps one escape worldly corruption but that person succumbs again, then that person is worse off than ever.$_{1Pe\ 2:20}$ Better not to know righteousness than to have known but turned one's back on its sacred command.$_{1Pe\ 2:21}$ Those who know righteousness but then turn back to sin are like a dog returning to its vomit or a washed sow wallowing again in the mud.$_{1Pe\ 2:22}$ Watch that sensual desires do not overcome dedication to Christ, bringing judgment.$_{1Ti\ 5:11\text{-}12}$

Spirit. Death to the flesh released us from the law so that we serve in the Spirit's new way rather than the written code's old way.$_{Ro\ 7:6}$ Those who live for the flesh set their minds on what the flesh desires, while those who live for the Spirit set their minds on what the Spirit desires.$_{Ro\ 8:5}$ Flee the evil desires of youth.$_{2Ti\ 2:22}$ Do not get drunk on wine, which leads to debauchery.$_{Eph\ 5:18}$ The flesh kills the mind, but the Spirit gives the mind life and peace.$_{Ro\ 8:6}$ When we walk by the Spirit, no longer doing whatever we want, we no longer gratify the flesh's contrary desires, with which the Spirit's desires conflict.$_{Gal\ 5:16\text{-}17}$ We must put to death the body's misdeeds to live, rather than live for the flesh, in which case we die.$_{Ro\ 8:12\text{-}13}$ In the last times, scoffers without the Spirit will follow their natural instincts into their own ungodly desires, while dividing you.$_{Jude\ 17\text{-}18}$ Shun and expose the fruitless deeds of darkness that the disobedient do in secret.$_{Eph\ 5:11\text{-}12}$ Fear judgment, hating even the clothing stained by corrupted flesh.$_{Jude\ 23}$

Curse

The letters address God's curse, which follows depravity, especially that of rejecting Christ's gospel. God's curse follows his wrath, wrought from judgment. See how the letters address God's curse. Does your fear for God's wrath lead you to reach out to others who do not know Christ and thus face a cursed existence?

Depravity. Let a curse be on anyone who does not love the Lord.$_{1Co\ 16:22}$ Let God curse anyone, even an angel, who preaches a false gospel.$_{Gal\ 1:8}$ Again, let God curse those who preach a false gospel different from the true gospel that you accepted.$_{Gal\ 1:9}$ Those who rely on the works of the law are under a curse because they do not do everything that the law requires.$_{Gal\ 3:10}$ Christ redeemed us from law's curse when crucifixion cursed Christ, who died for us.$_{Gal\ 3:13}$ God gives a depraved mind to those who do not think knowing him worthwhile, so that they do what they should not do, filling with every wickedness, evil, greed, and depravity.$_{Ro\ 1:28-29}$ Have great sorrow and unceasing anguish for the cursed and cut off from Christ, who are of your own people.$_{Ro\ 9:2-5}$ Whoever does not have godly qualities is nearsighted and blind, forgetting that they have been cleansed from their past sins.$_{2Pe\ 1:9}$ Those accursed experts in greed, whose eyes fill with adultery, never stop sinning and seducing.$_{1Pe\ 2:14-16}$

Wrath. God hardens whom he wants to harden, to display his power and see his name proclaimed in all the earth.$_{Ro\ 9:17-18}$ Non-believers who oppose you heap up their sins to the limit, facing God's wrath.$_{1Th\ 2:16}$ Sinners are springs without water and mists driven by a storm, for whom God reserves blackest darkness.$_{1Pe\ 2:17}$ Immorality is disobedience, bringing God's wrath.$_{Eph\ 5:6}$ One reaps no benefit from sin, only shame and death, because sin's wage is death.*Ro 6:21-22* God did not spare angels when they sinned, but sent them to hell, putting them in chains of darkness to be held for judgment.*1Pe 2:4* God reveals his wrath against all godlessness and wickedness of people suppressing the truth.*Ro 1:18* Stubbornness and unrepentant hearts store up God's wrath for judgment day.*Ro 2:5* God has wrath and anger for those who are self-seeking, reject the truth, and follow evil.*Ro 2:8* Everyone who does evil faces trouble and distress.*Ro 2:9* God judges people's secrets.*Ro 2:16* God is just in bringing his wrath on us and judging the world.*Ro 2:5-6* God's wrath is coming for sin.*Col 3:6* Idolatry brings God's wrath.*Eph 5:6* God reveals his wrath from heaven.*Ro 1:18*

Spirits

The letters caution against following false spirits of the antichrist. We must test spirits to see if they acknowledge Christ and must follow only the Father's spirits. The Spirit in us is greater than the spirits of the world's antichrist. See how the letters address spirits. Are you examining spirits for their testimony to Christ?

Rather than trust spirits from the many false prophets, test them to see if God sent them._{1Jn 4:1} Spirits that acknowledge Jesus Christ are from God, while spirits that do not acknowledge Jesus are not from God but from the antichrist about whom you have heard and who is now already here._{1Jn 4:2-3} Followers of Jesus are from God and have overcome false spirits, because God in his followers is greater than the world's antichrist._{1Jn 4:4} False spirits from the world speak from the world's viewpoint, to which those who don't know Jesus readily listen._{1Jn 4:5} God gives to some the gift of distinguishing between spirits._{1Co 12:8-10} Those who know God listen to those of us who are from God, while those who are not from God do not listen to us, which is how we distinguish the Spirit of truth from false spirits._{1Jn 4:6} God makes his angels spirits and his servants flames of fire._{Heb 1:7} Angels are ministering spirits sent to serve those who inherit salvation._{Heb 1:14} The Spirit warns against following deceiving spirits and demons._{1Ti 4:1} We should submit only to the Father of spirits to truly live._{Heb 12:9} You have come to the God who is the Judge of all and to spirits of the righteous he made perfect._{Heb 12:23}

Doubt

The letters confirm that doubt makes persons unstable in everything that they do. God does not answer the doubter's prayers. We have no reason to doubt, given how plain God has made what we should know of him. Indeed, we should help others overcome their doubt to save them from God's fire. See how the letters address doubt. Do you respond to doubt with the letters' approach?

When you ask God, believe rather than doubt, because the one who doubts tosses about like a wave that the wind blows on the sea.*Jas 1:6* Those who doubt should not expect to receive anything from the Lord. *Jas 1:7* Doubters are double-minded and unstable in all they do.*Jas 1:8* God makes plain to non-believers what they should know of him.*Ro 1:19* All have seen and understood God's invisible qualities including his eternal power and divine nature from what he made, so that all are without excuse.*Ro 1:20* Let God handle your anxiety because he cares for you.*1Pe 5:7* Non-believers know God, but their thinking is futile and their foolish hearts darkened, and so they neither glorify him as God nor give him thanks.*Ro 1:21* They claim wisdom but are fools*Ro 1:22* Whoever has doubts is condemned if they eat because their eating is not from faith, and everything that does not come from faith is sin.*Ro 14:23* Be merciful to those who doubt, saving them by snatching them from the fire.*Jude 22*

Favoritism

The letters caution against favoritism because God does not show favoritism. God welcomes and blesses all who call on his name. We should treat others as God treats us, each alike. See how the letters address favoritism. Do you treat others alike, avoiding favoritism?

God does not show favoritism.$_{Ro\ 2:11}$ God shows no favoritism when paying back for wrongs.$_{Col\ 3:25}$ God treats each alike because all are under sin's power.$_{Ro\ 2:8-11}$ God has no insiders and outsiders because the same Lord is Lord of all, saving and richly blessing all who call on his name.$_{Ro\ 10:12-13}$ Followers of our glorious Lord Jesus Christ must not show favoritism.$_{Jas\ 2:1}$ Give the poor person just as good a seat and just as much attention in meetings as the rich person, or you will have let evil judge among you.$_{Jas\ 2:2-4}$ God chose the world's poor to be rich in faith, loving him, and to inherit his promised kingdom.$_{Jas\ 2:5}$ Why should you dishonor the poor when the rich are the ones exploiting you, dragging you into court while blaspheming God?$_{Jas\ 2:6-7}$ You do right by keeping God's royal law to love your neighbor as yourself rather than by showing favoritism, which convicts you as a lawbreaker.$_{Jas\ 2:8-9}$ Remember that if you break one law you break them all.$_{Jas\ 2:10-11}$ We must not seek approval of others but of God because people pleasers do not serve Christ.$_{Gal\ 1:10}$ That some gain high esteem without encouraging you in carrying the gospel message should make no difference to you because God does not show favoritism.$_{Gal\ 2:6}$ Instruct without partiality or favoritism, as in the sight of God and Christ Jesus, and the elect angels.$_{1Ti\ 5:21}$

Judgment

The letters address at length how we should regard both judging and judgment. All should fear God's judgment, even the angels, because God indeed judges. God, however, judges justly, reserving his wrath for those who rebel against him, whom he rightly condemns. Although we may take our disputes before other believers, we should not judge others, or take revenge, but should instead repay wrongs with kindness. Christ will return to judge all, for which we should be ready. See how the letters address judgment. Do you avoid judging while preparing to submit to God, with Christ as your advocate?

God. Fear with dread to fall into the living God's hands.$_{Heb\ 10:31}$ God has wrath and anger for those who are self-seeking, reject the truth, and follow evil.$_{Ro\ 2:8}$ The Lord will sentence earth with speed and finality.$_{Ro\ 9:28}$ God is both kind and stern, kind to you while you remain in his kindness but stern to those who fall, which could be you if you are not careful.$_{Ro\ 11:22}$ The word says that every knee will bow before the Lord and every tongue will acknowledge God.$_{Ro\ 14:11}$ Each of us must account to God.$_{Ro\ 14:12}$ Keep the attitude of a foreigner, living here in reverent fear, because your Father judges each person's work impartially.$_{1Pe\ 1:17}$ Judgment begins with God's people but will be far harder for the ungodly sinners.$_{1Pe\ 4:17-18}$ God judges anyone who does wrong.$_{Col\ 3:25}$ God will especially judge those who follow the corrupt desire of the flesh and despise authority.$_{1Pe\ 2:10}$ God reveals his wrath against all godlessness and wickedness of people suppressing the truth.$_{Ro\ 1:18}$ The Lord punishes all who commit sins, as others have warned you.$_{1Th\ 4:6}$ Judgment will come suddenly even while people assume that they are safe, but they will not escape.$_{1Th\ 5:3}$

Justice. God is just in bringing his wrath on us and judging the world.~Ro 2:5-6~ God sees everything in all creation, uncovered and laid bare before him to whom we must give account.~Heb 4:13~ God judges people's secrets.~Ro 2:16~ God's judgments one cannot search or trace out.~Ro 11:33~ We have plenty of evidence that God's judgment is right.~2Th 1:5~ God repays each person for what they do.~Ro 2:6~ God said he avenges and repays, judging his people.~Heb 10:30~ God pays back for the harm sinners do, as they feast, carouse, and revel in pleasures in broad daylight.~1Pe 2:13~ The person with the Spirit judges all things with Christ's mind, while not subject to merely human judgments because no one knows the Lord's mind to instruct.~1Co 2:15-16~ Care little if a person or human court judges you, indeed as you do not even judge yourself.~1Co 4:3~ Even if your conscience is clear, you may not be innocent, because the Lord judges you.~1Co 4:4~ The Lord brings to light what one hides in darkness, and exposes the heart's motives, after which each will receive their praise from God.~1Co 4:5~

Rebellion. If we deliberately keep on sinning after learning the truth, then no sacrifice for sins remains and instead only fearful judgment and raging fire that consumes God's enemies.~Heb 10:27~ Those who rejected Moses's law died without mercy on two or three witnesses' testimony.~Heb 10:28~ Those who trample on the Son of God, treating as unholy the covenant's blood that sanctified them, and insulting the Spirit of grace, deserve much more severe punishment.~Heb 10:29~ Be humble rather than arrogant, and be careful, because if God rejected his chosen people, then he can reject you, too.~Ro 11:21~ Everyone who does evil faces trouble and distress.~Ro 2:9~ God judges adulterers and the sexually immoral.~Heb 13:4~

Condemned. God did not spare the ancient world when he brought the flood on its ungodly people while protecting Noah, a preacher of righteousness, and seven others.~1Pe 2:5~ God condemned the cities of Sodom and Gomorrah by burning them to ashes and made them an example of what is going to happen to the ungodly.~1Pe 2:6~ God has doomed to destruction the lawless man who opposes and exalts himself over everything connected with God, trying to take God's place and make himself God.~2Th 2:3-4~ Non-believers blaspheme in matters they don't even understand, like unreasoning creatures of instinct whom God catches and destroys.~1Pe 2:12~

Angels. The Lord who delivers also destroys in eternal fire those who do not believe and instead give themselves up to sexual immorality and perversion, even binding for judgment day angels who refuse his authority.*Jude 5-7* God did not spare angels when they sinned, but sent them to hell, putting them in chains of darkness to be held for judgment.*1Pe 2:4* Dreams and animal instincts lead ungodly people to pollute their bodies, reject authority, heap abuse on angels, and slander whatever they do not understand, when even the archangel Michael did not dare condemn the devil's slander but said instead that the Lord would rebuke him.*Jude 8-10* Bold and arrogant non-believers heap abuse even on angels who, although stronger and more powerful, do not heap abuse on non-believers when bringing the Lord's judgment on them.*1Pe 2:10-11* Believers will not only judge angels but how much more the things of this life.*1Co 6:3*

Judging. You have no excuse when you judge someone else because wherever you judge another, you condemn yourself because you do the same things.*Ro 2:1* God judges based on truth, so when mere humans judge others for doing the same things, they do not escape God's judgment.*Ro 2:2-3* Just because your faith is strong, don't judge the one who has weak faith, because God accepts them.*Ro 14:2-3* You are no one to judge another's servant, when each servant depends on their own master's judgment, and the Lord will help the one of weak faith stand.*Ro 14:4* Neither judge your brother or sister nor treat them with contempt because we will all stand before God's judgment seat.*Ro 14:10* Stop passing judgment on one another.*Ro 14:13* No more slandering others because speaking against another judges the law rather than keeps the law.*Jas 4:11* We have no grounds to judge another because only God, who is both Lawgiver and Judge, can save or destroy.*Jas 4:12* God is just in paying back trouble to those who trouble you, while relieving you from trouble.*2Th 1:6-7* Non-believers who oppose you heap up their sins to the limit, facing God's wrath.*1Th 2:16*

Disputes. Take your disputes with other believers before the Lord's people for judgment, not before non-believers.*1Co 6:1-2* The Lord's people will judge the world and so can competently judge trivial cases.*1Co 6:2* If you have disputes, then don't seek a ruling from those whose way of life church members scorn.*1Co 6:4* You should have someone among you wise enough to judge a dispute between believers.*1Co 6:5* Do not let one brother take another to court in front of unbelievers.*1Co 6:6* Lawsuits among you have already completely defeated you, when you should instead have preferred that others wrong and cheat you.*1Co 6:7* Rather than judge by appearances, know that one belongs to Christ just as much as another does.*2Co 10:7*

Revenge. Do not repay anyone evil for evil.*Ro 12:17* Do not take revenge, but leave it to God's wrath as the Lord says.*Ro 12:19* If your enemy is hungry, then feed him and if thirsty, then give him something to drink, having the effect of heaping coals on his head.*Ro 12:20* Do not be overcome by evil, but overcome evil with good.*Ro 12:21* Let no one pay back wrong for wrong.*1Th 5:15* Put up with one another, forgiving any against whom you have a grievance, just like the Lord forgave you.*Col 3:13* Forgive those who fail to come to your defense and instead desert you.*2Ti 4:16*

Return. In the last days, scoffers will follow their evil desires while questioning Jesus's return and any influence of God in the world.*2Pe 3:3-4* Those scoffers deliberately ignore that God's word created the heavens and the earth, God then deluged the earth with water, and God reserves the earth for fire and the ungodly for destruction on judgment day.*2Pe 3:5-7* God will judge all when the Lord Jesus returns.*2Th 1:7* When Jesus returns, God will punish with permanent destruction those who do not know God and do not obey the Lord Jesus's gospel, shutting them out from the Lord's presence.*2Th 1:8-10* God and Christ Jesus will judge the living and the dead.*2Ti 4:1* The Lord is the righteous Judge who rewards all who long for his appearing.*2Ti 4:8* The Lord rescues the godly while holding the unrighteous for punishment on judgment day, just as God rescued Lot, a righteous man, whom the depraved conduct of the lawless distressed.*1Pe 2:7-9* Stubborn and unrepentant hearts store up God's wrath for judgment day.*Ro 2:5* Judge nothing before the appointed time, but wait until the Lord comes.*1Co 4:5* We must all appear before Christ's judgment seat to receive our due for things we did in the body, whether good or bad.*2Co 5:10* No one condemns those who are in Christ Jesus.*Ro 8:1*

Part III: Direction

Obedience. Authority. Discipline. Repentance. Humility. Forgiveness. Unity. Action. Service. Fellowship. Elders. Church. Love. Joy. Sowing. Teaching. Building. Discerning. Wisdom. Trials. Rulers. Encouragement. Families. Body. Gifts. Giving. Prayer. Gratitude.

While the Bible tells the great story of light overcoming the continuing threat of darkness, the Bible also gives us abundant direction for following the light. We must obey those directions, remaining unified in their active pursuit. We need one another's fellowship to do so, in which we must not show favoritism. Above all, we must love, sowing generously the good seed of Christ. We should accept sound teaching and listen to wise counsel, especially in trials to forestall doubt. We should resist judging others and pursuing elaborate schemes for worldly riches but instead encourage one another while persisting in prayer. We should give, accept and exercise our gifts, and show gratitude for all that God does and is. See what sound and life-giving direction the letters give us.

Obedience

The letters give clear direction that we should obey. We should discern what God's word requires and then do as it commands, just as Christ kept his Father's word. We should do likewise in our conduct respecting others. Our goal should be to run the race to get the prize at the end. See how the letters address obedience. Do you listen for God and read his word to obey?

Choose. You may have the right to do anything, but not everything benefits you or is constructive.$_{1Co\ 10:23}$ Obeying God's word makes our love for God complete in us.$_{1Jn\ 2:5}$ Do not be fickle in intent or make worldly plans so that in the same breath you say both yes and no.$_{2Co\ 1:17}$ As God is faithful, let your message be consistent rather than contradictory.$_{2Co\ 1:18}$ Guard what others entrust to your care.$_{1Ti\ 6:20}$ Keep your head in all situations, discharging all the duties of your ministry.$_{2Ti\ 4:5}$ We must put to death the body's misdeeds to live, rather than live for the flesh in which case we die.$_{Ro\ 8:12-13}$ Do not be overcome by evil, but overcome evil with good.$_{Ro\ 12:21}$ You do well when you bear unjust suffering because conscious of God.$_{1Pe\ 2:19}$ Suffering for wrongdoing is nothing, but suffering for good commends you to God because Christ suffered for you as example.$_{1Pe\ 2:20-21}$

God. Even though Jesus was God's Son, Jesus learned obedience from what he suffered.$_{Heb\ 5:8}$ Those with faith obey the good news proclaimed to us, while those who do not share the faith do not obey.$_{Heb\ 4:2}$ Keeping Jesus's commands proves we know him, while failing to keep his commands proves that we don't know him and don't have the truth.$_{1Jn\ 2:3-4}$ As Christ's soldier, do not entangle yourself in other affairs, but instead please your commanding officer.$_{2Ti\ 2:4}$ When we live as Jesus lived, we know we are in him._{1Jn 2:6} We belong to the truth and set our condemning hearts at rest when we acknowledge that God is greater than our hearts and knows everything._{1Jn 3:19-20} When we keep God's commands by doing what pleases him, our hearts do not condemn us, and we receive from God anything we ask._{1Jn 3:21-22} God's command is to believe in his Son Jesus Christ and then to love one another._{1Jn 3:22} When we keep God's commands, we live in him and he in us, as the Spirit he gave us tells us._{1Jn 3:24} Obeying the law, not just hearing the law, makes one righteous in God's sight._{Ro 2:13}

Others. Be careful to do right in everyone's eyes._{Ro 12:17} Obey human authority whom God sends to punish those who do wrong and commend those who do right._{1Pe 2:13-14} Respect everyone, love the family of believers, fear God, and honor the ruler._{1Pe 2:17} Fearing God, obey your employer, not only when your employer is good and considerate but also when harsh._{1Pe 2:18} Workers should fully respect their supervisors so that no one slanders God's name and our teaching._{1Ti 6:} Those who work for believing supervisors should not show disrespect just because they are fellow believers but should instead serve them even better, as dear fellow believers devoted to the worker's welfare._{1Ti 6:2} Let your affection for one another be all the greater when you remember others' obedience._{2Co 7:15} Charity belongs to older, faithful widows, well known for good deeds like raising children, showing hospitality, and washing the feet of the Lord's people, helping those in trouble._{1Ti 5:9-10} Note and avoid anyone who does not obey instruction, that they may feel shame, while warning them rather than treating them as an enemy._{2Th 3:14-15} Christ appointed leaders to call non-believers to the obedience that comes from faith._{Ro 1:5} Be ready to punish every act of disobedience, once you complete your own obedience._{2Co 10:6}

Strive. Watch carefully that you keep your full reward and do not lose that for which you worked._{2Jn 8} Compete by the rules so that you win._{2Ti 2:5} When you feel poured out like a drink offering with the time for your departure near, be sure to have fought the good fight, finished the race, and kept the faith._{2Ti 4:6-7} Everyone who hears about your obedience rejoices because of you._{Ro 16:19} Run to get the prize because all racers run the race, but only one gets the prize._{1Co 9:24} Everyone in competition does strict training to get a temporary crown, but you train to get a crown that lasts forever._{1Co 9:25} Don't run aimlessly like others or fight like a boxer beating the air.*1Co 9:26* Instead, strike a blow to your body to make it your slave so that after you preach to others, God will not disqualify you for the prize.*1Co 9:27* Stand the test, obedient in everything.*2Co 2:9* Celebrate when followers testify about one another's faithfulness to the truth.*3Jn 3-4* Live a life worthy of the Lord, pleasing him in every way, bearing fruit in every good work, and growing in the knowledge of God.*Col 1:10-11*

Authority

The letters address the authority that God granted Christ over all. The letters confirm that God institutes other authorities under Christ, whom we should obey. We should also pray for those in authority. See how the letters address authority. Do you recognize and respect authority, especially that of Jesus Christ?

Christ. God's power for believers is the same as the mighty strength he exerted when he raised Christ from the dead and seated him at his right hand in the heavenly realms, over all rule, authority, power, and dominion, and every name not only now but in the future._{Eph 1:19-21} God gave Jesus Christ our Lord glory, majesty, power, and authority._{Jude 24-25} Christ is the head over every power and authority._{Col 2:10} The law has authority over someone only as long as that person lives._{Ro 7:1} The Lord who delivers also destroys in eternal fire those who do not believe, even binding for judgment day angels who refuse his authority._{Jude 5-7} The end will come when Christ hands God's kingdom to the Father after destroying all dominion, authority, and power._{1Co 15:24}

Instituted. Those in authority are God's servants for your good, wrath's agents to punish wrongdoers, and so if you do wrong, then you should fear the ruler's sword for good reason._{Ro 13:4} The Lord gives some authority to build you up rather than tear you down._{2Co 10:8} Anyone rebelling against the authority rebels against what God instituted, bringing judgment on themselves._{Ro 13:2} Instruct one another by the Lord Jesus's authority how to live to please God, urging one another more and more to live as you are living in the Lord Jesus._{1Th 4:1-2} Write to correct others when absent so as not, when present, to be harsh with the authority the Lord gave you for building up others, not for tearing them down.*2Co 13:10* Pay your taxes because the authorities, who are God's servants, give their time to governing.*Ro 13:6* Dreams and animal instincts lead ungodly people to reject authority, when even the archangel Michael did not dare condemn the devil's slander but said instead that the Lord would rebuke him.*Jude 8-10* Obey human authority, whom God sends to punish those who do wrong and commend those who do right.*1Pe 2:13-14*

Others. Pray for all people including those in authority, that you may live peaceful lives.*1Ti 2:1-2* Women should learn in submission, quietly, without assuming authority over those who teach or giving in to deception.*1Ti 2:11-13* God did not create man for woman but woman for man, so that women should, for the angels, have authority over their own head.*1Co 11:9-10* Share intimacy with your spouse, yielding to one another as the other wishes, giving your spouse authority over your own body.*1Co 7:3-4* Make petitions, prayers, and intercession for all people, including for those in authority, that you may live peaceful and quiet lives in all godliness and holiness.*1Ti 2:1-2* Encourage others with all authority.*Tit 2:15*

Discipline

The letters recognize that God disciplines his children. As hard as discipline is, especially in our arrogance, we should gladly accept it for our good. We should toughen up under discipline, incorporating rather than rejecting it, while taking encouragement from the discipline that we observe in our fellow believers. See how the letters address discipline. Do you express a godly attitude toward discipline?

The Lord disciplines those whom he loves and chastens those whom he accepts as his child._{Heb 12:6} Endure hardship as discipline because God is treating you as his child, as any good father disciplines a child._{Heb 12:7} If God did not discipline you, as he does every believer, then you would be illegitimate rather than a true son or daughter._{Heb 12:8} Because we respect our human father for disciplining us, we should submit all the more to the Father of spirits, to truly live._{Heb 12:9} Our human fathers disciplined us briefly as they thought best, but God disciplines us for our good so that we share in his holiness._{Heb 12:10} Discipline is not pleasant but painful when it happens yet later produces a harvest of righteousness and peace for those who accept it._{Heb 12:11} So strengthen your weak arms and knees._{Heb 12:12} Walk level paths so that the paths do not disable you but rather heal you._{Heb 12:13} God's Spirit gives us self-discipline._{2Ti 1:7} Avoid arrogance, or the teacher will bring a rod of discipline rather than love and a gentle spirit._{1Co 4:21} Delight at how disciplined are your fellow believers._{Col 2:5} An elder must be self-disciplined._{Tit 1:8} If you lack discernment, then the Lord will judge and discipline you so that God will not finally condemn you with the world._{1Co 11:32} Listen to this encouragement like a child listening to its father, not to make light of the Lord's discipline and not to lose heart when he rebukes you._{Heb 12:5}

Repentance

The letters encourage believers to repent, regretting and turning from sin, to pursue and accept Christ's righteousness. We should gently encourage others to repent and should be glad to see them do so. The Lord waits patiently, wanting all to repent, but no one who turns away from the Holy Spirit's sweetness repents again. See how the letters address repentance. Is the Spirit guiding you to repent?

Godly sorrow brings repentance, leading to salvation without regret, while worldly sorrow brings only death.₂Co 7:10 Godly sorrow produces earnestness, eagerness to clear oneself, indignation, alarm, longing, concern, readiness to see justice done, and effort to establish innocence.₂Co 7:11 Do not show contempt for the riches of God's kindness, forbearance, and patience, because he intends his kindness to lead you to repentance.Ro 2:4 Stubborn and unrepentant hearts store up God's wrath for judgment day.Ro 2:5 Purify the heart, stop sinning, and stop the double-mindedness, while ruing your former sin.Jas 4:8-9 Repent of impurity, sexual sin, and debauchery in which others indulge.₂Co 12:21 As obedient children of God, reject the evil desires you had when you didn't know God, and instead be holy in all you do like God is holy.1Pe 1:14-16 Regret hurting one another, but don't regret causing sorrow with the truth.₂Co 7:8 Be happy not for bringing sorrow to others or harming others but when that sorrow leads others to repent as God intends.₂Co 7:9 Gently instruct opponents in the hope that God will grant them repentance, leading them to a knowledge of the truth, and that they come to their senses.₂Ti 2:25-26 Foundational teaching in Christ includes repenting from acts leading to death.Heb 6:1-2 The Lord waits patiently to return, wanting everyone to repent rather than any to perish.₂Pe 3:9 No one repents again whom the Holy Spirit has already enlightened and has tasted the heavenly gift, goodness of God's word, and coming age's power, but has nonetheless fallen away.*Heb 6:4-6*

Humility

The letters emphasize the humility that the Lord expects us to bear in the knowledge of his righteousness and glory. We must avoid conceit, boasting only in the Lord and the service that he assigns us. Our judgments of ourselves should be frank and clearheaded. Our ambition should be to lead a quiet life that the Lord commends. See how the letters address humility. Do others recognize your humility?

Arrogance. Some of you have become arrogant, as if a teacher were not on the way soon to correct you, Lord willing.*1Co 4:18-19* Don't be arrogant, or the teacher will bring a rod of discipline, rather than come in love and with a gentle spirit.*1Co 4:21* Those who are rich materially should not be arrogant.*1Ti 6:17* Give others opportunity to take pride in you, so that they can answer those who take pride in the seen rather than in the unseen heart.*2Co 5:12* Show the humility and gentleness of Christ in your appeals to one another, especially face to face.*2Co 10:1* Don't compare yourself with others who commend themselves, because they unwisely measure themselves by themselves and compare themselves with themselves.*2Co 10:12* Some with great revelations will suffer a thorn in their flesh from Satan, to torment them and keep them from conceit.*2Co 12:7*

Boasting. Rid yourself of boasting that, like leavened yeast, works its way through everything, so that you may be without sin, as you really are in Christ, our sacrificed Passover lamb.*1Co 5:6-7* God chose the world's foolish things to shame the wise and weak things to shame the strong.*1Co 1:27* God chose the world's lowly things, despised things, and even things that are not, to nullify the things that are, so that no one may boast before him.*1Co 1:28-29* Do not boast beyond proper limits, but confine your boasting to the service that God assigns to you.*2Co 10:13* One doesn't boast too far when boasting in those who accept from you Christ's gospel.*2Co 10:14* One doesn't boast too far about work others do, while the faith of those others continues to grow, expanding your own preaching sphere into other regions.*2Co 10:15-16* When boasting, boast in the Lord.*1Co 1:31* Let our only boast be in the cross of our Lord Jesus Christ that crucified the world to us, and us to the world.*Gal 6:14* Boast in the Lord.*2Co 10:17* Many boast in the way the world does.*2Co 11:18* If you must boast, then boast of things showing your weakness.*2Co 11:30* Boast only about your weaknesses.*2Co 12:5* Refrain from boasting, so that no one thinks more of you than what you do and say warrants.*2Co 12:6* Boast all the more gladly about weaknesses, so that Christ's power rests on you.*2Co 12:9*

Clearheaded. Do not think too highly of yourself, but instead use sober judgment with the faith God gave you.*Ro 12:3* Do not deceive yourself by thinking you are something you are not, but instead test your own actions, taking pride in doing the best you can, without comparing yourself to someone else.*Gal 6:3-4* Do not claim that you have all you want, are already rich, and have begun to reign, when you have not.*1Co 4:8* Know the truth so that you remain humble.*Ro 11:25-26* Do not be proud or conceited, but instead be willing to associate with people of low position.*Ro 12:16* Humble yourselves under God, that he may lift you up in due time.*1Pe 5:6* Be completely humble, gentle, and patient, bearing with one another in love.*Eph 4:2* God saved us out of his own purpose and grace, not because of anything we have done.*2Ti 1:9* Remember what you were like when God first called you, neither wise nor influential, and not many of noble birth.*1Co 1:26*

Ambition. Your ambition should be to lead a quiet life, minding your own business while working with your hands, as instructed, to win outsiders' respect and not to depend on anyone.*1Th 4:11* Take pride when humbling and humiliation instead lift you up, because all things pass away quickly even as we go about our business.*Jas 1:9-11* You may not be inferior to esteemed others, and may deserve commending, even though you are nothing.*2Co 12:11* The Lord's commending approves, rather than commending that comes from oneself.*2Co 10:18* Show no selfish ambition or vain conceit but instead humbly value others above yourselves, looking to the interests of others over your own interest.*Php 2:3-4* Women who profess God should dress modestly, adorned not with elaborate hairstyles or jewelry, or expensive clothes, but with good deeds.*1Ti 2:9-10* Women should learn in submission, quietly, without assuming authority over those who teach and without giving in to deception.*1Ti 2:11-13* Do not puff yourself up as a follower of one teacher over another.*1Co 4:6* You are no different from anyone else in having only what you received, so that you cannot boast.*1Co 4:7*

Forgiveness

The letters address God's forgiveness of us and the forgiveness we should show for others. When we forgive, we do as the Lord does for us. See how the letters address forgiveness. Do you forgive as you should, knowing the cost of the forgiveness that God granted you?

God. God forgives our wickedness and remembers our sins no more.$_{Heb\ 8:12}$ Our redemption and forgiveness of sins is in Jesus Christ.$_{Col\ 1:14}$ If we say we are without sin, then we lie and deceive, while suggesting Christ lies, and while rejecting his word, but if we admit sin, the faithful and just Christ forgives and purifies us.$_{1Jn\ 1:8-10}$ In forgiving our sins, God canceled the indebtedness that stood against us and condemned us.$_{Col\ 2:14}$ Christ redeems us through his blood, the forgiveness of sins, as God lavished his grace's riches on us.$_{Eph\ 1:7-8}$ God forgives our sins and blesses us with righteousness apart from our works.$_{Ro\ 4:6-7}$ The law required that nearly everything be cleansed with blood, without which God would not forgive.$_{Heb\ 9:22}$ Sacrifice for sin is no longer necessary, where God has forgiven.$_{Heb\ 10:18}$

Others. Be kind and compassionate to one another, forgiving each other, just as God forgave you in Christ.$_{Eph\ 4:32}$ Put up with one another, forgiving any against whom you have a grievance, just like the Lord forgave you.$_{Col\ 3:13}$ If you forgive, then others will also forgive, all in Christ's sight for your sake, so that Satan, of whose schemes we know, does not outwit us.$_{2Co\ 2:10-11}$ Forgive those who fail to come to your defense and instead desert you.$_{2Ti\ 4:16}$ The majority may punish the one causing grief, but then forgive, comfort, and reaffirm your love so that excessive sorrow does not overcome that one.$_{2Co\ 2:6-8}$ Pray for the sinner so that through faithful prayer God will forgive the sinner.*Jas 5:13-15* Have nothing to do with people who are unforgiving.*2Ti 3:2-5*

Unity

The letters emphasize the unity that the Lord expects among believers. The Lord desires harmony among us, especially when believers gather as a church. Christ brings us that unity in one heart and one mind, indeed one body in Christ. See how the letters address unity. Are your words and actions unifying the body of believers?

Harmony. Live in harmony with one another.*Ro 12:16* As much as possible, live at peace with everyone.*Ro 12:18* Let your actions show and reputation be that you stand firm in the one Spirit, striving together as one for gospel faith.*Php 1:27* All followers should be like-minded, sympathetic, compassionate, and humble, while loving one another.*1Pe 3:8* Make every effort to keep the Spirit's unity through the bond of peace.*Eph 4:3* You have only one Lord, one faith, and one baptism.*Eph 4:5* And you have only one God and Father of all, who is over, through, and in all.*Eph 4:4-6* Plead with one another to be of the same mind in the Lord.*Php 4:2* Live peacefully with each other.*1Th 3:13* To unite with the Lord is to be one with him in spirit.*1Co 6:17* Avoid discord, jealousy, fits of rage, selfish ambition, slander, gossip, arrogance, and disorder.*2Co 12:20* Warn the disruptive, and be patient with everyone.*1Th 5:14* Let no bitter root grow up to cause trouble and defile many.*Heb 12:15* Men should pray and lift holy hands without disputing.*1Ti 2:8* Be of one mind, and God will be with you.*2Co 13:11*

Meeting. Your meetings do more harm than good when you come together as a church, with divisions among you.*1Co 11:17-18* Your disputes cheat and do wrong to yourself and your brothers and sisters.*1Co 6:8* Your differences will show which of you have God's approval.*1Co 11:19* You are not eating the Lord's Supper together because some of you have your own private suppers, leaving one hungry while another gets drunk.*1Co 11:20-21* Eat and drink in your own homes if you must, but don't despise God's church by humiliating those who have nothing.*1Co 11:22* When you gather to eat, you should all eat together.*1Co 11:33* Anyone who is hungry should eat at home so as to avoid judgment when you gather.*1Co 11:34* From one elder to another, I say shepherd God's flock eagerly as the example that God wants you to be, not because you must or for pride or dishonest gain, but so that the Chief Shepherd can give you an eternal crown of glory.*1Pe 5:4* The younger should submit to their elders, all clothing themselves with humility toward one another, because God opposes the proud while favoring the humble.*1Pe 5:5*

Christ. We are all together in Christ Jesus, not the insider or outsider, slave or free, or male or female.*Gal 3:28* In uniting with Christ, comforted by his love, have the same minds, spirit, tenderness, compassion, and love, while sharing with one another in the Spirit.*Php 2:2* Live such good lives among those who do not follow Christ that even as they condemn you, they see your good deeds and glorify God.*1Pe 2:12* Accept one another just as Christ accepted you, to bring praise to God.*Ro 15:7* In our Lord Jesus Christ's name, you should all agree with one another in what you say so that no divisions exist among you and you are in perfect unity in mind and thought.*1Co 1:10* May the God who gives endurance and encouragement give you the same attitude of mind toward each other that Christ Jesus had, so that with one mind and voice you glorify the God and Father of our Lord Jesus Christ.*Ro 15:6-7* Peace and love with faith from God the Father and the Lord Jesus Christ, to the brothers and sisters.*Eph 6:23*

Body. Just like a natural body has parts, in Christ we form one body belonging to one another, but with different gifts, as God gave each of us grace.*Ro 12:5-6* We must build up the body of Christ until we all reach unity in the faith, knowing the Son of God, becoming mature, and attaining to the whole measure of Christ's fullness.*Eph 4:12-13* Put off falsehood and speak truthfully to your neighbor, for we are all members of one body.*Eph 4:25* You have only one body and one Spirit, just as God called you to one hope.*Eph 4:4* Let the peace of Christ rule in your hearts because as members of one body God called you to peace.*Col 3:15*

Action

The letters emphasize that faith involves more than belief and attitude but also action. Our faith should produce deeds, or our faith is dead. See how the letters compel a believer to action. Can others see actions that you take in the name and Spirit of Christ, confirming your faith?

Deeds. Do more than listen to God's word, while deceiving yourself; instead do what the word says. *Jas 1:22* If you only listen but don't act, then you forget what you look like in not acting as the word says. *Jas 1:23-24* Instead, when you look deeply into God's perfect word that gives freedom and then do what the word says, God will bless you in what you do. *Jas 1:25* You do no good when you wish well someone without clothes and daily food but do nothing to help them. *Jas 2:15-16* We sin when we know the good that we ought to do but don't do it. *Jas 4:17* We must love with truthful actions rather than just words. *1Jn 3:17-18* Be an example in conduct for believers. *1Ti 4:11* Good deeds are obvious, while even those that are not obvious cannot remain hidden forever. *1Ti 5:25* Simply believing in God is not enough because even shuddering demons do that. *Jas 2:19* You avoid harm when eager to do good, but God blesses you even if you suffer for doing right, so that you need not fear threats. *1Pe 3:13-14*

Faith. Claiming faith when that faith produces no deeds won't save you. *Jas 2:14* Better, if God wills, to suffer for doing good than for doing evil, just like the righteous Christ, killed in body while raised in Spirit, suffered to take our sin away and bring us to God. *1Pe 3:17-18* Your good deeds should prove your faith. *Jas 2:18* It works both ways that while the body dies without the spirit, so, too, faith dies without deeds. *Jas 2:26* When you merely wish someone well who has needs, you only show your faith without action to be dead.*Jas 2:17* If you still need evidence that faith without deeds is useless, then look at the reward that God gave to Abraham for offering his son, his faith making complete what he did.*Jas 2:20-22* The good life of deeds done in humility will prove the wise and understanding among you.*Jas 3:13* God wills that you do good to silence foolish people's ignorant talk.*1Pe 2:15* Never lack zeal, instead keeping your spiritual fervor while serving the Lord.*Ro 12:11* Do not receive God's grace in vain.*2Co 6:1*

Service

The letters treat at length the topic of service in Christ. We should be charitable, remembering the poor. We should serve others over ourselves, using the gifts that we each possess. We should especially help God's people, and we are to help others especially to spread the gospel. When we serve others, we witness to Christ. We should also share in the work and strive while doing so. See how the letters address service. Are you serving as you should?

Charity. Remember the poor, being eager to help.$_{Gal\ 2:10}$ Help orphans and widows when they need it, while refusing to let the world pollute you, and God our Father will judge your religion pure and faultless.$_{Jas\ 1:27}$ Recognize widows who are really in need.$_{1Ti\ 5:3}$ Children and grandchildren should put their religion into practice by caring for their family, especially a widow.$_{1Ti\ 5:4}$ Anyone who does not provide for their relatives, especially their own household, denies the faith and is worse than an unbeliever.$_{1Ti\ 5:8}$ Followers must learn to devote themselves to doing good, to provide for urgent needs and live productive lives.$_{Tit\ 3:14}$ Do something useful with your own hands, that you may share with those in need.$_{Eph\ 4:28}$ Spur one another on toward good deeds.$_{Heb\ 10:24}$

Others. Risk your life to help others whom others cannot help.$_{Php\ 2:30}$ Supply what others fail to supply, refreshing others' spirit, while also recognizing those who do.$_{1Co\ 16:17-18}$ Though free and belonging to no one, make yourself a slave to everyone to win as many as possible.$_{1Co\ 9:19}$ To those under the law become as if under the law to win those under the law.$_{1Co\ 9:20}$ To those not having the law become like one not having the law, even though under Christ's law, to win those not having the law.$_{1Co}$

9:21 To the weak become weak to win the weak, just as you should become all things to all people so as by all possible means to save some.*1Co 9:22* Workers, obey your earthly supervisors in everything, not only when they watch you and to curry favor but with sincere heart, out of reverence for the Lord.*Col 3:22* Supervisors should treat workers the same way, without threats, because God in heaven is over both supervisor and worker, favoring neither over the other.*Eph 6:9* Provide your workers with what is right and fair because you, too, have a Master in heaven.*Col 4:1*

Gifts. If your gift is telling the future, then do so faithfully.*Ro 12:6* If your gift is serving, then serve faithfully.*Ro 12:7* If your gift is teaching, then teach faithfully.*Ro 12:7* If your gift is to encourage, then encourage faithfully.*Ro 12:8* If your gift is giving, then give generously.*Ro 12:8* If your gift is to lead, then lead diligently.*Ro 12:8* If your gift is to show mercy, then do so cheerfully.*Ro 12:8* The same Lord accepts different kinds of service.*1Co 12:5* The same God works in everyone and in different kinds of work.*1Co 12:6* Use your gifts to serve others, stewarding God's manifold graces.*1Pe 4:10* Serve with the strength God provides, so that everyone praises God.*1Pe 4:11* When in need, do not desire another's gifts, but desire that God credit more to the giver's account.*Php 4:17* Treat gifts of support as fragrant offerings and acceptable sacrifices pleasing to God.*Php 4:18*

God. You serve God.*2Ti 1:3* Cleanse yourself from articles of common use in favor of articles for special purposes so that you are your Master's holy instrument for good work.*2Ti 2:20-21* God breathed all Scripture for training so that God's servant is ready for every good work.*2Ti 3:16-17* God is just to remember your work and loves you to reveal him as you help his people.*Heb 6:10* Help others in their ministry.*2Ti 4:11* Do not seek your own good but the good of others.*1Co 10:24* Try to please everyone in every way, seeking the good of many rather than your own good, that God may save them.*1Co 10:33* Stay on where great doors for effective work open to you, even though many oppose you.*1Co 16:9* See that those who do the Lord's work have nothing to fear while with you.*1Co 16:10* No one should treat the Lord's workers with contempt but send them on their way in peace to return to their mentors.*1Co 16:11* Devote yourselves to the service of the Lord's people.*1Co 16:15* Submit yourselves to the Lord's people and everyone who joins in and labors at the work.*1Co 16:16*

Christ. Anyone who serves Christ pleases God and receives human approval.*Ro 14:18* Glory in Christ Jesus in your service to God.*Ro 15:17* Speak of no service other than what Christ accomplished through you in leading others to obey God by what you said and did through the Spirit of God's power.*Ro 15:18-19* We are God's handiwork, created in Christ Jesus to do good works that God prepared in advance for us to do.*Eph 2:10* Show Jesus Christ's genuine concern for one another's welfare rather than just looking out for your own interest.*Php 2:20-21* Christ himself gave the apostles, the prophets, the evangelists, the pastors and teachers to equip his people for works of service, so that they may build up the body of Christ.*Eph 4:11-12* Workers should obey earthly supervisors sincerely just as they would obey Christ, not to win favor only when watched but instead wholeheartedly as if working for Christ, doing God's will for God's reward.*Eph 6:5-8* Our Lord Jesus Christ and God our Father strengthen us in every good deed and word.*2Th 2:16-17* God equips you with everything good for doing his will, while working in you to please him, through Jesus Christ.*Heb 13:21*

Gospel. Do everything for the gospel's sake to share in its blessings.*1Co 9:23* We become the gospel's servants by the gift of God's grace given us through his power.*Eph 3:7* We should count ourselves less than the least of all the Lord's people, serving him by grace.*Eph 3:8* Work with all your heart as working for the Lord, not for others.*Col 3:23* Prove yourself serving with others in gospel work.*Php 2:22* Send co-workers and fellow soldiers to care for one another's needs.*Php 2:25* Help those who contend as co-workers in the gospel's cause.*Php 4:3* Churches may praise one for service to the gospel.*2Co 8:18* Let co-workers in God's service of spreading Christ's gospel strengthen and encourage you in your faith.*1Th 3:2*

Share. Share in giving and receiving, sending aid whenever you see a believer in need.*Php 4:15-16* Do good and share with others, pleasing God with your sacrifices.*Heb 13:16* Share in one another's struggles.*Php 4:14* Share every word and deed in the Lord Jesus's name.*Col 3:17* We serve the gospel.*Col 1:23* Work hard for one another.*Col 4:13* Acknowledge those who work hard among you, who care for you in the Lord and who admonish you, holding them in highest regard because of their work.*1Th 5:12-13* Help the weak.*1Th 5:14* Share with the Lord's people who are in need, practicing hospitality.*Ro 12:13*

Strive. Strive to do what is good for each other and everyone else.*1Th 5:15* You know how to follow a good example, working hard not to burden anyone, so that you, too, are a model for others to imitate.*2Th 3:7-10* Be busy rather than an idle and disruptive busybody who needs to settle down and earn the food they eat.*2Th 3:11* Never tire of doing good.*2Th 3:13* Each should show the same diligence to the very end, so that you realize that for which you hope.*Heb 6:11* Do not be lazy, but instead imitate those who through faith and patience inherit the promised reward.*Heb 6:12* Those who do not work will not eat.*2Th 3:10*

Fellowship

The letters emphasize at length the fellowship that believers share in Christ. We are family, brothers and sisters, and partners together, and should thus greet, show kindness to, and benefit one another as family. Christ calls us into this fellowship of believers. We should thus exhort and encourage one another as soldiers and workers in the faith. See how extensively the letters address fellowship. Do you participate in, support, and enjoy the fellowship of believers?

Family. In fellowship with one another, keep Christ Jesus's humble and obedient servant mindset.*Php 2:5-8* We appeal for those who join us as children in the family of faith, who were formerly useless to us but have become useful to all.*Phm 9-11* We do not withhold others, even those who are our very heart, from one another in the family of faith but share their fellowship, even when we are in special need.*Phm 12-13* When we do separate from one another for a little while, we do so that we may have one another back forever, no longer as slaves but as dear brothers and sisters in the Lord.*Phm 15-16* If one in the family of faith does another any wrong or owes another anything, then let the charge be to you and you pay it back, even if the person you pay owes you.*Phm 18-19* Pray to restore one another to the family of faith, while you prepare a guest room for the one for whom you pray.*Phm 22* Be like young children in humble innocence among other believers.*1Th 2:7* We are apostles, disciples, and followers of Christ Jesus by God's will, faithful brothers and sisters in Christ, a holy people.*Col 1:1-2* Give your right hand in fellowship to those in whom you recognize God's grace.*Gal 2:9*

Greeting. Welcome and comfort co-workers for God's kingdom when they visit.*Col 4:10-11* Greet and encourage those who love one another in the faith._Tit 3:15_ Greet all God's people in Christ Jesus, carrying the greetings of other brothers and sisters._Php 4:21-22_ Greet all God's people with a holy kiss._1Th 5:26_ Greet those who work very hard for you._Ro 16:6_ Greet fellow believers who suffer with you and were outstanding apostles in Christ before you were._Ro 16:7_ Greet dear friends in the Lord._Ro 16:8_ Greet co-workers and dear friends in Christ._Ro 16:9_ Greet those whose fidelity to Christ stands the test, and greet believing households._Ro 16:10_ Greet those in households who are in the Lord._Ro 16:11_ Greet women friends who work very hard in the Lord._Ro 16:12_ Greet those chosen in the Lord and those mothers who have been a mother to you, too._Ro 16:13_ Greet brothers and sisters and all the Lord's people who are with them._Ro 16:15_ Greet one another warmly in the Lord, with a holy kiss._1Co 16:19-20_ Greet one another with a holy kiss._2Co 13:12_ Send greetings to one another._2Co 13:13_ Greet the Lord's people._Heb 13:24_

Kindness. Be kind and compassionate to one another, forgiving each other, just as God forgave you in Christ._Eph 4:32_ Be hospitable to one another without complaint._1Pe 4:9_ As God's people, clothe yourselves with compassion, kindness, humility, gentleness, and patience._Col 3:12_ Conduct yourselves in the world, and especially with other believers, with integrity and godly sincerity, not relying on worldly wisdom but on God's grace._2Co 1:12_ Speak freely to one another, opening wide your hearts._2Co 6:11_ Don't withhold affection from one another._2Co 6:12_ As a fair exchange, open wide your hearts._2Co 6:13_ Make room for one another in your hearts, especially those who wrong, corrupt, and exploit no one._2Co 7:2_ Have such a place in your hearts for one another that you would live and die with them._2Co 7:3_ Take great pride in one another._2Co 7:4_ Tell one another about your longing for one another, your deep sorrow and ardent concern for one another, so that your joy may be greater than ever._2Co 7:7_ Prove your love to one another and reason for your pride in one another._2Co 8:24_ When visiting another, try to be as they wish you to be and find them as you want them to be, without discord, jealousy, fits of rage, selfish ambition, slander, gossip, arrogance, or disorder._2Co 12:20_

Benefit. Benefit one another in the Lord by refreshing one another's heart in Christ._Phm 20_ Do even more than another in the family of faith asks._Phm 21_ Don't desire the possessions of another but desire their benefit, as parents save up for their children rather than children for parents._2Co 12:14_ Do not burden another, especially if it helps you capture them.*2Co 12:16* Don't exploit anyone through others whom you send.*2Co 12:17-18* We resist doing anything without one another's consent, so that we do not force any favor one does for another but ensure that every favor is voluntary.*Phm 14* Hesitate to grieve one another, lest you have no one to make you glad.*2Co 2:2* Strive to make one another rejoice rather than distressed, having confidence that you will share one another's joy.*2Co 2:3* Your deep love for one another should lead you to great distress, anguish of heart, and many tears, when one grieves another.*2Co 2:4* The one caused grief grieves all together more so than just one.*2Co 2:5* The majority may punish the one causing grief, but then forgive, comfort, and reaffirm your love so that excessive sorrow does not overcome that one.*2Co 2:6-8* Don't intercede just for wrongdoers or injured parties but instead that they see their own devotion before God.*2Co 7:12*

Christ. God called you into fellowship with his Son, Jesus Christ our Lord.*1Co 1:9* Submit to one another out of reverence for Christ.*Eph 5:21* We thank our God every time we remember one another as brothers and sisters in Christ.*Php 1:3* Our hearts rejoice in Christ Jesus's affection for one another and in our common salvation in God's grace, no matter our own preaching or persecution.*Php 1:7-8* While we prefer to die to join Christ, we live instead to help one another progress in faith and joy until our boasting in Christ Jesus abounds.*Php 1:24-26* When away from your fellow believers, be present with them in spirit, delighting at how firm in faith in Christ they are.*Col 2:5* Among believers we see no insider or outside, sinner or saint, slave or free, but Christ is everything and in everyone.*Col 3:11* Fellow believers are your hope, joy, and crown, in which you will glory when our Lord Jesus comes.*1Th 2:19-20* Walk with fellow believers in the same footsteps by the same Spirit.*2Co 12:18* Avoid defending yourself to others, and instead speak in God's sight as those in Christ, doing everything to strengthen the other.*2Co 12:19* May the fellowship of the Holy Spirit be with you.*2Co 13:14*

Encouragement. Exhort one another, those believers whom you love, for whom you long, and who are your joy and crown, to stand firm in the Lord as dear friends.*Php 4:1* Renew your concern for fellow believers, looking for opportunities to show it.*Php 4:10* Be dear fellow servants in the Lord, sharing news of one another and events to encourage your hearts.*Col 4:7-9* Others long to know that you remain strong in your faith, that their labors for you have not been in vain.*1Th 3:5*

Bring good news about others' faith and love, recalling pleasant memories of one another whom you long to see.*1Th 3:6* Impart spiritual gifts to one another to encourage each other's faith and make you strong.*Ro 1:11-12* Make every effort, out of intense longing, to see again fellow believers from whom you separate for a short time, in person rather than thought, even when Satan blocks your way.*1Th 2:17* Long to see other believers, so that joy may fill you.*2Ti 1:4* Pray that God's will is that you rejoin one another.*Ro 1:9-10*

Workers. We are together prisoners of Christ Jesus, brothers and sisters, dear friends, fellow workers, and fellow soldiers, meeting in church and home, as we wish to one another grace and peace from God our Father and the Lord Jesus Christ.*Phm 1-3* Greet one another as fellow workers and prisoners in Christ Jesus, that the grace of the Lord Jesus Christ is with one another's spirit.*Phm 23-25* Regard one another as servants of Christ, entrusted with the mysteries that God has revealed.*1Co 4:1* Be partners and co-workers, an honor to Christ.*2Co 8:23* Welcome the friend of a partner in faith as you would welcome the partner.*Phm 17* Let your affection for one another be all the greater when you remember others' obedience.*2Co 7:15* Be glad when you can have complete confidence in another.*2Co 7:16* Prove your zeal to one another in many ways, while having great confidence in one another.*2Co 8:22*

Elders

The letters address the role of elders, deacons, and other leaders in the church. We should observe, appreciate, and model godly leaders. We should also support church leaders, making their work joyful. We should choose elders and deacons wisely based on solid evidence of their faith. We should also respect and value those who administer the church. See how the letters address elders. Do you conduct yourself and support your church's leaders as the letters direct?

Model. Join together in following good models, keeping your eyes on those who live right.*Php 3:17* As God's witnesses, see how holy, righteous, and blameless your leaders are among you as they deal with you like their own children.*1Th 2:10-11* God sets apart leaders for the gospel.*Ro 1:1* God chose apostles of Christ Jesus to address the faithful in Christ Jesus, bringing messages of grace and peace from God our Father and the Lord Jesus Christ.*Eph 1:1-2* An apostle of Christ Jesus is by the will of God.*2Ti 1:1* Gospel heralds, apostles, and teachers suffer without shame, believing and trusting Jesus.*2Ti 1:11-12* An apostle's true marks include signs, wonders, and miracles. *2Co 12:12* Those who serve well gain excellent standing and great assurance in their faith in Christ Jesus.*1Ti 3:13* No boasting about human leaders.*1Co 3:21* Follow the life and adopt the faith of your leaders who spoke God's word to you.*Heb 13:7* Everything is yours, whether that of one teacher or another.*1Co 3:21-23* Leaders who are away physically may still be with you in spirit, passing judgment in the Lord Jesus's name on those among you who practice a sexual immorality that not even non-believers practice.*1Co 5:1-4*

Support. Help leaders on their journeys wherever they go.*1Co 16:6* Share with one another how your leaders are and what they are doing, for encouragement.*Eph 6:21-22* Pray that God restores your leaders to you soon.*Heb 13:19* You benefit from supporting and submitting to your leaders, making their work a joy rather than burden, because while they lead, they also must account.*Heb 13:17* Greet your leaders.*Heb 13:24* Give double honor to elders who direct the church's affairs, especially those who preach and teach, because they deserve their wages.*1Ti 5:17-18* Do not entertain accusations against elders unless by two or three witnesses.*1Ti 5:19* Reprove sinning elders before everyone, so that others get the warning.*1Ti 5:20* Do not be hasty in laying on hands.*1Ti 5:22*

Elders. Establish order by appointing elders who are blameless and faithful, and who have believing children who are not wild and disobedient.*Tit 1:6* Elders managing God's household must not be overbearing, quick-tempered, given to drunkenness, or violent, or pursue dishonest gain.*Tit 1:7* Rather, an elder must be hospitable, one who loves what is good, who is self-controlled, upright, holy, and disciplined.*Tit 1:8* While our leaders in Christ could be bold, ordering us to do what we should, yet they should prefer to appeal to us on based on love.*Phm 8-9* An elder must hold firmly to the gospel's trustworthy message just as they learned it, so that the elder can encourage others with sound doctrine and refute those who oppose the message.*Tit 1:9* Elders face daily pressing concerns for the churches.*2Co 11:28* Elders feel weak for the weak, and burn inwardly for those led into sin.*2Co 11:29*

Deacons. Deacons are also to be worthy of respect, sincere, not indulging in much wine, and not pursuing dishonest gain.*1Ti 3:8* First test deacons, letting them serve only if having nothing against them.*1Ti 3:10* Deacons must hold onto the deep truths of the faith with a clear conscience.*1Ti 3:9* A deacon must be faithful to his wife and manage his children and household well.*1Ti 3:12* Be faithful ministers in the Lord.*Col 4:7* Complete the ministry you have received in the Lord.*Col 4:17*

Administrators. Administrators of God's grace are willing prisoners of Christ Jesus for the sake of the rest of us.*Eph 3:1-2* Overseers are to be above reproach, faithful to one's wife, temperate, self-controlled, respectable, hospitable, able to teach, not given to drunkenness, not violent but gentle, not quarrelsome, and not a lover of money.*1Ti 3:2-3* An overseer must manage his own family well and see that his children obey him, and must do so worthy of respect.*1Ti 3:4* He who can't manage his own family can't manage God's church.*1Ti 3:5* An overseer must not be a recent convert, or he may become conceited and fall under the same judgment as the devil.*1Ti 3:6* An overseer must also have a good reputation with outsiders, so that he will not fall into disgrace and into the devil's trap.*1Ti 3:7* Trust that aspiring to oversee a church is to desire a noble task.*1Ti 3:1*

Church

The letters address at length the nature and role of God's church to make his gospel wisdom known. The church is Christ's body, over which Christ is the head. We are his household, supporting one another in faith. God gives church members different gifts, which we should exercise in order and unity. Above all, we should not give up meeting together as the church. See how the letters address the church. Do you support the church consistent with the role and significance that the letters treat it?

Role. God's intent was that the church make known God's manifold wisdom to the rulers and authorities in the heavenly realms, as is God's eternal purpose already accomplished in Christ Jesus our Lord.*Eph 3:10-11* God's church is those whom he sanctifies in Christ Jesus and calls as his holy people, those everywhere who call on the name of our Lord Jesus Christ.*1Co 1:2* God the Father and the Lord Jesus Christ bring grace and peace to the church in God our Father and the Lord Jesus Christ.*2Th 1:1-2* God gives grace to the churches.*2Co 8:1* God's household, the church of the living God, is the pillar and foundation of the truth.*1Ti 3:15* The church helps widows with real need.*1Ti 5:16* Churches may praise one for service to the gospel.*2Co 8:18* Be church representatives honoring Christ.*2Co 8:23* Christ loved the church so much that he gave himself up for her, making her holy by cleansing her with his word so that he could present her to himself as radiant, without stain, wrinkle, or other blemish, but instead blameless.*Eph 5:25-27* Christ and the church are a profound mystery.*Eph 5:32* Imitate God's churches in Christ Jesus, even when suffering from your own people the same things those churches suffer.*1Th 2:14*

Body. The Son is the head of the body, the church._{Col 1:18} Christ heads his body the church, of which he is the Savior._{Eph 5:22-23} Christ is the head from whom the whole body grows as God causes it to grow._{Col 2:19} From Christ the whole body, held together by everyone, grows in love, as each part does its work._{Eph 4:16} God placed all things under Christ's feet and appointed him head over everything for the church, which is his body, the fullness of him who fills everything in every way._{Eph 1:22-23} Speaking the truth in love, we will grow to become in every way the mature body, with Christ as the head._{Eph 4:15} Christ feeds and cares for the church as his own body, of which we are members._{Eph 5:29-30} We are members of one body, sharing the promise in Christ Jesus._{Eph 3:6} Christ created in him one body, reconciled to God through the cross._{Eph 2:15-16} We are all members of one body._{Eph 4:25} God's people serve to build up the body of Christ._{Eph 4:11-12} God calls us to get along as members of one body._{Col 3:15}

Household. In Christ, you are no longer foreigners and strangers but fellow citizens with God's people, members of his household built on the foundation of those who went before you, with Christ Jesus as the chief cornerstone._{Eph 2:19-20} In Christ, the whole building joins and rises to become a holy temple in the Lord._{Eph 2:21} In Christ, we join to become a dwelling in which God lives by his Spirit._{Eph 2:22} Only those who can manage their own family can manage God's church._{1Ti 3:5} A church may meet in your house._{1Co 16:19-20}

Support. Commend servants of the church to one another, receiving them in the Lord in a way worthy of the Lord's people and giving them any help they may need from you, when they have benefited many people, including you._{Ro 16:2} Greet co-workers in Christ Jesus who risk their lives for you, for whom the churches are grateful._{Ro 16:3-4} Greet members of house churches, and greet the first in their area to convert to Christ._{Ro 16:5} Greet one another with a holy kiss, sending greetings from all the churches of Christ._{Ro 16:16} Greet one another warmly in the Lord, with a holy kiss._{1Co 16:20} Accept and enjoy with the whole church the hospitality of a generous believer among you._{Ro 16:23} Let the churches see your love for one another._{2Co 8:24}

Funds. Collect in the churches for the Lord's people._{1Co 16:1} The first day of every week, set aside and save money based on your income, for the collection._{1Co 16:2} Designate approved persons to collect and distribute your collection gifts.*1Co 16:3* Churches choose individuals to carry the offering, administered to honor the Lord and show eagerness to help.*2Co 8:19* Avoid any criticism of the way you administer giving.*2Co 8:20* Take pains to do right with giving, not only in the Lord's eyes but also in human eyes.*2Co 8:21*

Gifts. God placed in the church first apostles, second prophets, third teachers, then miracles, and then gifts of healing, helping, guidance, and different tongues.*1Co 12:28* Not all are apostles, prophets, or teachers, nor do all work miracles.*1Co 12:29* Not all have gifts of healing, speak in tongues, or interpret.*1Co 12:30* Eagerly desire greater gifts.*1Co 12:31* Unknown languages are a sign for non-believers, not for believers, while foretelling the future is for believers, not non-believers.*1Co 14:22* If everyone in church speaks in unknown languages, then inquirers and non-believers will think you are out of your mind.*1Co 14:23* But everyone foretelling the future convicts a non-believer or inquirer of sin and brings them under judgment, laying bare their secrets so they fall down to worship God among you.*1Co 14:-2425* In church, each of you should share a hymn, word of instruction, revelation, language, or interpretation to build up the church.*1Co 14:26*

Order. God is not over disorder but peace, as in all congregations of the Lord's people.*1Co 14:33* No more than three at most should speak in an unknown language, while someone must interpret.*1Co 14:27* Without an interpreter, the speaker should keep quiet in church, speaking only to himself and God.*1Co 14:28* Two or three may foretell the future, while others weigh carefully their words.*1Co 14:29* If someone sitting down has a revelation, then the first speaker should stop.*1Co 14:30* Speak in turn so that everyone receives instruction and encouragement.*1Co 14:31* You control your spirit as to when to speak.*1Co 14:32* Women should remain silent in the churches, in submission.*1Co 14:34* They should ask questions of their own husband at home, for speaking in church disgraces a woman.*1Co 14:35* Do everything in fit and orderly way.*1Co 14:40* Elders face daily pressing concerns for the churches.*2Co 11:28*

Unity. Let teaching on the good way of life agree in every church.*1Co 4:17* While you should not associate with sexually immoral people, you must inevitably associate with the world's immoral and greedy people, swindlers, and idolaters, because otherwise you would have to leave this world.*1Co 5:10* But still don't associate and eat with any immoral or greedy person or idolaters, slanderers, drunkards, or swindlers, when they claim to be a believer.*1Co 5:11* In other words, don't judge those who are outside the church, whom God will instead judge, but do judge and expel the wicked person inside the church among you.*1Co 5:12-13* Don't come together as a church with divisions among you.*1Co 11:17-18* You are not eating the Lord's Supper together because some of you have your own private suppers, leaving one hungry while another gets drunk.*1Co 11:20-21* Eat and drink in your own homes if you must, but don't despise God's church by humiliating those who have nothing.*1Co 11:22* Do not assume your church inferior to other churches or that your teachers think your church so.*2Co 12:13* God's churches persevere in faith through persecutions and trials.*2Th 1:4* Keep meeting together, rather than giving up, so that you encourage one another, and all the more as the last day approaches.*Heb 10:25*

Love

The letters address at length the love that we should show for one another. The letters exhort to love, just as God commands, and show how we should express love. God is love, and he expressed his love in sacrificing his Son for us. We should take care to love as God expresses. See how richly the letters treat our opportunity to love. Are others seeing the love of Christ in you?

Exhortation. Do everything in love.$_{1Co\ 16:14}$ Spur one another on toward love.$_{Heb\ 10:24}$ Love one another as brothers and sisters.$_{Heb\ 13:1}$ Devote yourselves to one another in love, honoring one another above yourselves.$_{Ro\ 12:10}$ Put on love over all other virtues because love binds all virtues together in perfect unity.$_{Col\ 3:14}$ You've heard from the start: love one another, and you will go from death to life.$_{1Jn\ 3:11-14}$ Wear love as a breastplate.$_{1Th\ 3:8}$ Love comes from a pure heart, good conscience, and sincere faith.$_{1Ti\ 1:5}$ Be an example in love for believers.$_{1Ti\ 4:11}$ Thank God for brothers and sisters whose love for one another increases.$_{2Th\ 1:3}$ Pursue love with those who call on the Lord out of a pure heart.$_{2Ti\ 2:22}$

Expression. Love each other deeply to cover many sins.$_{1Pe\ 4:8}$ Care for one another like a nursing mother cares for her children, out of love, delighted to share your lives.$_{1Th\ 2:7-8}$ Be sincere with your love, hating evil while clinging to good.$_{Ro\ 12:9}$ Love does no harm to a neighbor and thus fulfills the law.$_{Ro\ 13:10}$ Show hospitality to strangers because some have unknowingly shown hospitality to angels.$_{Heb\ 13:2}$ Remember those in prison as if you were with them, and remember the mistreated as if you suffered, too.$_{Heb\ 13:3}$ Be faithful in helping followers even when they are strangers to you, so that they may tell the church about your love.$_{3Jn\ 5-6}$ Now that your obedience to the truth has purified you so that you love one another, love deeply, from the heart.$_{1Pe\ 1:22}$ Show your gentleness to all because the Lord is near.$_{Php\ 4:5}$ Although we all have knowledge, knowledge only puffs up while love instead builds up.$_{1Co\ 8:1}$ Love those to whom you preach.$_{2Co\ 11:11}$

    God. Because God is love, whoever lives in love lives in God, and God in them.$_{1Jn\ 4:16}$ Whoever loves God, God knows.$_{1Co\ 8:3}$ We love because he loved us.$_{1Jn\ 4:19}$ To love God is to keep his commands.$_{1Jn\ 5:3}$ God sums up the commandments not to commit adultery, not to murder, not to steal, and not to covet, and any other command, by commanding to love your neighbor as yourself.$_{Ro\ 13:9}$ We have had from the beginning the command to love one another, when love is itself obedience to God's commands. $_{2Jn\ 5-6}$ God loves his holy people.$_{Ro\ 1:7}$ One only has the love of God in one if one shares one's possessions with brothers and sisters in need.$_{1Jn\ 3:17}$ We should love one another because love comes from God and loving shows we know our Father.$_{1Jn\ 4:7}$ Those who do not love do not know God who is love.$_{1Jn\ 4:8}$ We should love one another because God loved us.$_{1Jn\ 4:11}$ Even though no one has seen God, if we love one another, then God who lives in us makes his love complete in us.$_{1Jn\ 4:12}$ Anyone claiming to love God but who nonetheless hates a brother or sister lies because anyone who does not love one whom they have seen cannot love God whom they have not seen, which is why God commands us to love brother and sister.$_{1Jn\ 4:20-21}$ God taught you to love each other, as you do love God's family, as you should more and more.$_{1Th\ 4:9-10}$ The Lord directs the heart into God's love.$_{2Th\ 3:5}$ Believers in God should pursue love.$_{1Ti\ 6:11}$ God poured his love into our hearts through the Holy Spirit.$_{Ro\ 5:5}$ God's Spirit gives us love.$_{2Ti\ 1:7}$ Love is the Spirit's fruit.$_{Gal\ 5:22}$ May the love of God be with you.$_{2Co\ 13:14}$

    Christ. To love God, we must love his Son Jesus Christ and those who follow his Son, too.$_{1Jn\ 5:1-2}$ When God did not spare his own Son but gave him up for us, he showed that he graciously gives us everything.$_{Ro\ 8:32}$ No one and nothing separates us from the love of Christ, even though we face death all day long.$_{Ro\ 8:35-36}$ In everything, we are more than conquerors through him who loved us.$_{Ro\ 8:37}$ Neither death nor life, angels nor demons, present nor future, nor any powers, neither height nor depth, nor anything else in all creation, can separate us from God's love in Christ Jesus our Lord.$_{Ro\ 8:38-39}$ Follow God's example as dearly loved children by walking in love's way, like Christ loved and gave himself up for us as a fragrant offering and sacrifice to God.*Eph 5:1* Carry each other's burdens, fulfilling Christ's law.*Gal 6:2* By laying down his life for us, Jesus Christ showed us that we should lay down our lives for our brothers and sisters.*1Jn 3:16* God showed his love among us by sending his only Son to us that we might live through him.*1Jn 4:9* Our loving him matters little next to his loving us by sending his Son as a sacrifice to atone for our sins.*1Jn 4:10* Love one another in Christ Jesus.*1Co 16:24* Let Christ's love compel you, convinced that one died for all and thus all died.*2Co 5:14*

Cautions. If you speak in other languages, even of angels, but without love, then you only make an instrument's loud noise.*1Co 13:1* If you foretell the future and fathom every mystery, and your faith moves mountains, but without love, then you are nothing.*1Co 13:2* If you give everything to the poor and your body to hardship just to boast, but without love, you gain nothing.*1Co 13:3* Love is patient and kind, does not envy or boast, and is not proud.*1Co 13:4* Love does not dishonor others, seek itself, easily anger, or keep record of wrongs.*1Co 13:5* Love does not delight in evil but instead rejoices in truth.*1Co 13:6* Love always protects, trusts, hopes, and perseveres.*1Co 13:7* Love never fails, even though prophecies cease, speaking stops, and knowledge disappears.*1Co 13:8* We know and we prophesy only in part, but when things are finally complete, parts disappear.*1Co 13:9-10* We were once children, talking, thinking, and reasoning like children, but when we grew up, we stopped acting childishly.*1Co 13:11* We now see only a rough reflection but then will see face to face, just as we now know only a little but then will know everything, even as others will know us fully.*1Co 13:12* Only faith, hope, and love remain, with love the greatest.*1Co 13:13*

Joy

The letters confirm that joy should follow our faith. We should experience the joy that is the Spirit's fruit. We also should find joy in the faith of other believers. Joy centers not on circumstance but on the faith of one another. See how the letters describe the joy of our faith. Do you express the Spirit's joy in your own salvation and the salvation of others?

You. Your faith rewards you with inexpressible and glorious joy in salvation.$_{1Pe\ 1:9}$ Give joyful thanks to the Father for sharing in the kingdom of light.$_{Col\ 1:12}$ Joy is the Spirit's fruit.$_{Gal\ 5:22}$ We take great joy in Jesus Christ our Lord presenting us before his glorious presence.$_{Jude\ 24\text{-}25}$ Rejoice in the Lord always, rejoice!$_{Php\ 4:4}$ Show the Holy Spirit's joy when suffering for the gospel message.$_{1Th\ 1:6}$ Rejoice always.$_{1Th\ 5:16}$ Be joyful in hope.$_{Ro\ 12:12}$ May the God of hope fill you with all joy as you trust in him.$_{Ro\ 15:13}$ Everyone who hears about your obedience rejoices because of you.$_{Ro\ 16:19}$ Rejoice as you strive for full restoration.$_{2Co\ 13:11}$ God set the Son above, anointing him with the oil of joy.$_{Heb\ 1:9}$ Brothers and sisters, rejoice in the Lord!$_{Php\ 3:1}$ Sing and make music from your heart to the Lord.$_{Eph\ 5:19\text{-}20}$

Others. Our greatest joy is when followers testify about one another's faithfulness to the truth.$_{3Jn\ 3\text{-}4}$ Unity in Christ makes one another's joy complete.$_{Php\ 2:2}$ Even when suffering in faithful sacrifice and service, be glad and rejoice with other believers.$_{Php\ 2:17\text{-}18}$ The love of believers for one another gives us great joy and encouragement, refreshing the hearts of the Lord's people.$_{Phm\ 7}$ We take heartfelt joy in our common salvation in God's grace.$_{Php\ 1:7\text{-}8}$ We take great joy when our children walk in the truth. $_{2Jn\ 4}$ We pray with joy for other believers.$_{Php\ 1:4\text{-}5}$ Let news of one another cheer you.$_{Php\ 2:19}$ Welcome a fellow believer in the Lord with great joy and honor, especially when they almost die for Christ's work.*Php 2:29-30* Rejoice greatly in the Lord when renewing your concern for a fellow believer.*Php 4:10* Rejoice in suffering for others as Christ suffered.*Col 1:24* Fellow believers are your joy.*1Th 2:19-20* Take joy in others' faith.*1Th 3:9* Long to see other believers, so that joy may fill you.*2Ti 1:4* Pray that the Lord's people favorably receive contributions that you share, so that you have joy and refreshing company.*Ro 15:31-32* Enjoy the hospitality of a generous believer among you.*Ro 16:23* Take such great pride in one another that in all your trouble, your joy knows no bounds.*2Co 7:4* Tell one another about your longing, sorrow, and concern for one another, so that your joy may be greater than ever.*2Co 7:7* Rejoice with those who rejoice, while mourning with those who mourn.*Ro 12:15*

Sowing

The letters encourage that we sow generously, expecting a harvest of righteousness. Yet we must sow good rather than evil, for each bring their own different harvest. And God is the one who makes things grow, not the planter nor the harvester. See how the letters address sowing. Are you sowing good seed, expecting a righteous harvest?

Good. The thing is to persevere in doing good because the harvest is indeed coming for those of us who do not give up.*Gal 6:9* Do good wherever the opportunity arises but especially among the family of believers.*Gal 6:10* Support and work together with followers who go out sharing Christ's name because they'll get no help from those who don't follow Christ.*3Jn 7-8* Be pleased to make a contribution for the poor among the Lord's people because you may owe them material blessings to repay spiritual blessings.*Ro 15:26-27* Keep doing good in the faithful Creator's name even as you suffer for it.*1Pe 4:19* Plan visits to have a harvest among others.*Ro 1:13* Whoever sows generously reaps generously.*2Co 9:6*

Evil. God won't let us get away with it: we reap what we sow.*Gal 6:7* When we sow pursuing desires, we reap destruction.*Gal 6:8* One reaps no benefit from sin, only shame and death, because sin's wage is death.*Ro 6:21-22* Call to account and put out of the church those who spread malicious nonsense, who refuse to welcome other followers, and who stop other followers who want to help.*3Jn 9-10* Repay evil with blessing rather than evil, so that you inherit blessing.*1Pe 3:9* Whoever sows sparingly reaps sparingly.*2Co 9:6*

God. One reaps holiness and eternal life as a slave to God because God's gift is eternal life in Christ Jesus our Lord.*Ro 6:21-22* The Lord assigns each teacher to his task, some planting, some watering, but God making it grow.*1Co 3:5-6* Teachers are co-workers in God's service, while you are God's field.*1Co 3:9* Neither the planter nor the waterer is anything, but only God, who makes things grow.*1Co 3:7* The planter and waterer have one purpose, each rewarded for their own labor.*1Co 3:8* The plant must die to sow the seed that comes to life.*1Co 15:36* When we sow to please the Spirit, we reap from the Spirit eternal life.*Gal 6:8* Having godly qualities in increasing measure keep us from being ineffective and unproductive in knowing our Lord Jesus Christ.*2Pe 1:8* Stress trustworthy doctrine so that those trusting God excel in doing good, profiting everyone.*Tit 3:8* Sowing is not planting what will be but instead planting only the seed of what will be.*1Co 15:37* God gives the seed a body as he determines, giving each seed its own body.*1Co 15:38* God who supplies seed to the sower and bread for food also supplies and increases your store of seed to enlarge your righteousness harvest.*2Co 9:10*

Teaching

Teaching comprises more of the letters' direction than any other topic. Teaching is plainly critically important. The letters are, in effect, a teaching manual. They address the call to preach with courage. God calls preachers and teachers to share the power of Christ's cross. The purpose of teaching is to share Christ's gospel and only the true gospel, not false doctrine, to save the lost while to strengthen believers. Preachers and teachers deserve a wage, yet volunteers earn their own reward. See how the letters address teaching. Are you prepared in season and out to teach the gospel accurately?

Preaching. Preach the word, prepared in season and out of season, correcting and rebuking with great patience and careful instruction.$_{2Ti\ 4:2}$ Preach your message not with wise and persuasive words but demonstrating the Spirit's power.$_{1Co\ 2:4}$ No one preaches unless sent to bring the good news.$_{Ro\ 10:15}$ The commanded preaching of a godly servant leader who follows Jesus Christ must further the faith of God's elect in the truth, fostering godliness leading to the promised eternal life.$_{Tit\ 1:1-3}$ Some preach Christ out of envy, rivalry, and selfish ambition to make trouble for those who preach Christ out of goodwill and love, in the gospel's defense.$_{Php\ 1:15-16}$ But whether one preaches from false or true motives, what matters is that we preach Christ and rejoice.$_{Php\ 1:18}$ Read scripture publicly, preaching and teaching diligently with your whole self and showing progress, rather than neglect your gift given to you through prophecy in elders' laid-on hands.$_{1Ti\ 4:13-15}$ A preacher serves God in the preacher's spirit when preaching the gospel of God's Son.$_{Ro\ 1:9}$

Courage. God may give Christ Jesus's ministers grace to boldly remind others of important points.$_{Ro\ 15:15}$ Teach and rebuke with all authority, not letting anyone despise you.$_{Tit\ 2:15}$ Do not let the sufferings of a teacher discourage you because they are your glory.$_{Eph\ 3:13}$ Repeat your admonitions as safeguards for one another.$_{Php\ 3:1}$ We proclaim Christ, admonishing and teaching everyone with all wisdom and all the energy Christ so powerfully works in us, strenuously contending so that we may present everyone fully mature in Christ.$_{Col\ 1:28}$ Contend hard not only for those whom you know but even those whom you have not met.$_{Col\ 2:1}$ Look for results when courageously preaching the gospel with God's help to fellow believers, even when facing strong opposition.$_{1Th\ 2:1-2}$ Remember the toil and hardship of fellow believers who work day and night not to be a burden to anyone while preaching God's gospel.$_{1Th\ 2:9}$ Be confident in the Lord that others will do as commanded.$_{2Th\ 3:4}$ Have confidence through Christ before God.$_{2Co\ 3:4}$ Pray that God keeps preachers safe from persecuting non-believers.$_{Ro\ 15:31-32}$ Join in one another's struggles to proclaim the gospel by praying for one another.$_{Ro\ 15:30}$ Death works against our teachers so that life works in us. $_{2Co\ 4:12}$

God. God commissions gospel servants to present his word in its fullness.$_{Col\ 1:25}$ God appoints true and faithful teachers.$_{1Ti\ 2:7}$ No prophecy is by the prophet's own interpretation because prophecy never originated in human will, but prophets instead spoke from God as the Holy Spirit carried them along.$_{2Pe\ 1:20-21}$ Speak as approved by God and entrusted with the gospel, to please God rather than people.$_{1Th\ 2:4}$ Urge one another to live worthy of God.$_{1Th\ 2:10-12}$ Instruct one another by the Lord Jesus's authority how to live to please God, urging one another more and more to live as you are living in the Lord Jesus.$_{1Th\ 4:1-2}$ Do not claim competence in yourself but instead competence from God.$_{2Co\ 3:5}$ God makes us competent ministers of a new covenant not of the letter but of the Spirit, for the letter kills while the Spirit gives life.$_{2Co\ 3:6}$ State the truth plainly, and so commend yourself to everyone's conscience in God's sight.$_{2Co\ 4:2}$ Because God's mercy grants us this teaching ministry, we do not lose heart.$_{2Co\ 4:1}$ Persuade others out of your own fear of the Lord, because you are plain to God, and thus keep your conscience clear.$_{2Co\ 5:11}$ Be out of your mind for God but in your right mind for others.$_{2Co\ 5:13}$ We are Christ's ambassadors, God as if appealing through us, imploring on Christ's behalf to reconcile to God.$_{2Co\ 5:20}$

Christ. We do not preach ourselves but Jesus Christ as Lord, with ourselves as your servants for Jesus.$_{2Co\ 4:5}$ Wise and eloquent preaching must not empty Christ's cross of its power.₁Co 1:17 Proclaim God's testimony not with eloquence or human wisdom but instead knowing only Jesus Christ crucified, and that in weakness with great fear and trembling.₁Co 2:1-3 Our grace is to preach to Christ's boundless riches, making plain to everyone the mystery that our creator God hid in himself for ages past.Eph 3:8-9 Persist in Christ's teaching, rather than running ahead without it, that you may retain both Father and Son.₂Jn 9 Be ready at all times to gently and respectfully tell others that Jesus is the reason for your hope, even as your good behavior contradicts and shames those who slander you.₁Pe 3:15-16 Take as your goal that you encourage hearts and unite in love, for the full riches of knowing God's mystery, namely, Christ.Col 2:2 Let Christ's message dwell among you richly as you teach and admonish one another with all wisdom through psalms, hymns, and songs from the Spirit.Col 3:16 Teachers should thank Christ Jesus our Lord, who strengthens them, that he considers them trustworthy, appointing them to his service.₁Ti 1:12

Doctrine. Sound doctrine conforms to the gospel concerning the blessed God's glory.₁Ti 1:11 Stand firm and hold fast to sound teachings by word of mouth or writing.₂Th 2:15 Everything in the Scriptures is to teach us.Ro 15:4 Speak God's words.₁Pe 4:11 Speak the truth in Christ, conscience confirming through the Holy Spirit.Ro 9:1 Command and teach right things, without letting anyone look down on you because you are young.₁Ti 4:11 Teach only sound doctrine.Tit 2:1 Demolish arguments and pretensions against knowing God, to capture every thought for obedience to Christ.₂Co 10:5 If the Spirit so encourages, then meet privately with esteemed leaders to ensure that you preach the true gospel rather than run your race in vain.Gal 2:2 Do your best to present yourself to God for approval as a worker who correctly handles the word of truth.₂Ti 2:15 Teach using everyday examples.Ro 6:19 My believing brothers and sisters are filled with knowledge and competent to instruct one another.Ro 15:14 Send to one another faithful sons in the Lord that they may remind you of the good way of life in Christ Jesus, agreeing with the teaching in every church.₁Co 4:17 Who preaches doesn't matter because what gets preached matters, and what we believe matters.₁Co 15:11

Evangelism. Do the work of an evangelist.₂Ti 4:5 Fully proclaim Christ's gospel.Ro 15:19 To call on the Lord one must believe in him, while to believe in him one must hear of him, and to hear of him someone must preach._{Ro 10:14} Preach Christ's gospel where the Lord opens a door for you._{2Co 2:12} Make your ambition to preach Christ's gospel where not known, so that you do not build on someone else's foundation, and those whom no one told about Christ may see, hear, and understand._{Ro 15:20-21} Thank God, who always leads us as captives in Christ's triumphal procession, using us to spread the aroma of the knowledge of him everywhere._{2Co 2:14} To God, we are Christ's pleasing aroma among those whom he is saving and those who perish._{2Co 2:15} To one we are an aroma bringing death, while to the other an aroma bringing life, but who is equal to such a task?_{2Co 2:16}

Sinners. Turning a sinner from the error of their way saves them from death while covering over many sins._{Jas 5:19-20} We preach the gospel even to those who are still dead in sin, so that while they live according to human standards as to the body, they might come to live by God as to the spirit._{1Pe 4:6} Put no stumbling block in anyone's path, to discredit your ministry._{2Co 6:3} Some must preach to the non-believer, while others to the believer, the same Spirit at work in each._{Gal 2:7-8} A preacher's obligation is both to the wise and foolish, which is reason to be eager to preach._{Ro 1:14-15} Gently instruct opponents in the hope that God will grant them repentance leading them to a knowledge of the truth and that they come to their senses._{2Ti 2:25-26} One may take pride in ministry to outsiders in the hope that insiders will envy enough to turn to salvation._{Ro 11:13-14}

Others. Help older men to be temperate, worthy of respect, self-controlled, and sound in faith, loving, and enduring, and older women to be reverent, not to slander or to drink much wine, and to teach the good._{Tit 2:1-3} Older women should urge younger women to love their husbands and children and be self-controlled, pure, busy at home, kind, and subject to their husband, so that no one maligns God's word._{Tit 2:4-5} Older men should set a good example for young men to be self-controlled._{Tit 2:6-7} Teaching should have integrity, seriousness, and soundness that no one can condemn, shaming opponents who thus have nothing bad to say._{Tit 2:7-8} Teach workers to obey their supervisors in everything, to please them, not to talk back to them, and not to steal from them, instead showing their trustworthiness, to make attractive teaching about God our Savior._{Tit 2:9-10} Teach the people to submit to rulers and authorities, obey, do good, slander no one, be peaceable and considerate, and be gentle toward everyone._{Tit 3:1-2} Instruct how people should conduct themselves in the church.*1Ti 3:15* Instruct the people so that no one may be open to blame.*1Ti 5:7* Instruct without partiality or favoritism, as in the sight of God and Christ Jesus and the elect angels.*1Ti 5:21* Write to correct others when absent, so as not when present to be harsh with the authority the Lord gave you for building up others, not for tearing down.*2Co 13:10*

Teachers. Hesitate to teach because God judges teachers more strictly.*Jas 3:1* Share all good things with the one who instructs you in God's word.*Gal 6:6* Sound teachers back up their writings with actions.*2Co 10:11* Training as a speaker does not matter next to knowledge.*2Co 11:6* Follow a teacher's example, as the teacher follows Christ's example.*1Co 11:1* You may imitate those believers whose gospel message you welcome, even as you imitate the Lord, even when suffering severely.*1Th 1:6* You may also become a model to other believers who learn of your faith in God.*1Th 1:7-8* Do not take into your house or welcome anyone who teaches incorrectly, or you will share in their wicked work. *2Jn 10-11* Speak to sensible people, letting them judge for themselves what you say.*1Co 10:15* The Lord's servant must be kind to everyone and able to teach.*2Ti 2:24*

Wages. Those who preach and teach deserve their wages.*1Ti 5:17-18* Teachers could reasonably claim food, drink, and other support from you so that they need not work, and could take along with them a believing wife, just as soldiers do not serve at their own expense, vineyard planters get to eat their own grapes, and those tending flocks get to drink the flock's milk.*1Co 9:4-7* Human authority and the Law say the same thing, not to muzzle an ox while treading the grain, when we're not talking about oxen here.*1Co 9:8-9* God says so for human teachers that whoever plows and threshes should share the harvest.*1Co 9:10* Those who sow spiritual seed should reap a material harvest.*1Co 9:11* If others get your support, then teachers of the word should also, even if they choose to decline it and instead accept anything rather than hinder Christ's gospel.*1Co 9:12* Those who serve in the temple get their food from the temple, and those who serve at the altar share in the offering.*1Co 9:13*

Volunteers. The Lord commands that those who preach the gospel should receive their living from the gospel, even if some choose not to use these rights and prefer to die for the ability to so boast.*1Co 9:14-15* The Lord compels some to preach.*1Co 9:16* Those who preach voluntarily have a reward, but those whom the Lord compels to preach simply discharge their trust._1Co 9:17_ Preaching the gospel for free rather than claiming a gospel preacher's rights creates a reward._1Co 9:18_ Unlike so many, some do not peddle God's word for profit but in Christ speak before God with sincerity, as sent from God._2Co 2:17_ Appreciate rather than condemn those who preach God's gospel to you free of charge._2Co 11:7_ Other churches pay when preachers serve some, perhaps you, for free._2Co 11:8_ Teachers remove an obstacle when they keep from burdening those to whom they preach._2Co 11:9_ Respect the teaching of the free apostle who saw Jesus our Lord and wrote you letters, making you the result of his work and seal of his apostleship in the Lord._1Co 9:1-3_

Building

The letters address the topic of building. God is the master builder who lays the foundation and sets the cornerstone and capstone in Christ. You, too, should be a builder both of yourself and others, for we are God's temple when we hold to the hope that he placed in us. See how the letters address building. Are you participating with and relying on the Master builder?

Foundation. Look forward to the city with foundations, whose architect and builder is God.*Heb 11:10* You are God's building, on which, by God's grace, another laid a foundation as a wise builder, after which someone else builds on it but should build with care.*1Co 3:9-10* No one can lay any foundation other than the one already laid, which is Jesus Christ.*1Co 3:11* If anyone builds on this foundation using gold, silver, costly stones, wood, hay, or straw, then judgment day's fire will test and show their work for what it is.*1Co 3:12-13* Make your ambition to preach Christ's gospel where not known, so that you do not build on someone else's foundation, and those whom no one told about Christ may see, hear, and understand.*Ro 15:20-21* As you approach the living stone Jesus whom God chose as precious but humans rejected, God is building you like living stones into a spiritual house and ministry offering sacrifices God accepts through Jesus.*1Pe 2:4-5*

Builder. Don't say anything unwholesome but only what builds others up as they need, benefitting those who listen.*Eph 4:29* Build each other up just as you are doing.*1Th 5:11* The strong should bear the weak's failings not to please themselves but to please their neighbors for their good, to build them up.*Ro 15:1-2* When you build yourself up in your most holy faith and pray in the Holy Spirit, you keep yourself in God's love.*Jude 20-21* When the building survives, then the builder receives a reward.*1Co 3:14* If the building burns, then the builder loses but God still saves, even while the builder escapes through the flames.*1Co 3:15*

Temple. You are God's temple, with God's Spirit dwelling in your midst.*1Co 3:16* If anyone destroys God's temple, then God will destroy that person, because God's temple is sacred, and you together are that temple.*1Co 3:17* We are the living God's temple, God living with us and walking among us, he our God, and we his people.*2Co 6:16* The Lord gives some persons authority to build you up rather than tear you down.*2Co 10:8* Jesus was faithful to God who appointed him, just as Moses was faithful in God's house.*Heb 3:2* Jesus gets greater honor than Moses, just as a house's builder has greater honor than the house.*Heb 3:3* Someone builds every house, but God builds everything.*Heb 3:4* Moses was a faithful servant in God's house, witnessing what God would say in the future.*Heb 3:5* Christ is the faithful Son over God's house, where we are God's house, if we hold firmly to our confidence and the hope in which we glory.*Heb 3:6*

Discerning

Just as the letters address teaching, they also address learning and discerning. Teachers have one responsibility, while learners have another, which is to be discerning. Listen only to sound instruction, and then obey it. Be mature in your thought, listening with care and attention. Strive to know Christ. See how the letters address discerning. Does the Spirit guide you when you listen to teaching?

Sound. Entrust to reliable and qualified teachers the sound teaching that you learn.$_{2Ti\ 2:2}$ Hold, with faith and love in Christ Jesus, to the sound teaching that you learned, guarding the good deposit entrusted you, with the help of the Holy Spirit living in you.$_{2Ti\ 1:13-14}$ Praise to you for remembering your teacher in everything and for holding to the teaching just as taught.$_{1Co\ 11:2}$ Remember the lessons you learned from teachers who were with you.$_{2Th\ 2:5}$ Don't make a teacher have to be bold toward you in person by living under the standards of this world.$_{2Co\ 10:2}$ Don't let hard teaching frighten you unduly, even when weighty and forceful.$_{2Co\ 10:9-10}$ Some receive visions and revelations from the Lord.$_{2Co\ 12:1}$ Some God catches up to paradise to hear inexpressible things that no one may tell.$_{2Co\ 12:4}$ Believers cannot do anything against the truth but only for the truth.$_{2Co\ 13:8}$

Obedient. Thank God that you now obey the teaching from your heart.$_{Ro\ 6:17}$ You should rely completely on the gospel prophecy, paying attention to it as to a light shining in a dark place, until the day dawns in your heart.$_{2Pe\ 1:19}$ Do not be foolish, but know the Lord's will.$_{Eph\ 5:17}$ Others taught you to put off your former way of life and old self corrupted by its deceitful desires.$_{Eph\ 4:22}$ Teachers taught you to be made new in the attitude of your minds while putting on the new self, created to be like God in true righteousness and holiness.*Eph 4:23-24* Even while you obey God, whether your teachers are present or absent, continue to work out your salvation with fear and trembling, so that God may work in you to fulfill his good purpose.*Php 2:12-13* Anyone who rejects instruction rejects not just a person but God.*1Th 4:8* Keep away from idle believers who do not live as taught.*2Th 3:6* Do not refuse God who warned you from heaven because those who refused his earthly warning did not escape, and how much less you will escape.*Heb 12:25* Then, his voice shook the earth, but now he promises that his voice will shake earth and heaven, leaving only what does not shake.*Heb 12:26-27* The angels' message bound those who heard it, so that every violation and disobedience received just punishment.*Heb 2:2*

Mature. Move beyond elementary teachings about Christ, to maturity, not just to foundations like repenting from acts leading to death, having faith in God, cleansing rites, laying on of hands, resurrection of the dead, and eternal judgment.*Heb 6:1-2* God will permit you to reach maturity.*Heb 6:3* Stop thinking like children, except as to evil, but otherwise think like adults.*1Co 14:20* Like babies, crave pure spiritual milk, growing up in your salvation while knowing that the Lord is good.*1Pe 2:2-3* Be a good minister of Christ Jesus, nourished on the faith's truths and good teaching.*1Ti 4:6* Get ready for solid spiritual food, not just milk.*1Co 3:2* If you must live on milk, as still a spiritual infant, then you will not learn about righteousness.*Heb 5:13* Desire solid food for the mature, constantly training yourself to distinguish good from evil.*Heb 5:14* Aspire to teach rather than to need someone to teach you again elementary truths of God's word.*Heb 5:12*

Listening. Pay the most careful attention to what you have heard so as not to drift away.*Heb 2:1* Some people do not listen even when the Lord speaks to them in other languages and through foreigners.*1Co 14:21* Listen first before speaking.*Jas 1:19* Unless you who believe yourself religious hold your tongue, your religion is worthless.*Jas 1:26* All of us fail in many ways, but if you speak only without fault, then you do better keeping yourself from failing.*Jas 3:2* Just as a bit turns a horse, a rudder turns a ship, and a small spark sets a forest on fire, so, too, does the tongue turn and enflame us in evil with its great boasts.*Jas 3:3-6* We tame many animals but cannot tame our own tongue, the restless evil from which spreads deadly poison.*Jas 3:7-8* Even though we praise our Lord and

Father, we immediately curse others whom God made in his likeness, proving our praise corrupt because one spring cannot produce two different waters or one tree two different fruit.*Jas 3:9-12* You did not harden your heart when you heard about Christ and learned from others the truth that is in Jesus.*Eph 4:20-21* Listen to what benefits you and builds you up.*Eph 4:29*

Christ. You must accept the preaching that God raised Christ from the dead, rather than say resurrection doesn't happen.*1Co 15:12* Only those who are perishing do not see the gospel.*2Co 4:3* This age's god has blinded the minds of non-believers, so that they cannot see the gospel's light displaying the glory of Christ, who is the image of God.*2Co 4:4* Regard no one from a worldly perspective, as you once regarded Christ but no longer do.*2Co 5:16* Do not ignore the Lord's greater salvation message, confirmed by those who heard him.*Heb 2:3* God testified to the salvation message by signs, wonders, miracles, and the Holy Spirit's gifts distributed at his will.*Heb 2:4* Holy brothers and sisters, share in your heavenly calling by fixing your thoughts on Jesus, our apostle and high priest.*Heb 3:1* Your teachers need not commend themselves or have letters of recommendation because you are written on their hearts, a letter that everyone knows and reads.*2Co 3:1-2* You are a letter from Christ, the result of another's ministry, written not with ink but with the Spirit of the living God, not on stone tablets but on tablets of human hearts.*2Co 3:3*

Striving. Train yourself to be godly, for while physical training is of some value, godliness has value for all things in the present life and life to come.*1Ti 4:7-9* Labor and strive, having put your hope in the living God.*1Ti 4:10* Watch your life and doctrine closely, persevering in them to save both yourself and your hearers.*1Ti 4:16* The teaching and way of life you should know involves purpose, faith, patience, love, and endurance.*2Ti 3:10-11* Continue in what you learned and are convinced because you know those from whom you learned it and its source in the Holy Scriptures.*2Ti 3:14-15* Apply these things to yourself to benefit others, so that they may learn from you not to go beyond the writing.*1Co 4:6* God said that if you hear his voice, then not to harden your heart.*Heb 4:7* You will be hard to teach if you no longer try to understand.*Heb 5:11*

Wisdom

The letters address the source and pursuit of wisdom. We should desire wisdom and should speak wisdom to others. We must, though, be able to distinguish God's wisdom from the world's wisdom, which is foolishness in God's sight. See how the letters address wisdom. Are you both sharing and heeding godly wisdom?

Desiring. If you want wisdom, then ask God who will give you lots of it whether you have faults or not.$_{Jas\ 1:6}$ As long as you live, think of these words rather than just know them, and help others do likewise, so that you remain firmly established in the truth you now have.$_{2Pe\ 1:12\ -14}$ Think about true, noble, right, pure, lovely, admirable, excellent and praiseworthy things.$_{Php\ 4:8}$ Practice whatever you learn, receive, or hear from the wise, or see in them, so that the God of peace is with you.$_{Php\ 4:9}$ You are in Christ Jesus, who is our wisdom from God, our righteousness, holiness, and redemption, because of God.$_{1Co\ 1:30}$ The Lord gives insight.$_{2Ti\ 2:7}$ The Holy Scriptures make you wise for salvation through faith in Christ Jesus.$_{2Ti\ 3:14-15}$ Remember what you were like when God first called you, neither wise nor influential, and not many of noble birth.$_{1Co\ 1:26}$

Speaking. Speak wisdom among the mature, but not the wisdom of this age or of the rulers of this age, who are coming to nothing.$_{1Co\ 2:6}$ Declare God's wisdom, a hidden mystery that God destined for our glory before time began.$_{1Co\ 2:7}$ Rulers did not understand it, or they would not have crucified the Lord of glory.$_{1Co\ 2:8}$ Stimulate one another to wholesome thinking so that you recall the prophets' words and our Lord and Savior's commands shared through the apostles.$_{2Pe\ 3:1-2}$ Be wise in the way you interact with outsiders, making the most of every opportunity to season with salt your graceful conversation, knowing how to answer everyone._{Col 4:5-6}

Distinguishing. Bitter envy and selfish ambition that somehow pass for wisdom are not God's wisdom but are instead earthly and demonic, sowing disorder and evil._{Jas 3:14-16} God's wisdom is pure, peace-loving, considerate, submissive, full of mercy and good fruit, and impartial and sincere, helping you sow in peace and reap righteousness._{Jas 3:17-18} Do not treat prophecies with contempt but test them all._{1Th 5:19-22} Be wise about what is good and innocent about what is evil._{Ro 16:19} Although we all have knowledge, knowledge only puffs up while love instead builds up._{1Co 8:1} Those who think they know don't know as they should know._{1Co 8:2} Jews demand signs and Greeks look for wisdom, but we preach Christ crucified, a stumbling block to Jews and foolishness to other non-believers but God's power and wisdom to those whom God called._{1Co 1:22-24}

World. God makes foolish the world's wisdom._{1Co 1:20} God's wisdom is that the world not know him through its own wisdom, but instead, seemingly foolish gospel preaching pleased God to save those who believe._{1Co 1:21} God's foolishness is wiser than human wisdom, and God's weakness is stronger than human strength._{1Co 1:25} God chose the world's foolish things to shame the wise and weak things to shame the strong._{1Co 1:27} Rest your faith not on human wisdom but on God's power._{1Co 2:5} The message we speak is not human wisdom but as the Spirit taught us, explaining spiritual realities with Spirit-taught words._{1Co 2:13} The world's wisdom is foolishness in God's sight because he catches the wise in their craftiness._{1Co 3:19} The Lord knows that thoughts of the wise are futile._{1Co 3:20}

Trials

The letters address at length the trials that believers face. We persevere through trials and challenges, knowing that they test and refine our faith. In trials, we draw on the Lord's great strength. When suffering, we draw on the Lord's great comfort. We know that nothing separates us from the love of Christ. We thus delight in our weakness, which only reveals Christ's strength while strengthening our faith. See how the letters address trials. Are you facing, indeed welcoming, trials with the courage and strength that Christ supplies?

Persevering. Trials and challenges that test your faith should make you happy over the perseverance that they produce because perseverance makes you mature and complete._{Jas 1:2-4} When you persevere through test and trial, still loving the Lord, you receive life's crown that the Lord promised._{Jas 1:12} The Lord blesses those who persevere, as the Lord blessed Job, because the Lord is full of compassion and mercy._{Jas 5:11} The grief you suffer now in many trials, lasting only a little while, must not keep you from rejoicing over salvation._{1Pe 1:6} Trials prove your faith genuine, worth more than gold, resulting in praise, glory, and honor on Christ's return._{1Pe 1:7} We forget the past to strain toward the prize for which God called us heavenward in Christ Jesus._{Php 3:13-14} We should persevere in what we have already attained._{Php 3:16} Let the faith of others encourage you when distressed and persecuted._{1Th 3:7-8} Boast among God's churches about others' perseverance in faith through persecutions and trials._{2Th 1:4} The Lord directs the heart into Christ's perseverance._{2Th 3:5} Believers in God should pursue endurance._{1Ti 6:11} Endure hardship._{2Ti 4:5} Suffering produces perseverance, perseverance produces character, and character sustains hope._{Ro 5:3-4} Be patient in affliction._{Ro 12:12} We draw hope from the endurance the Scriptures depict.*Ro 15:4* God gives endurance.*Ro 15:6*

Strength. Be strong in the Lord in his mighty power.*Eph 6:10* Stand firm with the belt of truth buckled around your waist, with the breastplate of righteousness in place, and with your feet fitted with the readiness that comes from the gospel of peace.*Eph 6:14-15* In prayer, receive God's strength with all power according to his glorious might so that you endure with great patience.*Col 1:10-11* Do not let trials unsettle you, for you know quite well that your destiny is in them, as others keep telling you and has already occurred.*1Th 3:3-4* Recall prophecies others made about you to help you fight the battle well.*1Ti 1:18* Persecutions and sufferings come to sound teachers, but the Lord rescues from all of them.*2Ti 3:10-11* The Lord stands at our side and gives us strength, so that through us the message might reach all.*2Ti 4:17* Be on guard, standing firm in faith, strong and courageous.*1Co 16:13* The Lord rescues from every evil attack.*2Ti 4:18*

Comfort. God comforts us in all our troubles, so that we can comfort those in any trouble with the comfort we ourselves receive from God.*2Co 1:4* Just as we share abundantly in the sufferings of Christ, so also our comfort abounds through Christ.*2Co 1:5* Suffer distress for the comfort and salvation of one another, so that comfort in distress produces patient endurance of suffering.*2Co 1:6* Hope firmly for one another, knowing that just as you share in one another's suffering, you also share in comfort.*2Co 1:7*

Christ. No one and nothing separates us from the love of Christ, even though we face death all day long.*Ro 8:35-36* In everything we are more than conquerors through him who loved us.*Ro 8:37* Neither death nor life, angels nor demons, present nor future, nor any powers, neither height nor depth, nor anything else in all creation, can separate us from God's love in Christ Jesus our Lord.*Ro 8:38-39* Our suffering does not compare with the glory that God will reveal in us.*Ro 8:18* Don't treat your fiery ordeals as something strange, but instead rejoice for suffering with Christ.*1Pe 4:12* Insults because of Christ bless you, showing that God's glorious Spirit is on you.*1Pe 4:14* Don't murder, steal, or meddle, and suffer, but instead suffer gladly as a Christian, praising God that others know you follow Christ.*1Pe 4:15-16* After you suffer a little while, God who is all grace and who called you to eternal glory in Christ will restore you, making you strong and steadfast.*1Pe 5:10* Join with others in suffering for the gospel, by the power of God.*2Ti 1:8* Join with others in suffering, like a good soldier of Christ Jesus.*2Ti 2:3* Others will persecute everyone living a godly life in Christ Jesus.*2Ti 3:12* Endure everything so that the elect may also obtain salvation in Christ Jesus, with eternal glory.*2Ti 2:10* Those who endure with Christ will also reign with him.*2Ti 2:12*

Weakness. We have the gospel treasure in jars of clay to show that all-surpassing power is from God and not us.*2Co 4:7* Opposition presses us hard on every side without crushing us, perplexing us but not despairing us, persecuting us but not abandoning us, striking us down but not destroying us.*2Co 4:8-9* We always carry around in our body Jesus's death, so that our body may also reveal Jesus's life.*2Co 4:10* We face death for Jesus' sake, so that our mortal body may reveal his life.*2Co 4:11* Do not lose heart because, while you may waste away outwardly, inwardly God renews you daily.*2Co 4:16* Our eternal glory far outweighs the light and momentary troubles achieving that glory for us.*2Co 4:17* As God's servants, conduct yourself appropriately whether in great endurance, troubles, hardships, distresses, beatings, imprisonments, riots, hard work, sleepless nights, and hunger.*2Co 6:4-5* Some apostles will labor and toil without sleep, know hunger and thirst, often go without food, and be cold and naked.*2Co 11:27* Delight in weaknesses, insults, hardships, and difficulties for Christ's sake because when you are weak, you are strong.*2Co 12:10* Be glad whenever you are weak but strong, while praying that God fully restores you.*2Co 13:9*

Faith. The Holy Spirit says that if you hear his voice, then do not harden your hearts in rebellion, even under testing in the wilderness.*Heb 3:7-8* Fix your eyes on the unseen rather than what you see because what you see is temporary, while the unseen is eternal.*2Co 4:18* We share in Christ when we hold our original conviction firmly to the very end.*Heb 3:14* Remember your earlier days after receiving the light, when you endured despite great conflict full of suffering.*Heb 10:32* Others may publicly expose you to insult and persecution, or you may stand side by side with those whom others so treat.*Heb 10:33* Suffer along with the imprisoned, and joyfully accept your property's confiscation, because you know that you have better and lasting possessions.*Heb 10:34* Do not throw away your confidence, but instead expect rich reward.*Heb 10:35* Persevere so that when you have done God's will, you receive what he promised.*Heb 10:36*

Be confident that with the Lord helping you, you need not fear, because mere mortals cannot oppose God.*Heb 13:6*

Rulers

The letters briefly address how believers should treat rulers. God establishes authorities, whom we should therefore respect. Authorities are for our good, and so we should expect punishment when doing wrong and have no fear when doing right. See how the letters address rulers, including to give them their due. Are you exhibiting the proper respect for governing authorities?

Submit to the authorities not just to avoid punishment but also out of conscience.*Ro 13:5* Subject yourself to governing authorities because God established them.*Ro 13:1* Anyone rebelling against authority rebels against what God instituted, bringing judgment on themselves.*Ro 13:2* Rulers hold no terror for those who do right, only those who do wrong, and so do what is right to be free from fear and instead receive commendation.*Ro 13:3* Those in authority are God's servants for your good, wrath's agents to punish wrongdoers, and so if you do wrong, then you should fear the ruler's sword for good reason.*Ro 13:4* Pay your taxes because the authorities, who are God's servants, give their time to governing.*Ro 13:6* Give to everyone what you owe them, including taxes if you owe taxes, revenue if you owe revenue, respect when respect is due, and honor when honor is due.*Ro 13:7* Pay every debt, and let no debt remain outstanding except the continuing debt to love one another, out of which you fulfill the law.*Ro 13:8*

Encouragement

The letters address the encouragement that we draw from faith in Christ and that we accordingly owe one another as believers. As you read how often and clearly the letters speak to encouragement, consider why they do so. We must have greater need than we think. Are you drawing sufficient encouragement from Jesus while also encouraging others appropriately?

You. Look to Jesus, who endured such opposition from sinners, for encouragement when you are weary and losing heart.*Heb 12:3* With God for us, no one can be against us.*Ro 8:31* Let co-workers in God's service strengthen and encourage you in your faith.*1Th 3:2* Take comfort and encouragement from witnessing your holy, righteous, and blameless leaders.*1Th 2:10-11* The Lord gives some authority to build you up rather than tear you down.*2Co 10:8* The strong should bear the weak's failings not to please themselves but to please their neighbors for their good, to build them up.*Ro 15:1-2* Even Christ did not please himself but instead bore insults directed toward others.*Ro 15:3* Our Lord Jesus Christ and God our Father encourage our hearts.*2Th 2:16-17* We draw hope from the encouragement the Scriptures provide.*Ro 15:4* God gives encouragement.*Ro 15:6-7* God comforts the downcast, sending others whom God has comforted, to comfort you.*2Co 7:6-7*

Others. Encourage one another daily, so that sin's deceitfulness hardens none of you.*Heb 3:13* Encourage one another with how God treats believers on Christ's return.*1Th 4:18* Encourage those who love one another in the faith.*Tit 3:15* Be dear fellow servants in the Lord, sharing news of one another to encourage your hearts.*Col 4:7-9* Encourage one another, building each other up just as you are doing.*1Th 5:11* Encourage the disheartened.*1Th 5:14* An elder should encourage others with sound doctrine.*Tit 1:9* Share with one another how your leaders are and what they are doing, for encouragement.*Eph 6:21-22* The love of believers for one another gives us great encouragement, refreshing the hearts of the Lord's people.*Phm 7* Encourage with all authority.*Tit 2:15* Take as your goal that you encourage believers' hearts.*Col 2:2* Encourage with great patience and careful instruction.*2Ti 4:2* Encourage each other's faith, making one another strong.*Ro 1:11-12* Take great encouragement from one another.*2Co 7:4* Be encouraged for yourself but especially delighted to see how happy others are for spirits others have refreshed.*2Co 7:13* Encourage one another.*2Co 13:11*

Families

The letters address families at length. Marriage is right, but unmarried devotion to the Lord is better. Those who marry should remain married, although the believing spouse may let the non-believing spouse go. A husband should give himself up for his wife, like Christ for the church. A wife should likewise love her husband, women being the glory of men. Intimacy is for marriage. Children should obey and care for their family, while fathers should not discourage or exasperate their children. See how the letters address families. Are you conducting yourself within your family as you should?

Unmarried. The unmarried and widows should find remaining unmarried good, unless they cannot control themselves, in which case they should marry so as not to burn with passion.$_{1Co\ 7:9}$ Outside of any command, and instead as a trustworthy judgment, the unmarried should find remaining unmarried good.$_{1Co\ 7:25-26}$ Those who are already engaged to marry should not seek release, but if you are not yet engaged, then don't look for a spouse.$_{1Co\ 7:27}$ If you can, then avoid marriage concerns and needing to please one's spouse, thus avoiding the world's affairs, and focus instead on pleasing the Lord, involved in the Lord's affairs.$_{1Co\ 7:32-34}$ This advice is not to restrict you but for your own good, to live right in undivided devotion to the Lord.$_{1Co\ 7:35}$ Marrying is right, but not marrying is better.$_{1Co\ 7:38}$ The widow is probably happier if she stays unmarried.$_{1Co\ 7:40}$ Those who care for widows should not let them burden the church, so that the church can help widows with real need.$_{1Ti\ 5:16}$

Marriage. If you do marry, then you have not sinned, although those who marry face many troubles in this life that they could avoid.$_{1Co\ 7:28}$ You do not sin by marrying one toward whom you might not be acting honorably while engaged, because of strong passions, if you want to marry and feel you should.*1Co 7:36* But nothing compels you to do so if you make up your mind and control your will.*1Co 7:37* The Lord's command to the married is that wife must not separate from husband, and if separated must stay unmarried or reconcile, and husband must not divorce wife.*1Co 7:10* Outside of any command, if you marry a non-believer with whom you are willing to live, then don't divorce.*1Co 7:12-13* A believing spouse sanctifies a non-believing spouse, making the children holy.*1Co 7:14* But if the unbelieving spouse leaves, let that spouse go, because nothing binds the believing spouse then, God having called believers to live in peace.*1Co 7:15* A believing spouse doesn't know if their faith will save the other.*1Co 7:16* A woman must remain married to her husband while he lives, but if her husband dies, then she may marry whomever she wishes if he belongs to the Lord.*1Co 7:39*

Husbands. Husband, love your wife rather than be harsh with her.*Col 3:19* A husband should treat his gentler wife with respect, as fellow heir of God's gracious gift of life, so that nothing hinders the husband's prayers.*1Pe 3:7* Like Christ loved and gave himself up for the church, a husband must love and give himself up for his wife so that she is holy, cleansed by God's word, and pure, radiant, and blameless toward her husband.*Eph 5:25-27* A husband should love his wife as his own body and self because no one hates their own body.*Eph 5:28-29* A husband must leave father and mother, uniting to his wife to become one flesh.*Eph 5:31* A husband must love his wife as he loves himself, while the wife must respect her husband.*Eph 5:33* The head of every man is Christ, of woman is man, and of Christ is God.*1Co 11:3* Man did not come from woman, but woman from man.*1Co 11:8* Men who pray or prophesy with covered head dishonor the head.*1Co 11:4* Men should not cover the head because they are the image and glory of God.*1Co 11:7* The nature of things teaches you that long hair disgraces a man, while long hair is woman's covering glory.*1Co 11:14-15* No one need contend because God's churches have no other practice.*1Co 11:16*

Wives. Wife, submit yourself to your husband, as befits the Lord.*Col 3:18* A wife should win her husband to the word by her pure, reverent, and submissive behavior.*1Pe 3:1-2* A wife's beauty should not come from fancy hair and clothes, gold jewelry, and other outward adornment but from the inner unfading beauty of a gentle and quiet spirit in which God sees great worth, like holy women in the past.*1Pe 3:3-6* A wife should submit to her husband in everything as we all submit to the Lord, with the husband wife's head as Christ heads his body, the church submitting to Christ.*Eph 5:22-24* Women who pray or prophesy with uncovered head dishonor the head as if shaved.*1Co 11:5-6* God did not create man for woman but woman for man, so that women should for the angels have authority over their own head.*1Co 11:9-10* Still, in the Lord, women and men depend on one another because as woman came from man, so woman bears man, with everything coming from God.*1Co 11:11* Judge for yourselves whether women should pray to God with head uncovered.*1Co 11:13* Women should be worthy of respect, not malicious talkers but temperate and trustworthy in everything.*1Ti 3:11* Women are the glory of men.*1Co 11:7*

Intimacy. Having no sexual relations is good, but to avoid sexual immorality, have sexual relations only with one's own spouse.*1Co 7:1-2* Share intimacy with your spouse, yielding to one another as the other wishes, giving your spouse authority over your own body.*1Co 7:3-4* Avoid depriving one another when agreeing to devote yourselves to prayer for a time, but then come together again so that Satan does not tempt your lack of self-control.*1Co 7:5* Having spousal relations is a concession, not a command, because having no spouse or relations may be better, although each has one's own gift from God.*1Co 7:6-7* Honor marriage, and keep the marriage bed pure, because God judges adulterers and the sexually immoral.*Heb 13:4* A younger widow whom sensual desire tempts should remarry, have children, manage the home, and give the enemy no opportunity for slander, rather than turning away to follow Satan.*1Ti 5:14-15* Mourn and put out of your fellowship those among you who practice sexual immorality that not even non-believers practice, like a man sleeping with his father's wife.*1Co 5:1-2* Treat younger men as brothers, older women as mothers, and younger women as sisters, with absolute purity.*1Ti 5:1-2*

Children. Children should obey their parents in the Lord, honoring father and mother, as the first commandment with a promise says, that they may enjoy a long and good earthly life.*Eph 6:1-3* Children, obey your parents in everything to please the Lord.*Col 3:20* Fathers should not exasperate their children but instead teach and train them in the Lord.*Eph 6:4* Fathers, don't make your children bitter, discouraging them. *Col 3:21*

While many may guard you in Christ, few will be fathers to you in Christ Jesus, although one may through the gospel.*1Co 4:15* Imitate one who becomes like a father to you in Christ.*1Co 4:16* Do not rebuke an older man harshly, but exhort him as if your father.*1Ti 5:1* We celebrate that our children walk in the truth, just as the Father commanded. *2Jn 4* Children and grandchildren should put their religion into practice by caring for their family and so repaying parents and grandparents, because doing so pleases God.*1Ti 5:4*

Body

The letters address the body, both as the fellowship of believers as the body of Christ and how we should regard our own body. First, though, God gave Christ a body so that Christ could sacrifice his body to save us. In doing so, Christ became the head of the body, which is his church. The church body has many parts, the least parts still indispensable. God cares how you care for your body, which is his temple, bought at great price. While we do not follow useless rules for the body, we do keep the body pure for the Holy Spirit. We also do not fear the body's death, knowing instead that God has prepared a heavenly body for each of us. See how the letters address the body. Are you participating in the body of Christ, while treating your own body as you should?

Christ. When Christ came into the world, he said that God did not desire sacrifice and offering, which did not please God, but instead God had prepared a body for Christ.*Heb 10:5-6* And by God's will and Jesus Christ's sacrifice of his body once for all, God has made us holy.*Heb 10:10* Be confident entering the Most Holy Place by Jesus's blood, the new and living way he opened for us, that is, his body.*Heb 10:19-20* God's revealed mystery is that through the gospel we are heirs together with his chosen people, members of one body, sharing the promise in Christ Jesus.*Eph 3:6*

Church. The Son is the head of the body, the church.*Col 1:18* God placed all things under Christ's feet, appointed him head over everything for the church, which is his body, the fullness of him who fills everything in every way.*Eph 1:22-23* Let the peace of Christ rule in your hearts because as members of one body, God called you to peace.*Col 3:15* You have only one body and one Spirit, just as God called you to one hope.*Eph 4:4* The bread we break participates in Christ's body._{1Co 10:16} We who are many are one body because we share one loaf._{1Co 10:17} Just as one body has many parts, so it is with Christ._{1Co 12:12} One Spirit baptized all, whether insider or outsider, slave or free, to form one body, giving each the same Spirit to drink._{1Co 12:13}

Parts. Even so the body has many parts, not just one._{1Co 12:14} Just like a natural body has parts, in Christ we form one body belonging to one another but with different gifts as God gave each of us grace._{Ro 12:5-6} No body part stops being part of the body, without the body losing sense._{1Co 12:15-17} God placed each part in the body, just as he wanted them to be._{1Co 12:18} The body would be nowhere if all parts were the same._{1Co 12:19} The one body has many parts._{1Co 12:20} No part can reject another part._{1Co 12:21} On the contrary, the weaker body parts are indispensable._{1Co 12:22} The less-honorable parts we treat with special honor, while unpresentable parts we treat with special modesty._{1Co 12:23} Ordinary parts need no special treatment, but God assembles the body, giving greater honor to parts lacking honor._{1Co 12:24} The body should have no division, its parts instead having equal concern for each other._{1Co 12:25} If one part suffers, then every part suffers with it, while if one part receives honor, every part rejoices._{1Co 12:26} You are Christ's body, and each one of you is a part._{1Co 12:27}

You. Strike a blow to your body to make it your slave so that after you preach to others, God will not disqualify you for the prize._{1Co 9:27} Your body is a temple of the Holy Spirit, who is in you and whom you received from God._{1Co 6:19} Honor God with your body because you are not your own, and God instead bought you at a price._{1Co 6:20} Our old self's crucifixion with him killed the sinful body, setting us free from sin and making us no longer slaves to sin._{Ro 6:6-7} Because God is merciful, offer your body as a living sacrifice, holy and pleasing to God, as your true and proper worship._{Ro 12:1} Do not let sin reign in your body, obeying its evil desires._{Ro 6:12} Do not offer any part of yourself as an instrument of wickedness._{Ro 6:13} God's will is that you control your own body to be holy and honorable._{1Th 4:3-6} We must put to death the body's misdeeds to live, rather than live for the flesh in which case we die._{Ro 8:12-13}

Rules. Useless rules like those not to handle, taste, or touch certain things are merely human commands and teachings having only a false appearance of wisdom based on the body's harsh treatment._{Col 2:21-23} We preach the gospel even to those who are still dead in sin, so that while they live according to human standards as to the body, they might come to live by God as to the spirit.*1Pe 4:6* Yet God did not mean the body for sexual immorality but for the Lord, and the Lord for the body.*1Co 6:13* Never unite with a prostitute your body, which is a member of Christ, because the two bodies then become one flesh.*1Co 6:15-16* Flee sexual immorality because while all other sins are outside the body, sexual sin is against one's own body.*1Co 6:18* God did not mean the body for sexual immorality but for the Lord, and the Lord for the body.*1Co 6:13* A husband should love his wife as his own body and self because no one hates their own body.*Eph 5:28-29* A husband must leave father and mother, uniting to his wife to become one flesh.*Eph 5:31*

Heaven. If the earthly tent in which we live suffers destruction, God gives us an eternal house in heaven, not built by human hands.*2Co 5:1* If Christ is in you, then even though your body dies because of sin, the Spirit gives life because of righteousness.*Ro 8:10* May your whole spirit, soul, and body be blameless at our Lord Jesus Christ's return.*1Th 5:23* We long to be in our heavenly dwelling, which will not leave us exposed.*2Co 5:2-3* In our earthly tent, we groan with burden, fearing deadly exposure while wanting heaven's protection from death.*2Co 5:4* Know with confidence that to be at home in the body is to be away from the Lord.*2Co 5:6* Prefer to be away from the body and at home with the Lord.*2Co 5:8* Make your goal to please him, whether at home in the body or away from it.*2Co 5:9* We must all appear before Christ's judgment seat to receive our due for things we did in the body, whether good or bad.*2Co 5:10*

Gifts

The letters address the gifts that God gives each of us to strengthen his church. God's gifts are good, perfect, and irrevocable. Choose and use gifts to build up the church. Foretell the future to encourage the church. Speak in unknown languages only when praying for interpretation, to edify the church. See how the letters address gifts. Are you receiving, choosing, and using God's gifts as you should?

Giver. The Father in heaven, who does not change, gives the good and perfect gifts from above.*Jas 1:17* When Christ ascended, he took many captives while giving gifts to his people.*Eph 4:8* God's gifts are irrevocable.*Ro 11:29* Know the Spirit's gifts.*1Co 12:1* The same Spirit distributes different gifts.*1Co 12:4* God gives to each one the Spirit's manifestation for the common good.*1Co 12:7* The same Spirit distributes each gift to each one, just as he determines.*1Co 12:11* To one person, God gives wisdom through the Spirit, to another person knowledge by the same Spirit, to another faith by the same Spirit, to another gifts of healing by that one Spirit, and to others miraculous powers, prophecy, distinguishing between spirits, speaking in different tongues, or interpretation of tongues.*1Co 12:8-10* Just like a natural body has parts, in Christ we form one body belonging to one another but with different gifts as God gave each of us grace.*Ro 12:5-6* Because you eagerly desire the Spirit's gifts, choose and excel in those that build up the church.*1Co 14:12* If you think the Spirit has gifted you, then acknowledge the Lord's command because if you ignore the command, then others will ignore you.*1Co 14:37-38*

Foretelling. Love by eagerly desiring the Spirit's gifts, especially foretelling the future.*1Co 14:1* Foretelling the future strengthens, encourages, and comforts others.*1Co 14:3* Foretelling the future edifies the church.*1Co 14:4* Every one of you does well to speak in an unknown language, but the one who foretells the future is greater, unless someone interprets the unknown language to edify the church.*1Co 14:5* Be eager to foretell the future, but do not forbid speaking in unknown languages.*1Co 14:39* Use your gifts to serve others, stewarding God's manifold graces.*1Pe 4:10*

Languages. Anyone who speaks in an unknown language speaks only to God, not people, and so no one understands them as they utter mysteries by the Spirit.*1Co 14:3* Speaking in an unknown language edifies only yourself.*1Co 14:4* What good is speaking in an unknown language unless some revelation, knowledge, prediction, or word of instruction results?*1Co 14:6* No one knows the instrument's tune unless the musician distinguishes the notes.*1Co 14:7* The trumpet must sound a clear call to get soldiers ready for battle.*1Co 14:8* The world has many languages, each with meaning.*1Co 14:10* Speaking in a foreign language does not convey meaning.*1Co 14:11* Thus, unless you speak intelligibly, no one knows what you say, and you just speak into the air.*1Co 14:9* If you speak in an unknown language, then pray for interpretation.*1Co 14:13* Indeed, your spirit praying in an unknown language leaves your mind unfruitful.*1Co 14:14* Pray with your spirit while also praying with understanding, even as you sing with your spirit while also singing with understanding.*1Co 14:15* Praise God in ways that others can agree rather than so they don't know what you are saying, because otherwise, you may give thanks well enough but edify no one.*1Co 14:16-17* Be glad to speak unknown languages, but in the church prefer to speak five intelligible words that instruct others than ten thousand unknown words.*1Co 14:18-19*

Giving

The letters address not just gifts, talents with which we share the gospel and encourage believers, but also giving. The letters urge generosity in giving. The letters also give several other measures for when and how much to give. Giving's purpose is to supply others' needs so that thanks overflow to God. See how the letters treat giving. Are you giving in the abundance that the letters exhort, to God's praise?

Generosity. Even in very severe trial, let your overflowing joy and extreme poverty well up in rich generosity.*2Co 8:2* Our Lord Jesus Christ's grace was that although he was rich, he became poor for your sake, so that his poverty would make you rich.*2Co 8:9* Give as much as able, even beyond your ability, entirely on your own.*2Co 8:3* Urgently plead for the privilege of sharing in service to the Lord's people.*2Co 8:4* Exceed expectations, giving first to the Lord and then by God's will to others.*2Co 8:5* When you excel in everything, whether faith, speech, knowledge, earnestness, or love, excel also in the grace of giving.*2Co 8:7* Whoever sows sparingly reaps sparingly, and whoever sows generously reaps generously.*2Co 9:6* God can bless you abundantly, so that you always have all you need while abounding in good works.*2Co 9:8* As you scatter freely your gifts to the poor, your righteousness endures forever.*2Co 9:9* God, who supplies seed to the sower and bread for food, also supplies and increases your store of seed to enlarge your righteousness harvest.*2Co 9:10* God enriches you in every way so that you can always be generous, resulting in thanksgiving to God.*2Co 9:11*

Measure. Each give what your heart decides, not reluctantly or under compulsion, for God loves cheerful givers.*2Co 9:7* If you are willing to give, then your gift is good based on what you have, not what you do not have.~2Co 8:12~ The point is not to relieve others while pressing you hard but that equality exists.~2Co 8:13~ Let your present plenty supply others' need, so that their plenty can later supply your need, equally.~2Co 8:14~ Then, the one who gathers much will not have too much, and the one who gathers little will not have too little.~2Co 8:15~ Be eager to help, so that others can boast about your readiness to give and so your enthusiasm stirs others to action.~2Co 9:2~ Be ready, though, to meet the expectation of those who boast about you.~2Co 9:3~ Otherwise, you may make them ashamed for having had such confidence in you.~2Co 9:4~ Finish arrangements for the generous gifts you promise, being ready to give rather than giving grudgingly.~2Co 9:5~ Finish the charitable acts of grace that you start for others.~2Co 8:6~ When you are first to give and to have the desire to do so, still finish your giving, so that you match your eager willingness by completing it as you are able.~2Co 8:11~

Others. God puts into the heart concern for one another.~2Co 8:16~ Welcome appeals for one another, participating with enthusiasm and your own initiative.~2Co 8:17~ Your gifts not only supply the Lord's people's needs but also overflow expressions of thanks to God.~2Co 9:12~ The gifts by which you prove yourself lead others to praise God for your obedience in confessing Christ's gospel and generosity in sharing with them and everyone else.~2Co 9:13~ Without commanding giving, test your love's sincerity with the earnestness of others.~2Co 8:8~ Their hearts go out in prayers for you because of the surpassing grace God has given you.~2Co 9:14~ Gladly spend everything for another believer, and receive for yourself as well, showing that you love them and letting them love you.~2Co 12:15~

Prayer

The letters address at length the topic of prayer. We are to pray continually, constantly remembering others in our prayers. We should pray with confidence that God answers prayer, healing the sick, unifying believers, and forgiving sinners. We should pray that God enlarges our faith. And we should pray for the spread of the good news of Jesus Christ, for the salvation of others. See how the letters address prayer. Are you praying as God desires?

Continually. Pray in the Spirit on all occasions with all kinds of prayers and requests, remaining alert to pray continually for all the Lord's people.$_{Eph\ 6:18}$ Present your prayers, petitions, and requests to God with thanksgiving.$_{Php\ 4:6}$ We have not stopped praying that God fill you with knowledge of his will.$_{Col\ 1:9}$ Devote yourself to watchful and thankful prayer.$_{Col\ 4:2}$ Continually mention fellow believers in prayer, remembering before God our Father their faithful work, loving labor, and endurance inspired by hope in our Lord Jesus Christ.$_{1Th\ 1:2-3}$ Pray earnestly night and day that you may supply what others lack in faith.$_{1Th\ 3:10}$ Pray continually.$_{1Th\ 5:17}$ Brothers and sisters, pray for one another.$_{1Th\ 5:25}$ Constantly pray for one another that our God makes us worthy of his calling and by his power grants our every desire for goodness and every deed prompted by faith.$_{2Th\ 1:11}$ The widow alone and in need hopes in God, praying day and night for help.$_{1Ti\ 5:5}$ Night and day, constantly remember others in your prayers.$_{2Ti\ 1:3}$ Constantly remember one another in prayer while praying that God's will is that you rejoin one another.$_{Ro\ 1:9-10}$ Be faithful in prayer.$_{Ro\ 12:12}$

Confidence. The prayer of a righteous person is powerful and effective, like Elijah praying first for no rain and then for rain, both prayers that God answered._Jas 5:16-18_ We are rightly confident that if we ask anything according to God's will, then he hears us and we have whatever we ask of him._1Jn 5:14-15_ Make petitions, prayers, and intercession for all people, including for those in authority, that you may live peaceful and quiet lives in all godliness and holiness._1Ti 2:1-2_ Men everywhere should pray, lifting up holy hands._1Ti 2:8_ Receive anything consecrated by God's word and prayer._1Ti 4:5_ Pray for the sick so that faithful prayer will heal the sick._Jas 5:13-15_ Pray for each other for healing._Jas 5:16_ Our prayer for one another is to enjoy good health and that all go well, especially in the soul._3Jn 2_ Ask that our God and Father and the Lord Jesus help you gather with other believers._1Th 3:11_ Pray that the Lord make others' love increase and overflow for one another and everyone else, like your love increases and overflows._1Th 3:12_ Pray that the Lord's people favorably receive contributions that you share, so that you have joy and refreshing company._Ro 15:31-32_ Wrestle in prayer for one another, so that you may stand firm in all God's will, mature and fully assured._Col 4:12_

Sin. Pray for the sinner so that through faithful prayer God will forgive the sinner._Jas 5:13-15_ Pray for any brother or sister who sins, other than for sin that leads to death, because God will give them life._1Jn 5:16-17_ Pray that God strengthen hearts, so that others will be blameless and holy in the presence of our God and Father when our Lord Jesus comes._1Th 3:13_ Pray for one another that others have a clear conscience and desire to live honorably in every way._Heb 13:18_ Pray that God delivers us from evil people._2Th 3:2_ Pray that God keep preachers safe from persecuting unbelievers._Ro 15:31-32_ Pray for one another to help defeat persecution, in gracious favor._2Co 1:11_ Pray that God fully restores you._2Co 13:9_ Pray especially that God restores your leaders to you soon._Heb 13:19_

Faith. We pray that our partnership in faith is effective in deepening our understanding of every good thing we share for the sake of Christ._Phm 6_ Your faith in the Lord Jesus and your love for all God's people makes us remember you in our prayers._Eph 1:15-16_ We thank our God as we remember one another in our prayers because we hear about one another's love for the holy people and faith in the Lord Jesus._Phm 4-5_ Pray that the God of our Lord Jesus Christ, the glorious Father, may give one another the Spirit of wisdom and revelation, so that we may know him better._Eph 1:17_ Pray that the Spirit may enlighten our heart that we may know God's hope, his glorious inheritance in us, and his incomparably great power for us who believe.*Eph 1:18-19* We pray that out of God's glorious riches he strengthens you in your inner being with power through his Spirit, so that Christ dwells in your heart through faith.*Eph 3:16-17*

Christ. Pray that we may glorify the name of our Lord Jesus and receive his glory, by the grace of God and the Lord Jesus Christ.*2Th 1:12* When living on earth, Jesus prayed and petitioned fervently to God who could save him from death, and God heard Jesus because of his reverent submission.*Heb 5:7* Pray that you and all the Lord's holy people, rooted and established in love, can grasp how wide, long, high, and deep Christ's love is, and know his love surpasses knowledge, that God may fill you to his fullness.*Eph 3:17-19* Pray that the message of the Lord spreads rapidly.*2Th 3:1* Desire and pray to God that those who know of Jesus will turn to him for salvation.*Ro 10:1* Pray also for your teachers so that whenever they speak, the Spirit gives them fearless words making known the gospel's mystery. *Eph 6:19-20* In all prayers for believers, we always pray with joy for our partnership in the gospel.*Php 1:4-5* Join in one another's struggles to proclaim the gospel by praying for one another.*Ro 15:30* Always thank God, our Lord Jesus Christ's Father, when praying for those about whose faith in Christ Jesus and love for God's people you have heard.*Col 1:3-4* Pray that God opens doors for others to proclaim Christ's mystery clearly, as they should.*Col 4:3-4*

Gratitude

The letters address gratitude, that attitude of thanksgiving that believers should always carry in all circumstance. We thank God especially for the faith of believers and our own faith. See how the letters address gratitude. Do you wear gratitude as you should, evident to all?

God. Thank God for his indescribable gift.*2Co 9:15* Thank God that you receive his kingdom.*Heb 12:28-29* Thank God for the joy that the faith of others brings you.*1Th 3:9* Thank God with a clear conscience.*2Ti 1:3* Thank God for those whom God gives grace in Christ Jesus.*1Co 1:4* Thank God through Jesus Christ for believers whose faith others report all over the world.*Ro 1:8* Thank God continually when you receive the word of God from one another.*1Th 2:13* Always give thanks to God the Father for everything, in the name of our Lord Jesus Christ.*Eph 5:19-20* Give thanks in all circumstances, as God's will for you in Christ Jesus.*1Th 5:18* Give thanks to God the Father through Jesus Christ.*Col 3:17* Give joyful thanks to the Father for sharing the kingdom with his holy people.*Col 1:12* Present requests to God with thanksgiving.*Php 4:6* Sing to God with gratitude in your hearts.*Col 3:16*

Others. Always thank God for fellow believers.*1Th 1:2* Always thank God for brothers and sisters loved by the Lord.*2Th 2:13* Always thank God for brothers and sisters whose faith grows more and more, and whose love for one another increases.*2Th 1:3* Always thank God for others' faith in Christ Jesus and love for God's people, about which you hear.*Col 1:3-4* Your faith in the Lord Jesus and your love for all God's people makes us give thanks for you.*Eph 1:15-16* Make your prayer thankful.*Col 4:2* Teachers should thank Christ Jesus our Lord that he considers them trustworthy.*1Ti 1:12* Give thanks for all people.*1Ti 2:1-2* Share thanksgiving in place of coarse talk.*Eph 5:4* Everything God created is good, not to reject but to receive with thanksgiving.*1Ti 4:4* The thanksgiving cup for which we give thanks participates in Christ's blood.*1Co 10:16* Give thanks for answered prayers defeating persecution.*2Co 1:11* Thanksgiving overflows to God's glory, as grace reaches ever more people.*2Co 4:15*

Conclusion

The first thing that one draws from this study of the letters is that the letters have a *lot* to say to us, not just overall but also on any one given topic. The above seventy-six topics are more numerous than one might suppose from the letters. Most of those topics include two or more subtopics, making much larger the already-large number of matters that the letters address. If the subject is significant, then you are likely to find the subject in the letters. The topics do seem to naturally divide themselves into the great story of God's light overwhelming the still-formidable but nonetheless entirely lost influence of darkness, with much personal and corporate direction fruitfully mixed in. The letters in that way marvelously integrate doctrine and application. Yet the letters also treat each individual topic at some length and, in many cases, at great length. In the letters, one can read for the gospel's broad comprehension or instead, if one prefers, dive deep.

To what topics do the letters give the most attention? In the way that the above sections interpret the letters, some bigger topics include sanctification, sin, teaching, the gospel, the Lord's return, and of course the Father and Son. Topics with greater treatment do not necessarily deserve greater attention, although in the case of the gospel and our Lord, they certainly do deserve such attention. Effusive treatment of other topics may simply mean that the topics have more ins and outs to them, not that the topics have greater significance. Teaching is an example. Some of us do more teaching than others do. Those who teach have more to consider than those who do not teach but instead give or serve, when in any one instance giving or serving may have greater significance than teaching. The letters may treat other topics more extensively, like encouragement, grace, and peace, for their exhortatory value. Paul, for instance, wrote a great deal about the Lord's grace and his wish for peace among believers.

To what topics do the letters give little or no attention? Perhaps surprisingly, the letters barely mention fasting, tithing, foot-washing, and worship, practices and disciplines that certainly find support in other places in the Bible, even from the words and actions of our Lord. The letters say only a relatively little about baptism and communion, perhaps because of the Gospels' clarity around those topics. The letters say a lot about resurrection but only a little about the Lord's birth and culminating ascension. What topics surprised you? The letters address at some length the topics of God's power, sowing, authority, discerning, quarrels, and death. The major surprise, though, may simply have been how much the letters say about each of the seventy-six topics. Collectively, the letters are incredibly rich, not the afterthought with which some misguided critics treat them.

You can see from each section's organization that many of the topics begin with prosaic direction to do this or that, while avoiding the other thing, but then inevitably proceed to how the direction arises out of Christ. Sound direction is one thing, while close relationship with Christ is quite another thing. Thus, the letters are not primarily about living well, although they certainly do give helpful advice. Instead, the letters are primarily about preserving and improving your relationship with Christ. The Bible doesn't just give direction. Yes, the direction that it gives is alone good direction, bringing flourishing life. The Bible, though, is God's story and by extension the story of your relationship with God through Christ. Value the letters primarily for their instruction on growing closer to Jesus.

For each topic, the letters often also treat both you and others at some length. While the letters address themes like power, death, or the body, and doctrines like redemption and sanctification, the letters also provide abundant practical interpretation of those themes and that doctrine. The practical interpretation typically addresses things that you should or should not do, and attitudes that you should or should not maintain, and then how you should think about and treat others. Those others about whom the letters give direction include believers in the family of faith and non-believers, pagans, sinners, opponents, persecutors, and antichrists, as the letters variously refer to those who have not embraced and have instead rejected Jesus Christ.

The main thing that a reorganization of the letters by topic seems to accomplish, though, is the letters' veneration. Views on the letters vary. For me, they have always seemed a special treasure, while to others they have the character of an afterthought. I recall reading one Bible, cast as literature rather than holy scripture and published for a college audience, that explicitly omitted most of the letters as having little or no consequence. To the contrary, I suspect that most believers value the letters highly. Yet I also suspect that fewer believers fully grasp how deep, consistent, rich, profound, and glorious the letters truly are. That revelation of the living and life-giving character of the letters, like the same character of the rest of the Bible, is something that I am still pursuing with ardor. My hope is that you are doing so, too, and that this very modest work makes some contribution, however small, to your effort. Thank you, Lord, for your word, including the glorious letters. May the letters, like the rest of your word, penetrate most deeply into our hearts, minds, and souls, revealing your magnificent Spirit and bringing the endless life of Christ.

Abbreviations

Romans	*Ro*	Titus	*Tit*
1 Corinthians	*1Co*	Philemon	*Phm*
2 Corinthians	*2Co*	Hebrews	*Heb*
Galatians	*Gal*	James	*Jas*
Ephesians	*Eph*	1 Peter	*1Pe*
Philippians	*Php*	2 Peter	*2Pe*
Colossians	*Col*	1 John	*1Jn*
1 Thessalonians	*1Th*	2 John	*2Jn*
2 Thessalonians	*2Th*	3 John	*3Jn*
1 Timothy	*1Ti*	Jude	*Jude*
2 Timothy	*2Ti*		

Appendices

Authors

The Bible organizes the twenty-one New Testament letters by their authors. The first thirteen letters claim Paul's authorship, with a fourteenth letter Hebrews having no identified author but placed next in order after the thirteen letters attributed to Paul. These fourteen examples traditionally comprise the Pauline letters, notwithstanding substantial question over the authorship of some of the fourteen letters. The next letter identifies itself as having James as its author, followed by two letters claiming Peter's authorship, three letters claiming John's authorship, and a final letter claiming Jude's authorship. Questions also exist over the authorship of some of these last seven letters. Questions over authorship, as to letters claiming specific authors, in no sense imply that any anonymous authors meant to mislead readers as to attribution. To the contrary, devoted students, in the role of the attributed author's trusted scribe or memoirist, may have been the anonymous authors, in honorific attribution following a convention common to ancient schools. Thus, even if Paul, for instance, did not write several of the letters claiming his authorship, then the attribution still bears authority in tracing to Paul the experience that formed the thought, all under the Holy Spirit's inspiration. Keep that reassurance in mind when considering the following discussion of individual authors.

Paul

As just indicated, tradition recognizes the apostle Paul as the primary human author of the Bible's New Testament letters, acknowledging that the Holy Spirit is the divine author of each letter and all the Bible. Thirteen of the Bible's twenty-one letters attribute themselves by name to Paul, including Romans, 1 Corinthians, 2 Corinthians, Galatians, Ephesians, Philippians, Colossians, 1 Thessalonians, 2 Thessalonians, 1 Timothy, 2 Timothy, Titus, and Philemon. Some readers attribute a fourteenth letter Hebrews to Paul, although unlike the other thirteen letters, Hebrews does not claim Paul's authorship. Scholars show strong consensus that Paul wrote at least seven of the thirteen letters that claim his authorship, including Romans, 1 Corinthians, 2 Corinthians, Galatians, Philippians, 1 Thessalonians, and Philemon. Paul may have dictated the other six letters claiming his authorship, or other authors who sought Paul's mentoring and learned from Paul may have credited Paul with those other letters.

Paul had exquisite credit to author so many of the letters. Scholars generally attribute the apostle Paul's birth to Jewish parents in A.D. 6 in Tarsus. Tarsus would have been in the east of modern-day Turkey, also known as Asia Minor as the westernmost extension of the Asian continent. Paul, then known as Saul, was a Roman citizen from birth but spent his formative years in Jerusalem, studying the Jewish Torah under the prominent rabbinical scholar and Sanhedrin member Gamaliel. Paul was thus by his own claim or admission a Pharisee's Pharisee, so strict of a Jewish religious adherent that he persecuted the new Christians in Jerusalem and throughout Judea. Indeed, poignantly, Paul was present and approving at the first recorded Christian martyr Stephen's stoning, as the book of Acts documents.

Paul came to Christ around 33 A.D. in his dramatic encounter with the risen Lord on Paul's way to Damascus to persecute believers. The book of Acts records that Paul completed that trip blind, receiving his sight and the Holy Spirit when meeting the visiting convert Ananias. Paul then spent three years in Arabia before returning to Damascus briefly to preach Jesus, until persecution caused him to flee to Jerusalem. Paul met with the apostles in Jerusalem before returning home to Tarsus and the surrounding region, including Antioch, to preach for approximately the next decade from 36 A.D. to 46 A.D. Paul then spent another decade on three missionary journeys throughout the Eastern Mediterranean, from about 37 A.D. to 47 A.D., when he may have written about half of his letters. Paul spent much of his last seven years under arrest and imprisoned in Caesarea and Rome, guiding the churches and defending the faith even as he defended himself. He may have written the other half of his letters during this period, before his death by execution in Rome in A.D. 64.

James

Tradition holds that Jesus's brother James wrote the letter bearing that name, even though the letter itself refers to James only as a servant of God and the Lord Jesus Christ, not expressly Jesus's brother. Some readers prefer to call James a *half* brother of Jesus, holding that Jesus and James would have shared only Mary as their mother (Mary having other children, too). The Holy Spirit came on Mary when she conceived Jesus, while Mary's husband Joseph would have been James's father and the father of Mary's other children. Others prefer to treat James and his other siblings as Joseph's children from a prior marriage ending in his wife's death, and thus Mary's adopted children, or simply as cousins to Mary's Son Jesus, Mary thus maintaining her virginity. In any case, biologically related to Jesus or not, James until his death around 62 A.D. was a prominent leader in Jerusalem of the community of believers that the apostles formed and influenced. In dozens of places, the letter's text shows that its author was familiar with Jesus's sayings, before repetition spread and tradition fixed those sayings. Jesus's brother James could well have been the letter's author.

Yet others named James could instead have authored the letter. Interestingly, Jesus's two apostles James the son of Zebedee and James the son of Alphaeus were less likely the letters' author, Zebedee's son because of his early martyrdom as the book of Acts records, and Alphaeus's son because of his lack of prominence in the biblical record. The letter implies that the James who wrote the letter was prominent, as Jesus's brother James surely was. Paul's letters described James, the brother of the Lord, as one of three church pillars. Jude, the author of another letter by that name, referred to himself not only as a slave of Jesus Christ, as James likewise did in his letter, but also as a brother of James, again taken by some as further evidence that Jesus's brother wrote the letter.

If indeed, Jesus's brother James, the early Jerusalem church's leader, wrote the letter by his name, then we do have an extraordinary witness to the Holy Spirit's testimony. John's Gospel records that Jesus's brothers did not believe in Jesus, and so James' conversion likely followed the resurrection. Paul in 1 Corinthians records that the resurrected Lord appeared to his brother James. Confirming James's prominence, some historians identify Jesus's brother James as James the Just, James of Jerusalem, and the Bishop of Jerusalem. James, Peter, and Paul each played leading roles in the early church. The authority one attributes to each depends to some degree on one's perspective, whether Catholic, Reformed, liberal, or otherwise. All three would likely dismiss any special authoritative claim, in humility making themselves the least among the apostles, as Paul acknowledged in his own letters. The Jewish historian Josephus records outside the biblical record that James, Jesus's brother, had the Pharisees' respect for his pious observance of the law, despite that enemies had James put to death in A.D. 62 in a brief period between local Roman governors.

The three great witnesses James, Peter, and Paul certainly knew and supported one another, if at times also contesting in the faith, as the book of Acts records Paul doing openly in Peter's presence. Acts also records Paul receiving in Antioch a messenger from James carrying an instruction to local believers that Paul rejected. Yet Acts also records Peter leaving a message for James and the other apostles when Peter was preparing to leave Jerusalem, much as Acts mentions Paul's visiting James on Paul's last time in Jerusalem. James clearly supported both Paul and Peter. In Galatians, Paul notes his visit to Peter and James in Jerusalem after Paul's conversion and a second visit to Peter, James, and John, whom Galatians records Paul regarding as the church's pillars. So again, in Jesus's brother James, the letter would have an extraordinary author. Yet whoever wrote the letter James, we know from its inclusion in the Bible and the profound quality of its text that we have the most-extraordinary witness to the Holy Spirit.

John

Many readers attribute to Jesus's beloved disciple John the three letters 1 John, 2 John, and 3 John, on substantial internal and external evidence. John wrote the Gospel of that name, in which he identifies himself as the disciple whom Jesus loved, leaning on Jesus's breast at the

Last Supper the night of Jesus's betrayal. John and his brother James, also a disciple of Jesus, were sons of Zebedee, the three of them working as unschooled and ordinary fishermen on the Sea of Galilee, when Jesus called John and James to discipleship. John, his brother James (not Jesus's brother James), and Peter were Jesus's inner circle of disciples who witnessed Jesus's Mt. Hermon transfiguration, saw Jesus raise Jairus's dead daughter, and accompanied Jesus (but slept) while Jesus prayed in the Garden of Gethsemane. Some inference exists that John's mother was Salome, who could have been a sister of Jesus's mother Mary, which if so would have made John a cousin to Jesus.

John was especially close to Jesus in other ways. Mark's Gospel records that Jesus nicknamed John and his brother James the Sons of Thunder for their outspoken quick tempers. On the cross, Jesus appointed John to care for Jesus's mother Mary. John was the one to recognize the resurrected Jesus the moment of the miraculous catch of fish. Because John in his Gospel referred to himself in the third person, John may also have been the disciple who knew the high priest and thus accompanied Jesus into the high priest's courtyard for Jesus's trial, and who ran with Peter to the empty tomb. The book of Acts records that John was with Peter for the lame man's healing at the temple, to preach before the Sanhedrin about Jesus's crucifixion and resurrection, and for arrest, release by an angel, and flogging. In Galatians, Paul identifies John with Peter and Jesus's brother James (not John's brother James, whom King Herod Agrippa I beheaded around a decade after Jesus's resurrection) as a pillar of the early church in Jerusalem.

External evidence suggests that John left Jerusalem to serve Asia Minor's churches in his later years. The book of Revelation and external sources record John's exile to the island of Patmos in the Aegean Sea between Asia Minor (modern-day Turkey) and Greece, assuming, as many accept, that John indeed wrote the book of Revelation. John's exile likely took place around 95 A.D. near the end of the Christian persecutor Dominian's reign. Dominian's assassination a year later likely enabled John to return to Asia Minor to die there, probably near Ephesus, around 98 A.D., with his reputed tomb in the ruins of St. John's Church at Selcuk. If that history is correct, then John may well have been the only one of the twelve disciples to die of natural causes, as the end of his Gospel suggests and tradition holds. John, like Paul and

James, was plainly an extraordinary witness to author his letters, under the Holy Spirit.

Peter

Some hold that the prominent disciple Peter wrote the letters 1 Peter and 2 Peter. Others, noting substantial differences in the letters' styles, and the similarities of 2 Peter to the following letter Jude, attribute 2 Peter to another author who may have accompanied and learned from Peter. Some hold that a single author wrote both 2 Peter and Jude. Among those who believe that a single author wrote both 2 Peter and Jude, one theory holds that the author's reference in Jude to desiring to write another letter when needing instead to urgently write the letter Jude, was a reference to 2 Peter, a theory that would both answer and put a neat bow on the question of both letters' authorship. That theory would then make the reference in 2 Peter to an earlier letter already sent, a reference to the letter Jude rather than, as many assume, a reference to 1 Peter. In any case, if Peter did not write 2 Peter, then readers can still have confidence that 2 Peter's author knew Peter, his experiences, and his teaching well.

We do in any case know a great deal about Peter's life from the four Gospels and the book of Acts, and from external accounts, amplified by tradition, a little bit about his imprisonment and death. Peter's original name was Simon, according to Luke's Gospel a Galilean fisherman brother of another disciple Andrew. Luke suggests that Simon and Andrew were the first two disciples whom Jesus called, both promptly walking away from their boats and nets on Jesus's invitation to be fishers instead of men. The Gospels portray Simon as an outspoken and often-erring leader of the disciples in their communication and interaction with Jesus. For example, at the Last Supper, he initially refused Jesus's offer to wash his feet but then impulsively asked Jesus to wash his entire body. Simon, though, was the first to call Jesus the Son of the living God, the Messiah. Jesus on that occasion renamed Simon as Peter, meaning *the rock*, implying the confession of Christ on which all else stands. As indicated above, Peter witnessed Jesus's Mt. Hermon transfiguration and various miracles, and was with Jesus as Jesus prayed in the Garden of

Gethsemane, along with John and his brother James, the three comprising an inner circle of disciples.

While at the Last Supper, Peter professed willingness to die with Jesus, Peter then promptly denied Jesus three times outside the high priest's courtyard at Jesus's trial, as Jesus had predicted. Peter was nonetheless one of the two disciples who ran to the empty tomb immediately after Jesus's reported resurrection. Peter thereafter remained a leader among the disciples, especially after Jesus restored Peter along the Sea of Galilee's shores, three times telling Peter to feed Jesus's sheep. Peter preached boldly in Jerusalem at Pentecost, when the Spirit descended and thousands confessed Christ. As indicated above, Peter and John also preached boldly when brought before the Sanhedrin, for having healed another at the temple gate, and later suffered imprisonment before release by an angel, and flogging. As also indicated above, Peter was one of the three pillars of the early church in Jerusalem, along with John and Jesus's brother James. A vision brought Peter to eat with the gentile Cornelius, the event, with Paul's intercession, helping to enlarge Christianity's reach beyond Jewish converts to gentiles.

Many credit Peter with substantial contributions to Mark's Gospel. Mark, also known as John Mark, was not a disciple of Jesus but did travel extensively with Peter as Peter carried out Jesus's Great Commission. Mark's Gospel treats in detail events that only Peter and the other inner-circle members John and his brother James would have witnessed. No matter whether Peter dictated the Gospel to Mark, Peter may well have contributed to the Gospels' record over the course of the three-plus decades that Peter served as a witness after Christ's resurrection. Peter left Jerusalem carrying the gospel to other regions including likely Rome, where external accounts and tradition hold, consistent with Jesus's apparent prophecy at Peter's restoration, that Peter suffered death by crucifixion. Indeed, tradition holds that Emperor Nero granted Peter's wish to die crucified upside down, in humility to Jesus's glorious cross-borne victory. Tradition and external accounts further hold that Peter converted his jailers and dozens of others to Christ in the months before his death around A.D. 67, despite enduring horrible torture. Peter, like Paul, James, and John, was an extraordinary witness to author his letters, under the Holy Spirit.

Jude

As mentioned above in the treatment of the author James, the author of the letter Jude states that he is a brother of James, possibly intending the James who wrote the epistle by that name and thus indicating that Jude may be another of the Lord Jesus's half-brothers or step brothers, son of Joseph and possibly also of Mary. If that is so, that Jude was, like James, a member of Jesus's natural family, then Jude, like James, would not have been a follower of Jesus until after Jesus's resurrection, for the same reasons and based on the same accounts mentioned above as to James. The biblical record and other accounts give little more information about Jude, the brother of James and half-brother or step brother of Jesus, other than a reference in 1 Corinthians that the Lord's brothers and their wives made missionary trips. The author Jude, if the Lord's brother, thus served and traveled as a missionary like Paul, Peter, and James, and would, like those others, have been an extraordinary gospel witness.

Alternatively, the author Jude may, when writing that he is a brother of James, have meant that he was a spiritual rather than biological brother of James. The author Jude may also have referred to a different James entirely, rather than the Lord's brother. If so, then the biblical record includes several other Jude-brother candidates named James, although the record suggests no one candidate over another. Some believe that Jude could have been Jesus's disciple Judas, Jude being an equivalent name commonly substituted for Judas after the betrayal, understanding that two disciples went by that name and that the letter's author would have been the faithful Judas rather than the betrayer Judas who died shortly after the betrayal. The latter possibility raises another opportunity to believe Jude to be an extraordinary gospel witness. Given the questions over authorship and the little information that we have about any candidate author, the letter Jude is hard to date but probably followed Peter's writing 1 Peter around A.D. 65 and could have been between A.D. 67 and 80.

Anonymous

Again, you can see from the above uncertainties over the letters' authorship that a substantial chance exists that one or more of the letters had an author who remains anonymous to us. Hebrews may be the letter most likely to have had an anonymous author. Anonymity does not mean lack of prominence or credibility. For example, in addition to Paul, scholars speculate that Hebrews' author could have been Luke, Barnabas, Apollos, or Priscilla, among prominent others. While we should all appreciate the extraordinary experiences that the known authors had, we should also appreciate that the anonymity of any author makes no difference to writings that the Holy Spirit inspired. If God can talk through a donkey, as he did to the diviner Balaam, then God can talk to us through anonymous authors of exquisitely crafted letters, each of which clearly implies that the author, even if anonymous, had profound experiences, knew and interacted with historical figures, and above all heard and obeyed God's Holy Spirit. Thus, once again, have no concern over authorship, even as you take a healthy interest in the authors, their identities, and their experiences. The Bible, including each of its letters, is the inspired word of God.

Audiences

Because the Bible's twenty-one New Testament letters generally take the form of correspondence, they do presume certain audiences, from which we can learn more about the letters and their intended meaning. Appropriate to the prevailing conventions for correspondence, the letters typically begin with a greeting that identifies the letter's author and recipients. A thanksgiving prayer typically follows. The letters then devote their main content to practical instruction in tenets of Christian faith, often addressing specific challenges that the letter's recipients face. The letters tend to include relatively specific counsel and direction on conduct, drawn from the more-general doctrinal presentation. The letters typically conclude with personal information about the author and acquaintances, greetings, and pleas.

One can group the letters according to audience and attributes, beyond grouping the letters according to their stated or presumed authors, as shown in the foregoing appendix. For instance, four of the Pauline letters, including Ephesians, Philippians, Colossians, and Philemon, bear the mark of *captivity* letters, Paul having written from prison. Three other Pauline letters, including 1 Timothy, 2 Timothy, and Titus, we know as the *pastoral* letters because addressed to protégé pastors and carrying advice on how to guide the congregation. Aside from Hebrews, the other Pauline letters outside of the pastoral letters all had specific church communities as their audience. The last seven letters outside of the Pauline corpus, including James, 1 and 2 Peter, 1, 2, and 3 John, and Jude, we know as *catholic* or *universal* letters because not addressed to a specific church community. The universal letters have general application. The letters addressed to church communities facing specific challenges also have universal value and appeal for the warnings that they hold. Consider the following summary of each letter, in the order that the letters appear in the Bible.

Romans

Romans presents the gospel as clearly and forthrightly as any other letter, and with greater detail and comprehensiveness than most. For those reasons, many favor Romans as a first read for new Bible readers. Some evangelists use the so-called Roman Road to Salvation through the letter to lead explorers to Christ. Consensus is that in Romans, the author Paul wrote between A.D. 56 and A.D. 58 to a church in Rome that none of the apostles had yet visited. Jewish converts at Pentecost may have migrated to Rome ahead of any apostle, witnessing to new local Gentile converts, while establishing the church there. The letter appears to address both Jewish and Gentile believers. Despite that Paul expresses his deep love for the church's members, Paul was likely writing to believers whom he did not know, intending instead to introduce himself while also confirming with passion their remarkable and growing faith. Paul planned to visit the church but wanted in advance to confirm the gospel message that he would bring. Paul may have written Romans from Corinth while preparing to visit Jerusalem to deliver a collection, before heading to Rome and then on to Spain, having finished his work in the Eastern Mediterranean.

Although Romans includes greetings appropriate for a letter, the heart of Romans is a long and bold statement of faith and argument for the faith, much more so than correspondence addressed to a specific audience. Romans first declares the gospel's facts before confirming our desperate need to receive its salvation. Romans then presents the gospel as available to all, God having extended his grace to all, and anyone by faith alone able to accept God's grace. Romans next describes the freedom that salvation brings, before confirming God's plan for Christ's body to unite Jews with Gentiles. Romans then describes the service that follows submission to Christ, each believer having one's own spiritual gifts, exercised in unity to build one another up in faith. Romans ends with Paul describing his personal plans and extending greetings. The clear truths that Romans boldly expresses hold endless encouragement for readers at any point in their growing faith.

1 Corinthians

Paul wrote 1 Corinthians to the church in Corinth, a large and rich port city on the southern coastline of the western part of Greece, not far from Athens. Paul had founded the church in Corinth on his second missionary journey. Paul wrote 1 Corinthians around A.D. 55, on his third and last missionary journey, near the end of the three years that Paul was serving the church in Ephesus, a prominent city located on Asia Minor's westernmost coast across the Aegean Sea from Greece. The church in Corinth to whom Paul addressed 1 Corinthians was navigating an especially idolatrous and sexually corrupt culture. Rampant immorality threatened to undermine the spiritually immature church. Paul sought to fortify the church's faith with specific answers to the church members' immediate and quite-practical questions about how to conduct themselves in the face of such temptation, confusion, and opposition.

First Corinthians begins by stressing that the believers should remain unified around the faith's gospel tenets. Church leaders have specific roles that they should undertake with maturity. First Corinthians then addresses how the church should treat immoral members, the letter denouncing in the strongest terms the sexual sin that beset the church. The letter next addresses how to preserve and strengthen the weakened marriages typical in the corrupt culture. First Corinthians' spectacular love chapter breaks through other sections answering specific questions of conduct on worship, women, communion, and spiritual gifts. The long and rich letter next discusses death and the resurrection body, followed by parting thoughts, greetings, and benediction. First Corinthians remains a weighty and highly practical tool for preserving unity within a body of believers and instructing believers in how to relate to one another while resisting surrounding corruption. It also reveals priceless inspiration and comfort on death and the resurrected body.

2 Corinthians

Paul wrote 2 Corinthians to the same church in Corinth, largely in response to how the church had received his letter we know as 1 Corinthians. Paul wrote two other letters to the same church in Corinth, both of which are lost. In 2 Corinthians, Paul commends those who had taken to heart his 1 Corinthians counsel, thus maturing in their still-developing faith. But in 2 Corinthians, Paul felt compelled to defend himself against slanderous attacks of others, a small but dangerous number of false teachers, who had rejected his 1 Corinthians counsel. The letter is thus more personal than 1 Corinthians and plainly more painful for Paul to write. Paul had in effect to brag to establish his authority, which worked against Paul's godly humility. Paul not only defends himself in 2 Corinthians but also attacks false teachers. The letter also supplies additional practical counsel like that Paul wrote in 1 Corinthians, here though on how to collect money for the poor. The letter shows how intensely one ought to love the church and its members, and struggle for the truth. No doubt, 2 Corinthians will forever remain an inspired witness to that truth.

Galatians

Paul wrote the letter Galatians to the churches that Paul had founded on his first missionary journey through Galatia, the region in south-central Asia Minor. Because Paul did not address the letter to any specific church, he plainly intended that the Galatian churches circulate the letter among them. Paul wrote Galatians while in Antioch in central Asia Minor, just before Paul returned to Jerusalem in A.D. 50 for the council that settled an issue that Paul addressed in Galatians and elsewhere. As an early letter, Galatians addressed an issue that divided the early church, having to do with the relationship between Jewish and Gentile converts. Jewish leaders known as the Judaizers were advocating that Gentile converts to the new Christian faith must keep Jewish laws and traditions. To the Judaizers, faith in Christ was not enough. New Gentile converts must also comply with burdensome laws including those for circumcision. In Galatians, Paul rejected that position, opposing the apostle Peter, and advocating vigorously that faith in Christ was sufficient. The new faith-based covenant was one of life and liberty, whereas the old law-based covenant was one of demand and death. Galatians is a spectacular testimony that the gospel is authentic, superior, and sufficient.

Ephesians

Ephesians addresses itself both to the churches at Ephesus, on the western coast of Asia Minor across the Aegean Sea from Athens on the Greek peninsula, and to believers everywhere. Ephesus was a strategic, regional port city on the high order of Syria's Antioch and Egypt's Alexandria, while also on the main route between Rome and the East including Jerusalem. Paul, whom the letter credits as author, resided in Ephesus for three years, serving the local churches, supporting that the letter addressed close family and friends in the faith. The trusted Tychicus carried the letter to the Ephesians from Rome in about A.D. 60, where Paul was in prison. The letter does not address specific issues but instead supplies general encouragement, instructing believers in the church's nature and role. Its main message is that Christ unites believers in his life-giving body, which is the church, in one Spirit, under one God and Father over all. That broader perspective makes Ephesians one of the universal letters, a bright jewel in the King's crown and treasure to believers everywhere.

Philippians

Paul founded the church at Philippi on his second missionary journey. With Philippi located on the Aegean Sea's northern coast, outside of Asia Minor, the church was the first on the European continent. The church plainly held Paul in the highest regard because it had sent a gift for Paul whom Rome held in prison. Paul wrote Philippians around A.D. 61 to thank the church for the gift and encourage the church's members, and believers everywhere, in deepening their faith. Paul's one passion was to know Christ more for that opportunity's surpassing greatness, against which everything else, including all earthly riches, was loss, and any hardship meant nothing. Philippians is thus a letter of love, joy, and celebration, overflowing with the glorious Holy Spirit, a favorite of many believers, made even more encouraging by the fact that Paul was enduring such prison hardship while writing it.

Colossians

Colossians addresses itself to a church in Colosse, located inland in the southwestern part of Asia Minor. Paul, the letter's credited author, did not found or visit Colosse's church, which Epaphras, and others whom Paul's missionary preaching converted, seem instead to have founded. Paul was in prison in Rome in A.D. 60, the letter's approximate date. The letter indicates that misguided believers in Colosse's church were mixing their precious Christian faith with pagan and secular beliefs in a sort of religious relativism, the contemporary equivalent of which may be *cultural Christianity*. The letter thus directs its instruction to the sufficiency of faith in Christ alone. Given Christ's fullness and lordship, Christ *and* anything else is less than Christ and thus a loss and dangerous heresy. Colossians confronts that heresy with the truth that Christ is God and the head of the church, we are in Christ, and therefore we have no need for the world's legalism, philosophy's asceticism, or another world's mysticism. Christ has all power and authority. Colossians offers a timeless and precious grounding in the deepest reaches of our faith.

1 Thessalonians

Paul wrote 1 Thessalonians around A.D. 51 to the church in Thessalonica, an important land trade route and seaport located at the northern head of the Aegean Sea. Paul had founded the church on his second missionary journey. The letter came shortly later, to encourage the new believers in their growing faith. Indeed, Paul sent Timothy to encourage the church and confirm the members in their new faith. 1 Thessalonians thus carries ardent messages of assurance and reassurance, exhortation in the faith, and comfort in coming resurrection. Only toward the letter's end does Paul challenge the church to avoid sexual immorality while living righteously in a sinful world. Paul concludes the letter with specific counsel on preparing for Jesus's return, helping one another remain strong, and testing all teaching against the true gospel message, followed by benedictions and requests for prayer. First Thessalonians remains solid reassurance, especially to new believers needing encouragement in faith.

2 Thessalonians

The 2 Thessalonians letter from Paul in Corinth to the church in Thessalonica around A.D. 51 followed 1 Thessalonians by as little as a few months. Its brevity and content make clear that Paul wrote 2 Thessalonians to address confusion about the timing of Christ's return that 1 Thessalonians, and the church's continuing persecution, had raised. Some in the church had evidently misconstrued 1 Thessalonians' statement that Christ could come at any moment as an excuse for idleness. Those and others had also misconstrued their persecution as evidence that the Lord's day was indeed quite near, another excuse, those felt, for not pursuing more of the Lord's good work. Paul in 2 Thessalonians corrected the church, indicating that while Christ's return could be quite near, an expectation that is fully appropriate, his imminent return was no excuse for idleness. The Lord indeed desires patient and expectant waiting but also desires that the Lord's ministers, which includes all believers, should work as he desires. Evil will increase in the last days, bringing with it the believers' increased persecution, but those signs are simply greater reason to spread the gospel message, doing the Lord's commissioned work.

1 Timothy

In 1 Timothy, Paul addresses his young protégé, the son and grandson of godly Jewish women who had accepted Christ, raising Timothy in the faith as among the first second-generation Christians. Paul wrote the letter later in his ministry, around 64 A.D., just before his final Rome imprisonment. Timothy, though young, had substantial responsibility as the pastor of the church that Paul had served at Ephesus. Timothy thus faced considerable challenges both within the body of believers, to maintain the body's morality and unity, and from without, to resist the surrounding culture's pressure and help the members endure popular persecution. Paul begins 1 Timothy with fatherly counsel confirming Timothy in the faith while warning him about the peril of false teachers, a warning that Paul amplifies later in the letter. Paul next gives instructions for public worship in order and unity, followed by counsel on the qualifications of church elders or overseers, and deacons, thus coaching Timothy in how to build and maintain character and order in the church body. The letter includes substantial advice on pastoral care before concluding with exhortations to encourage the young pastor in his own motives, character, ministry, and faith. The letter remains core counsel for church leaders, surely as important of a witness to the Holy Spirit today as it was for the young Timothy.

2 Timothy

Paul wrote 2 Timothy just a couple of years later, around A.D. 66 or 67, during his second, short Rome imprisonment before execution. The letter is Paul's last. It thus constitutes a figurative passing of the torch from the apostolic generation, who met and knew the Lord, to those who would carry the church forward based instead on witness and faith. In 2 Timothy, Paul expresses the deep love the apostles had for their faith children on whose commission the gospel message would now depend. Paul urges Timothy to remember his calling and hold fast to the truth as he exercises his gifts to prepare the next generation's leaders. The letter warns again of deceivers and the word's power to expose and stand against them. Paul concludes with a final commission for Timothy to preach to the end, closing with a poignant request for some personal items and information. The letter stands as timeless testament to the strength of character and depth of love with which the Holy Spirit blesses enduring faith leaders.

Titus

Paul wrote the letter Titus around A.D. 64, between his two Rome imprisonments and about the time of 1 Timothy, to his special representative Titus who oversaw the churches on the island of Crete. Titus was a Greek protege whose faith Paul had long nurtured. Galatians records Titus meeting with the leaders of the Jerusalem church as evidence of the Holy Spirit's work among Gentile believers. Indeed,

Titus served as Paul's ambassador in other work. The letter Titus is another, and likely last, step in Paul's careful development of another outstanding servant of the faith. In the letter, Paul counsels Titus on church affairs, much like Paul had counseled Timothy in 1 Timothy. Paul's counsel on how to treat different age groups of believers is a touching example. While the letter Titus includes precious counsel, its greater witness may be to the care that established faith leaders should take in identifying and developing the next generation of leaders. It would then have taken not much more than just one missed generation for the church to have disappeared. The same remains true today, confirming the Holy Spirit's enduring power and purpose in the letter Titus.

Philemon

Paul wrote the letter Philemon in about A.D. 60 to a wealthy slaveowner of that name, who may have been a member of the church at Colosse. The letter would have been extraordinary for the time, in calling Philemon's slave Onesimus, then in Paul's service but a thief runaway from Philemon, Philemon's brother in Christ. In the letter, Paul makes a plea that the slaveowner take the runaway slave back free, as a brother, because as Paul so tactfully puts it in the letter, the slaveowner owes his own life to Paul. All are dead apart from Christ, while all are free together in Christ. The short and spare letter's profound implications for the equality of all in Christ thus go far beyond the letter's simple plea that Philemon take Onesimus back as a faith brother. The letter Philemon testifies that Christ removes all legal, economic, social, and other barriers among believers, uniting all in freedom as members of the one body of Christ.

Hebrews

The letter to the Hebrews addressed Jews who were examining Christianity or had converted to Christianity but questioned how the new faith related to the previously all-important Jewish law and traditions. This important but precarious Jewish-Christian audience faced double challenges, opposition and persecution from both Jews who rejected

Christ while demanding adherence to the religious laws and from Romans who perceived threats to their rule from the new faith. Hebrews thus addresses at length the supreme authority and complete sufficiency of Christ, and freedom from religious laws and traditions that Christian faith brings, while respecting that the same God instituted both the old and new covenants, for related reasons. Hebrews resolves in Christianity's favor critical theological issues, while still respecting the essential role of the old-covenant laws in preparing the ground for Christian faith. The letter, possibly written around A.D. 70 just before the Temple's destruction or perhaps as late as A.D. 90, must have been enormously heartening to Jewish converts who wondered at the seeming delay in Christ's return and who endured terrible persecution.

Hebrews first affirms at great length Jesus's superiority to angels, leaders, and priests, his new covenant's superiority to the old covenant, his body's superiority to the old Temple, and his sacrifice a better sacrifice than that of the priests. The Son radiates God's glory, as God's exact representation, the Son's word sustaining all things. The letter then examines the faith's practical implications including to hold onto one's confession and encourage one another in faith, while waiting patiently for Christ's return. Hebrews confirms the contrasting consequences, whether punishment or reward, of rejecting or persevering in the faith. The letter includes a rousing review of faith heroes that, again, must have deeply encouraged the letter's Jewish-Christian readers and hearers. The letter's high tone and sermon-like construction make it a unique read among the letters, a priceless message guaranteed to confirm and inspire Christian believers in every age and everywhere.

James

James wrote his letter from Jerusalem around A.D. 49 just before the Jerusalem council the next year, to Jewish Christians who had migrated outward from the Jerusalem church into surrounding Gentile areas. His Christian audience faced persecution, although the letter's content suggests that their greater threat may have been from their own hypocritical tendencies and poor behavior. James thus writes as their stern and authoritative former senior pastor, free to give frank counsel because of their close relationship and strong bond. James begins by telling them how Christians should live and act among others, next suggesting how faith moves into action. Faith, to be worthwhile, must make a difference in a believer's life. Behavior matters. James next cautions about holding one's tongue and warns against false earthly wisdom. James wants his former church members to avoid temptation in favor of godly living. He concludes the letter with encouragement to respect, support, and pray for one another. The letter James remains today an extraordinarily practical and direct manual for sound Christian living, invaluable to anyone earnestly practicing the faith.

1 Peter

The disciple Peter wrote his first letter around A.D. 62 to A.D. 64, possibly from Rome, just before Nero's awful persecution of Christians that included Peter's execution. Like James, Peter was writing to Jewish Christians whom persecution had driven from Jerusalem. Roman torture and execution of Christians throughout the empire was driving the Christian faith outward rather than extinguishing it. Peter's Jewish-Christian audience for his first letter had dispersed north into Asia Minor. The letter's purpose, then, was to bolster the fleeing Christians' faith against horrible persecution. The widely read letter opens with the revelation that persecution simply proves faith genuine, bringing not shame but rather, on Christ's return, glory and honor. God's blessings are what Christians seek, not human praise and honor. Peter's letter instructed the suffering believers in how to conduct themselves under terrible trial and how to guide other suffering believers. The comforting themes of 1 Peter include salvation as precious gift, persecution proving victory, the family of believers, and God's ultimate judgment. The letter continues to reveal to believers today the great weight of their coming glory.

2 Peter

If Peter was the author of his purported second letter, dated to around A.D. 67, rather than another author attributing Peter, then he wrote it shortly after his first letter and at the very end of his life just before his execution. The second letter's audience was the larger church, believers everywhere, rather than those of a certain ancestry or region. The assurances of 1 Peter are largely absent, replaced in 2 Peter with warnings against false teachers, a call to diligent action, a challenge to grow in faith, and an assurance of Christ's return in judgment against non-believers. The challenges that 2 Peter addresses are not external, such as Roman persecution, but internal, against heresy and spiritual malaise. Believers need comfort from suffering, but they also need reminders that faith involves moving forward confidently and responsibly, as 2 Peter continues to admonish.

1 John

The disciple John wrote the letter 1 John from Ephesus on the western coast of Asia Minor, likely between A.D. 85 and A.D. 90. The late date of John's letters would mean that Rome had already destroyed Jerusalem's Temple, Nero had already sought to rid Rome of its Christians, the other disciples had probably already been executed leaving John as the sole survivor, and Christians had followed the Jewish diaspora out of Jerusalem in all directions. John was thus writing not to any specific church or region but to believers everywhere, carrying the faith into the future. The letter opens without addressing itself to any audience, beginning instead with John's claim to have seen the Lord's incarnation. John portrays God as light and urges believers to walk in that light, obeying Christ and embracing the faith family while resisting antichrists opposing the gospel's truth. The letter next portrays God as love, irresistible and familial, God making us his children, while we reveal our family relationship with God through good deeds. Again, we must reject deceivers. The letter concludes with John portraying God as life, that life found in our relationship with his Son. The letter's clarity and succinctness beautifully reflect John's gospel, making the letter a pearl of incalculable value.

2 John

John wrote his very short second letter near the date of his first letter, probably around A.D. 90, still while in Ephesus and before his exile on the island of Patmos. John's second letter differs from his first in that he directs it to a *chosen lady* and her children, which might mean a member of a local church but could just as well mean a certain church and its members, or the broader church and believers everywhere. The letter, also different from his first letter in its instructional more so than inspirational emphasis, confirms that faith means following Christ, obeying his words. The letter both challenges and lifts readers. We must walk in obedience to Christ's commands, the primary one of which is to love one another. Christ is truth carried out in sacrificial love, set against false teachers and opposing popular culture's self-centeredness. John's second letter, like the first, lifts the face and opens the heart toward the glory of Christ.

3 John

John addresses his very short third letter, written from Ephesus around the A.D. 90 date of his second letter, to a dear friend Gaius to thank him for his hospitality. John and other traveling church leaders depended on believers like Gaius for food and shelter as they visited to preach and instruct the local congregation. In his third letter, John praises Gaius and another hospitable believer for their service and support, while disparaging another believer who had refused any hospitality and instead tried to commandeer and control the local church for his own benefit. John's letter thus serves as a brief reminder to care for leaders who serve the church faithfully, while the letter warns against false leaders who would instead have the church serve them. True to John's teacher's heart, though, the brief letter slips in a few short instructions to avoid evil, do good, and thus see God. John lets God's light shine even in a brief thank-you letter and reminder to support church leaders.

Jude

The short letter Jude, written around A.D. 65, addresses itself simply to those whom God called and Jesus kept, thus to believers everywhere. The whole of the letter urges that believers contend for the faith. The letter's first section documents the mendacious methods and corrupt characteristics of false teachers whom believers must identify, oppose, and reject. The letter's second section urges believers to fight for truth, persevere through trials, and stand firm in the faith. The letter ends with a stirring doxology to the God and Savior who keeps us and purifies us to present us to himself as witness to his glory. Jude's brevity, simplicity, and urgency make it a more-than-fitting conclusion to the letters, in anticipation of the Bible's concluding masterpiece Revelation.

Other Faith Books by Nelson Miller

Following Jesus

Looking to Jesus

Answered Prayers

Secret Devotion

The Faithful Lawyer

Facing Death

www.ingramcontent.com/pod-product-compliance
Lightning Source LLC
Chambersburg PA
CBHW052019070526
44584CB00016B/1821